Learning from Language

PITTSBURGH SERIES IN COMPOSITION,
LITERACY, AND CULTURE

David Bartholomae and Jean Ferguson Carr,
Editors

Learning from Language

Symmetry, Asymmetry, and Literary Humanism

WALTER H. BEALE

University of Pittsburgh Press

Published by the University of Pittsburgh Press, Pittsburgh, Pa., 15260
Copyright © 2009, University of Pittsburgh Press
All rights reserved
Manufactured in the United States of America
Printed on acid-free paper
10 9 8 7 6 5 4 3 2 1

Library of Congress Cataloging-in-Publication Data

Beale, Walter H.
   Learning from language : symmetry, asymmetry, and literary humanism / Walter H. Beale.
      p.   cm.
   Includes bibliographical references and index.
   ISBN-13: 978-0-8229-6038-6 (pbk. : alk. paper)
   ISBN-10: 0-8229-6038-9 (pbk. : alk. paper)
   1. English language—Rhetoric. 2. Symmetry in literature. 3. Language and languages—Philosophy. I. Title.
  PE1403.B43 2009
  808'.042—dc22   2009006974

UXORI VENUSTAE LEPIDAEQUE

Contents

Acknowledgments   ix

1. Symmetry, Asymmetry, and Literary Humanism   1
2. Two Famous Asymmetrists   18
3. Six Claims of Symmetry   37
4. Reading the World: Structural Analogy   67
5. Creating the World: The Performative Principle   83
6. Naming and Renaming the World   108
7. Figuring (Out) the World: Tropes and Tropology   126
8. Style and Virtue   151
   Conclusion: The Love of Words   174

   Works Cited   183

   Index   191

Acknowledgments

I appreciate the excellent advice and direction of my editors at the University of Pittsburgh Press, and also that of the wise and exacting scholarly consultants engaged by them. W. Barnes Tatum, professor of Greek and New Testament at Greensboro College, read portions of the manuscript directly relevant to his expertise, offering important suggestions, corrections, and encouragements. Dr. Laurie White, an astute rhetorician and literary humanist, discussed with me on many occasions this book's ideas and arguments, reading and commenting on a good deal of it in manuscript form. My colleagues and advanced students in language, rhetoric, and literary theory at the University of North Carolina at Greensboro provided an indispensable community of conversation. I am grateful to them all.

Learning from Language

1
Symmetry, Asymmetry, and Literary Humanism

This book is primarily for teachers and prospective teachers of English, although I believe it will interest scholars in the fields of language, rhetoric, and discourse generally. It is the result of many years of teaching courses in language and linguistics to students of literature and rhetoric, and one of its primary goals is to bring these fields into friendlier conversation with each other. I do not intend to survey every critical and philosophical issue in the extensive interface of these disciplines. This book is for the advanced student of literature, rhetoric, or composition studies, who may be taking that first course in linguistics or philosophy of language; the professor who may be rethinking the structure and content of that course in English language for prospective teachers; or the experienced teacher looking for a chance to reexamine those murky relations within the language, literature, and rhetoric triangle of English Studies.

Although some of my terminology is new, the basic questions are very old: Do words (does language) reflect reality? Can the study and practice of language itself—considered apart from the subjects and disciplines that language encodes and communicates—make you a smarter, wiser, and better person? Teachers of language and literature have always tended to think so, and this affirmative answer is what I will term *symmetry*. Many of these teachers now realize, however, that there are serious objections to symmetry, as well as a history of erroneous thinking and practice on the subject; and so they'd rather not be questioned too closely on particulars. In fact, many have lost confidence that the question can be answered affirmatively at all. A host of scientific and philosophical developments in the last half century, as well as a host of educational failures—in a civilization that wants earnestly to promise the extended benefits of literacy to all its citizens—have seriously eroded that confidence. My goal is to offer a prospect of restoration. Even though specific attributions of symmetry have often been wrong, sometimes resulting in ineffective practice, our basic intuitions of symmetry are valid, demonstrable, and usable. Language does teach us something, if we listen in the right places, and learn from it in the right ways.

For individuals in the field of English Studies, there are practical and personal as well as philosophical urgencies to the symmetry question, and the following conditions can be regarded as symptomatic:

- Most of us would describe ourselves as "lovers of words" or "lovers of language," but few of us have any distinct or communicable sense of what these phrases entail.

- Philology, conceived originally as the historical study of language, and oriented toward the establishment and understanding of early English texts, once held a secure place in the study of letters. But linguistics, understood broadly as the scientific study of language in general, has no such security. A national survey in 1969 discovered unanimity among American leaders in English Studies that the preparation of English teachers should include at least one course in "the English language"; however, that same study discovered no agreement about the content of such courses, and no agreement at all about the "points of application" of linguistic principles to the needs of English teachers (Pearson and Reese). No greater state of agreement has developed since that time.

- Although courses in "English Linguistics," "Linguistics for Teachers," and "History of the English Language" do exist in nearly every program of English education, the primary points of application upon which most would be found to agree are actually negative. That is to say: differences among spoken varieties of English, either geographical or social, are not indicative of accomplishment or intelligence, and efforts to modify them are not productive; the formal teaching of grammar does not result in better writing and speaking; the differences between prestigious and nonprestigious usage do not have anything to do with clarity of thought or true elegance of expression; and an educational emphasis on such matters has, in any case, little positive effect, even on usage itself (for an interesting critical perspective on "History of the English Language," see Crowley 11–42).

- Quite fortunately, a half-century's labors in sociolinguistics and language history, combined with other sources of critical consciousness, have led to forms of language instruction that celebrate (rather than worry about) the diversity of dialects, traditions of discourse, and modes of literacy that exist nationwide and worldwide in English (see Smitherman and Villaneuva; Graddol; Leith; and Swann). However, specific recommendations for teaching—things that may be thought to lead to better reading, writing, speaking, and citizenship—are still limited to by-now familiar liberations from (warnings against) the old enthronements of majority speech.

To any observer of this field from the outside, the immediate question might be an astonished, "Is there really a problem here? What two things could go more naturally and comfortably together than English Studies and the formal study of language?" To anyone on the inside, however, the disjunction is more apparent. For any college or university faculty in the English-speaking world, "English" primarily means the study of literature in English. The formal study of language has very little to do with it, and the place of linguists in most departments of English is marginal and precarious (see especially Robinson). Among faculties in secondary schools, the response might be more complicated, because here the responsibility for teaching competence in the use of language is felt more urgently, and issues of language, literacy, and language policy receive more daily attention. But here there are also sharp discontinuities. The formal study of language plays no role in the study of literature, and its relevance to effective writing and speaking is at best ambiguous—and, in fact, a subject of long-standing dispute. At every level, many of the most successful teachers do their best to minimize the formal study of language, while many of their best students are repelled by it.

In the past half century in America, roughly since the appearance of Edward P. J. Corbett's *Classical Rhetoric for the Modern Student,* university English faculties have taken on a much greater and more learned responsibility for all that "rhetoric," in the classical sense, can mean: the development of the effective use of language in the world, and the parallel development of a broader human character and sensibility. But even the most successful university programs of rhetoric and composition have remained separate from other parts of the English curriculum; and here too, in spite of strenuous efforts, the formal study of language has remained stubbornly marginal.

None of this signals a particular crisis in English Studies. It is simply a fact of life, albeit a curious one. Wherever language and rhetoric have been taught, the problem has cropped up in one way or another. The divisions we are talking about are related to a question that has fascinated philosophers, grammarians, poets, and theologians from Plato onward. I call it the *symmetry question*. In its simplest and earliest form, as I indicated at the beginning, this is the question of whether words reflect reality. The question is paraphrasable, however, in a variety of complicated ways and contexts: What is the relationship of language to the world, especially to our thoughts about the world and to our experience of it? Is language understandable as simply the medium through which we express our thoughts and experience? Or is there a relationship of symmetry between the two? Do forms and structures of language parallel (mimic, tie into, anticipate) or participate in the forms and structures of these other things—that is to say, the world, our consciousness of it, our experience of it? If they do not, should we worry about it? If they do, are there ways that we can use that knowledge?

I am now going to shift away from the term "English Studies" and take up the more historically inclusive notion of "literary humanism." As implied by its separate verbal components, the field of literary humanism was named originally for its devotion to "letters" on the one hand, and for its separateness from "divinity" or theological studies on the other hand. (In the Renaissance period of European history, whence the notion of humanism derives, this separateness did not imply hostility to religion, as some have thought, although the fact of separation did mean a good deal.) The term has been defined in a number of different ways, but in general literary humanism has come to name any conscious program of scholarship and teaching that combines the study of language, rhetoric, and literature, working toward greater competence, character, and wisdom in the individual and, hence, toward a better society. That is a rather cumbersome definition, but it does underscore both the complexity and the ambitiousness of the enterprise: scholarship, teaching, language, rhetoric, literature, competence, character, wisdom, and a better society. As literary humanists of the Renaissance understood quite well, such conscious programs were broader and more oriented toward civil society than the theologically oriented education of medieval Europe; and they had a much earlier origin, in pre-Christian Greece and Rome.

Looking at the various components of this definition of literary humanism, it becomes readily apparent that how the symmetry question is answered can have a powerful impact upon how any literary humanism is conceived, constructed, and put into practice. The medieval supporting structures of an eternal truth are no longer in the foreground. The credibility of the literary humanistic enterprise, and the viability of its hopes, are greater if there are correspondences or analogues between structures of language and those of human knowledge, character, and social aspiration. With this fact in mind, we can now pose the symmetry question in some different ways: Does language itself, and its study, have special things to teach you about the world? If you listen to language and practice its arts, are there important things about the world that you might expect to hear or learn? And if so, can literary humanism be organized to facilitate this listening and learning?

Historically, since its inception in the Greek city-state, most serious literary humanism has been animated by an intuition and a claim of symmetry. In modern times as well (that is, since the eighteenth century), literary humanists have been motivated by a strong conviction of symmetry, and that conviction has fueled a great deal of devoted research, both in language and in literature. However, when it has come actually to illuminating the study of literature with the study of language, or harnessing linguistic insights to the teaching of effective use, they have not really known what to do with this conviction. Moreover, some of the things they have done with it have been neither wise nor effective. Most strikingly, humanists have not been powerfully assisted by linguistic science, either in articulating the conviction itself or in giving it practical application.

A strong reason for this is that modern linguistic science has been animated by a different leaning altogether from the one that has fueled literary humanism. This is the view that I will call *asymmetry*. It is the view that, by and large, language is its own kind of system, operating with its own unique principles, hence the idea that linguistic structures are related to other kinds of structures is considered a mistake. For many literary humanists, the privileging of asymmetry, especially its characteristic expression as "arbitrariness," has caused linguistics to seem worse than not very helpful, much like an alien presence. And when students of literature have themselves embraced asymmetry, it has seemed like a defection to the dark side.

Advocates of literature might argue that, with or without symmetry, it's in the great works of literary art, not in everyday writing and speaking, that we witness the most compelling, beautiful, and revelatory articulations of language and the world. These displays are not on the surface of things, not to be purchased inexpensively with a sentence diagram or a right-branching nominalization transformation; they are bought dearly, with great struggle and sacrifice, through processes that are only dimly understood, by minds of extraordinary power and insight.

This is true enough, and every lover of literature will to some degree assent to it. It is one of the great positions—though not by any means the only possible one—of modern literary humanism. But it does not answer the question of why the study of language has contributed so little to the understanding and appreciation of these things. And it opens up a larger and fascinating theoretical question as well: Is the function of literature to mine the possibilities of language, discovering its deep participations in experience? Or is it rather to construct these things as artful and entertaining illusions, in ephemeral and perhaps suspect ways? Without a doubt, the answers to these questions for literary humanists—most especially English teachers—can be located by looking at the history of conflicts between symmetry and asymmetry (a history which reaches back much further than the advent of modern linguistics or literary criticism) and also by listening to and learning from language in some different ways.

The Marriage to Latin

For roughly the first eighteen hundred years of the Common Era, these questions about language were not make-or-break questions for teachers of language and literature. They were certainly not unknown to literary humanists, and different leanings did affect practice in one way or another; but they were not the basis for anxieties about how the whole enterprise fits together. Language, including the issue of competence in its use, was dominated by the study of one particular language, Latin. Literature was dominated by a particular literature: a list of great works in which the world's wisdom, beauty, and eloquence were deposited, primarily in Latin. Consequently, questions aside about how language and literature participate in the world and in each other, the case for literary humanism was bunkered on both sides by a common and necessary subject matter: the Latin language, considered a more elevated medium than the vernacular languages, and the great religious, philosophical, and literary texts composed in Latin.

For hundreds of years, in the Middle Ages and the Renaissance, the terms "grammar" and "Latin" were virtuously synonymous. It was understood that what a student was doing in the grammar stage of the curriculum—in later centuries the "grammar school"—was learning how to read, speak, and write in Latin. (The first books of English grammar did not appear until the sixteenth century, and these were neither scholarly books nor manuals of proper English, but rather primers for the study of Latin.) Latin was the nearly universal and exclusive medium of learning, of government, of religion and ecclesiastical affairs, right down to the church service, and all the important literature, including Holy Scripture, was written in it. Moreover, it was not anybody's native language, and virtually all study of "language" was aimed at learning how to read, write, and speak Latin.

Everyone who taught Latin and wrote manuals for its instruction did so in the confidence that Latin was a necessary acquisition. However, most had another kind of confidence as well: Latin was a superior language. And here is an important meeting place for the symmetry question and the practice of literary humanism. The idea of Latin's superiority over the various languages of the people (vulgar tongues, they were called, from the Latin "vulgus," meaning common people) is strongly connected to the idea that Latin is more symmetrical: it is closer to reality. It has a greater purchase on the truths and realities that language must represent. It is more appropriate, therefore, to the important communal functions (the sacraments of the Roman Catholic Church, the affairs of government and diplomacy, the conduct of teaching, learning, and scholarship) that language must perform.

For the most part during this period, the superiority of Latin was not so much advocated as it was assumed. The judgment of modern linguistics, of course, is that this assumption was wrong. It was based partly on superstition (Latin as divinely ordained) and partly on ignorance of historical facts. But more exactly, it was based on an imperfect understanding of fundamental linguistic processes and linguistic relationships: how languages are internally structured; how and why they change; what happens when they come into contact with one another; and what conditions make it possible for one variety of a language to become standardized and adapted for official use. The science of language acknowledges a blunt truth: there is no evidence that any language is better than any other language. However, the proposition that seems so dubious and outlandish to the modern linguist would have seemed obvious and uncontestable to the medieval schoolman.

It is important to keep in mind from the outset that the primary argument for the greatness of Latin was always its obvious association with greatness. It was the language of learned and holy people; and most of the wise, beautiful, and holy literature was written in it. However, if you asked an educated person to explain formally why Latin was superior, you would generally get some combination of the following:

> Latin is more logical and intellectually complex than the vulgar languages, and therefore (in addition to being more dignified), it is more in touch with ultimate reality.

> Latin is more highly structured and regular than the vulgar languages, and therefore (in addition to being more dependable), it is more in touch with the higher regularities of the cosmos.

> Latin is more permanent and stable, less subject to change and variation, than the vulgar languages, and therefore (in addition to being more widely accessible), it is more in touch with the permanent and stable realities of the universe.

> Latin is more elegant, dignified, and beautiful, and therefore (in addition to being a fitter medium for important occasions), it is more expressive of elegance, dignity, and beauty in general.

> Latin has a greater store of scientific, philosophical, and religious vocabulary, and therefore (in addition to being a necessary lingua franca), it is a more powerful medium for exploring these things.

In this history, no single individual would have endorsed with equal emphasis all of these formal justifications. Interestingly, by the end of the Renaissance period, some of the assumptions of Latin's superiority had eroded considerably, even as others were being asserted more vigorously. As early as the thirteenth century, poets were engaging in open and flamboyant relationships with their vernaculars (see *The Divine Comedy* and *The Romance of the Rose*), even as the Catholic church remained faithful. Dante wrote a treatise, *De Vulgari Eloquentia*, defending the vernacular in literature, but even here the superiority of Latin (which he calls "grammatica") is not seriously questioned. Dante in fact promoted the superiority of his own Tuscan dialect on the grounds that it was closer to Latin.

In the sixteenth century, leaders of the Protestant Reformation would tear asunder and denounce as superstition the hold of Latin on religious life, even while literary humanists in Protestant countries (notably England) were constructing a school curriculum that was more rigorously based on Latin than ever before: acquiring Latin, doing Latin exercises designed to improve thinking, absorbing the wisdom that was (still) stored in Latin, and preparing to conduct the world's business in Latin. Some of the masters of grammar schools in sixteenth- and seventeenth-century England initiated trial separations, so to speak—that is, attempts to teach logic and rhetoric in English—but these attempts were not immediately successful, and the study of grammar continued to mean, for the most part, the study of Latin and great books written in Latin. In this setting also, the presiding assumption was that Latin was a superior language, even if it was not inherently so, because the great classical authors had made it so. And so strong was Latin's hold that even by the time of the eighteenth century, when literary humanists were celebrating a rich and proud national literature, and the teaching of English was becoming an important part of the educational agenda, the old assumption remained. A project of English literary humanism would become to improve the language—in fact, to make it as logical, as regular, as stable, as dignified, and as beautiful as Latin.

It has been such a long time since anyone was signed on to this particular project that a good deal of the philosophy behind it has passed out of memory as well. For that reason, I want to take a closer look at some specifics, for what they may reveal about the symmetry question. Among the various justifications of Latin's superiority, the arguments about reason and stability were generally more compelling than those about beauty (hence the gorgeous infidelities of the poets). The first argument, regarding logic, would have been the most compelling of all. Here, for thinkers of the Middle Ages and the Renaissance, was the primary meeting ground of language and reality.

Although it is very little emphasized today, logic was an integral component of traditional language arts, the second in the "trivium" of basic preparatory studies: grammar, logic, and rhetoric. Its purpose, then as now, was to secure sound thinking, and it did this by teaching students how to perform specific dialectical operations: how to define terms properly; how to distinguish different concepts from one another; how to distinguish the different kinds of propositions or claims that are made in an argument; and how to join together propositions correctly in support of these claims.

Why would Latin be considered more logical than other languages? Primarily because its grammar seemed more complex and therefore more attuned to those logical differences named above. Latin did possess a more complex and comprehensive set of noun and verb endings (inflections), expressing different relationships of case and tense, than any European language. A student learning the name for boy ("puer"), for instance, would have to learn along with it ten different inflectional endings, depending upon the particular reality it represented in a given sentence and its logical relationship to other parts of a sentence: Was the boy singular or plural? The subject or object of a verb (nominative or accusative)? The owner or originator of something (genitive)? And so on through the case system: puer, pueri, puero, puerum, puero, pueri, puerorum, pueris, pueris. There is a much longer list for the various tenses and moods of a verb. And it is all far more complicated than this, of course, because there are different classes of nouns and verbs, each requiring a different set of inflectional endings. By contrast, the European vernaculars, including French, Italian, and Spanish (the living continuations of Latin), had evolved into languages with far simpler inflectional systems.

What linguists have long understood is that no language is really more complex or logical than another. What Latin accomplishes with its inflectional system is as readily accomplished in English by a battery of prepositional expressions and by a much more tightly regulated system of word order. However, the differences we are talking about were right there on the surface to see. Latin was indeed more complex on that surface, and the vernacular language did look grammatically and logically impoverished by comparison. Moreover, Latin is devilishly difficult to learn as a second language, requiring years of painstaking effort. For a variety of reasons, the grammar of the curriculum became the necessary boot camp, the portal to logic, rhetoric, literature, theology, the sciences, and the "higher" life.

More important than whatever combination of factors may have made Latin seem more logical than other languages was the prestige of logic itself. In contrast to modern times, medieval thinkers placed a much higher premium upon logic than upon observation, experiment, or feeling. In this predilection they combined Christianity's conviction of the fallenness of this world with a philosophy of knowledge inherited from Plato and Aristotle. The things of this world—nature as well as human life and human history—were in this view radically imperfect, unreliable, and transitory. More perfect, more permanent, and therefore more "real" and knowable, were the ideas or abstract categories of things, apprehensible through logic. From this premise it only took one more step of reasoning to think of these permanent things as more readily accessible through the more permanent medium—Latin. The down-to-earth vernaculars participated more in the impermanence and fallenness of the earth itself.

An entire school of medieval grammarians, the so-called modistae of the thirteenth and fourteenth centuries, devoted their labors to proving that grammatical concepts or modes (parts of speech, the categories of case, tense, and so on) provided direct links to permanent ideas built into the structure of reality and the human mind. In other words, a tripartite condition of symmetry was posited among modes of being (realities out there), modes of conceptualizing (ideas about them), and modes of signifying (words about them). In later medieval philosophy, the symmetry question appears prominently in attacks upon this position, resulting in the famous debate between realists and nominalists. Realists held that abstract ideas or universals—justice, love, freedom—have objective and permanent reality. In fact, they are more real than any historical fact or condition that they might name, and these realities are knowable, or at least partially so, through human language. Nominalists (from the Latin "nomen" or name) held that the general ideas of things are simply names for material (the real) things, or rather generalizations about them. These categories have no reality apart from their connections to material things, and these things are not really knowable in the abstract. The categories of language, therefore, have no special purchase upon them.

The realism versus nominalism debate, especially as the early modern world headed speedily in the direction of nominalism, held some potential for dissolving the marriage to Latin. However, this dissolution was not to occur for a very long time, and not without a host of real-world developments. As long as Latin remained the central repository of learning and literature, the lingua franca of scholars and diplomats, (still, for a great part of Europe) the language of the Church, and as long as formal education remained the possession of a very small part of the population, the hold of Latin would remain firm. Interestingly, from the sixteenth century onward, Protestant leaders would have powerful reasons for opposing the practical hegemony of Latin in religious life. Theoretically, they opposed the very idea that a particular language could possess special powers. (Here, at least in the popular imagination, was the basis for the power and necessity of the Church's sacraments.) However, even as Protestant leaders were promoting vernacular literacy for a wider segment of the population, the marriage of literary humanism to Latin remained strong, and in some ways it became stronger.

Literary humanists of the Renaissance (the first scholars and teachers actually to call themselves "humanists") mounted a new defense of what has come to be known as a "classical education." This education consisted essentially of a rigorous program of grammar, logic, and rhetoric in Latin, and after that, the great moral and philosophical literature in Latin. Humanists believed confidently in the superior logic, beauty, and expressiveness of Latin, especially in what they considered its purer classical form. They scoffed at what they considered the corrupted Latin of the medieval church (they also invented the very term "medieval"), and they promoted instead the Latin of the Roman republic, represented most exquisitely in the works of Cicero. They were the founders of the sixteenth- and seventeenth-century grammar schools mentioned earlier; and they constructed a curriculum that was more rigorous than had existed in medieval schools. Partly as a consequence, in both Protestant and Catholic Europe, nearly all preparatory education and all university education would remain in Latin. And for a long time to come, the best way to improve your native language would be considered to make it more like Latin (Knowles 107–14; Amsler 287–89).

This historical sketch is not meant to debunk traditional literary humanism, nor certainly to discredit the general idea of symmetry. The purpose has been to underscore that literary humanists, while admirable in their purposes, can be mistaken about particulars. Their work is fueled by an intuition and a leaning toward symmetry—an "enchantment," as the brilliant French linguist Gerard Genette has termed it. However, they have inherited a literary humanism that, because of its long marriage to Latin, is partial to ideas about symmetry that no longer stand up to rational scrutiny. The marriage to Latin produced some beautiful children, but it was nevertheless a bad marriage.

It is important to keep in mind that the symmetry question, and also its relevance to literary humanism, is much older than the Renaissance grammar school or the medieval trivium. What a broader historical view will uncover is that the struggle between symmetry and asymmetry is not merely a struggle between literary humanism and the science of language (or even, going back a little further, between literature and philosophy). It is a struggle within literary humanism itself. There can be (and have been) literary humanisms intelligently founded on a leaning toward asymmetry as well. And more importantly, there can be (and have been) humanisms that intelligently join the two.

Symmetry versus Asymmetry

If you dispense with the question of whether there is anything very special about the Latin language, there still remains the question of whether there is anything very special about any language at all. And obviously this turns out to be a more fascinating question. We can begin with two quotations that illustrate the two basic leanings, both of them from great literary figures and neither more or less sophisticated about language than the other. The first is from W. H. Auden's "In Memory of W. B. Yeats":

> Time that is intolerant
> Of the brave and innocent,
> And indifferent in a week
> To a beautiful physique,
> Worships language and forgives
> Everyone by whom it lives;
> Pardons cowardice, conceit,
> Lays its honours at their feet.
> Time that with this strange excuse
> Pardons Kipling and his views,
> And will pardon Paul Claudel,
> Pardons him for writing well. (46–57)

The next is from Samuel Johnson's Preface to the *Dictionary of the English Language*: "I am not so lost in lexicography as to forget that words are the daughters of earth, and that things are the sons of heaven" (7).

The first quotation expresses the view that language, properly and creatively used, is an organ not merely of clarity and beauty but of special revelation as well; that these things belong together and lead into each other. This is something that poets have always tended to believe. When William Wordsworth exclaimed (in "Lines Composed a Few Miles above Tintern Abbey") that nature "never did betray the heart that loved her," he meant also the natural language—the "language of the sense," which appears in the same poem as our primary way of connecting to nature (122–23). He is

> well pleased to recognize
> In nature and the language of the sense,
> The anchor of my purest thoughts, the nurse
> The guide, the guardian of my heart, and soul
> Of all my moral being. (107–11)

Wordsworth's statement is certainly more extravagant and unguarded than Auden's, but Auden's is strong enough. Yeats, Rudyard Kipling, and Paul Claudel are all figures whose political views he detests, but he believes that their special relationship to language (not just their command of it) gives them access to a truth that transcends politics. Would it not follow from this that the best education is the one that joins the love of wisdom to the love of words? This is symmetry.

Samuel Johnson's quotation—and please keep in mind that it comes from a great literary critic and student of language—stands for the equally cogent position that all of the above is basically not true. Individuals like Johnson are more likely to recognize that the common tongue (and the noble one too, in all its plumage and decoration) is a carrier of error, prejudice, and false gods. Francis Bacon, the seventeenth-century prophet of the scientific mind-set, termed them "the idols of the marketplace" (40–42). Such individuals may love the poets but be less inclined to forgive them simply for writing well. Language, they recognize, has no particular hold on the truth; in fact, by its very nature it tends to soak up prejudice and error like a sponge. Words "plainly force and overrule the understanding," says Bacon, "and throw all into confusion, and lead men away into numberless empty controversies and idle fancies" (40). No sentence that we speak can be coherent and comprehensible unless it lays its new information on a comfortable bed of old information—presupposition, that is—the already known. It is the old information, chiefly embedded in the existing vocabulary, that usually carries the error and prejudice. As an example, consider Johnson's own use of the words "sons" and "daughters" in the quotation above. No contemporary writer would use such a sexist metaphor; no editor would allow it.

Our ordinary speech is full of prejudice, inexactitude, and outright error. This is why anyone's first step in learning any new scientific or scholarly field will be to master its vocabulary—one that replaces the looseness and misconception of the old, the common language with the exactitude and fixity of the new. It is also why groups of individuals who have been oppressed or discriminated against have become vigilant about the ways that prejudices against them are carried unconsciously in ordinary speaking and writing.

These are among the great truths and lessons of asymmetry, and it would follow from them that every education, like every serious discourse, should begin with a set of procedures for washing and wringing dry the dirty sponge of language. In this view, individuals should be trained to learn from and listen to language for its characteristic ways of leading one astray, and to practice a discourse that surpasses ordinary usage. The traditional language art that takes on this project directly is dialectic (or practical logic), and there are forms of literary humanism that concentrate on dialectic for this very reason. Released from the marriage to Latin, dialectic might give very little attention to details of language at all; in fact, it might scorn such attention.

Individuals of a scientific and dialectical bent are drawn to asymmetry. However, it is important to remember that the devotion to logic is not the only form that a leaning toward asymmetry can take. One such was the program of "General Semantics," which gained some educational currency in the mid-twentieth century, chiefly through its two most prominent popularizers, Stuart Chase (*Science and Sanity*) and S. I. Hayakawa (*Language in Thought and Action*). This program sought to alert students not only to the dangers of ordinary speech and discourse (the ubiquitous tendency toward abstraction, generalization, prejudicial assumption, and the false lures of advertising and propaganda), but to what it considered the uncertain paths of traditional logic as well. The program lost currency because of its failure to understand the ways in which language does lead us to what is true and valuable and good.

Another, more traditional (and actually more embraceable) asymmetrist position is that the study of logic is too arid a procedure, even as the study of linguistic detail is too picayune and futile. The surer path, in this view, is to fill your head with substance. Being well-read—studying the best works of literature in the old, broad sense (philosophy, ethics, and history, as well as literary art works)—is the best way to learn sound thinking and, in the long run, the effective and responsible use of language. In which case, sing praise again that we are free from Latin! In fact, we are free from language itself, and we can go directly to the substance of communication and learning. Are translations of the great books OK? Certainly. Language does not encode wisdom, it simply transmits it. This is an ancient position, and it is explained cogently by Vivien Law in her magisterial *History of Linguistics in Europe*:

> If language turns out to mirror reality faithfully and inevitably, then we have no freedom to use it as we choose ... we must unavoidably speak in accordance with the truth inherent in the world. If, on other hand, language is arbitrary, we are cut off from reality—but at the same time we are free: free to speak and act in accordance with the truth of reality, or not. (20)

A value of the leaning toward asymmetry is its urgent understanding of our responsibility to use language with care: our natural language is prone to prejudice and error, and so we must scrub it clean. Just as importantly, however, asymmetry in the right hands can also celebrate and teach the art of language. Wordsworth, to be sure, believed that poetry works its wonders by finding the natural language, the one that connects to nature, and scraping away the excess. However, many lovers of poetry (Samuel Johnson included) have believed that the best poetry achieves what it achieves precisely by imparting to language a beauty, integrity, and clarity of thought that it does not naturally possess.

Symmetry and asymmetry, it should now be apparent, are not two forms of literary humanism but two contrary ways of thinking that have motivated and informed it. They connect to philosophical issues of a broader sort, and they connect to specific practices in the language arts. Historically, symmetry has been the more enchanting proposition and the more powerful motivator, though the more difficult to explain and defend. And there have been (and can be) specific views and practices that are plainly mistaken. Again, while specific intuitions of symmetry have often been inaccurate, they are never entirely wrong. The humanist love of language and confidence in language is neither unrequited nor misplaced. Language is a great teacher, but we must learn to listen carefully.

Suggested Reading

Conley, Thomas M. *Rhetoric in the European Tradition.* New York: Longman, 1990. A very good overview of the discipline of rhetoric from ancient to modern times, with an emphasis on competing traditions and the philosophical viewpoints behind them.

Genette, Gerard. *Mimologiques: Voyage en Cratylie.* Trans. Thais E. Morgan. Lincoln: University of Nebraska Press, 1995. The original, groundbreaking study of attempts to connect structures of language to realities outside of language, with an emphasis on French sources.

Grafton, Anthony, and Lisa Jardine. *From Humanism to the Humanities: Education and the Liberal Arts in Fifteenth- and Sixteenth-Century Europe.* Cambridge: Harvard University Press, 1986. Among the many available treatments of humanism in the Renaissance period, this book, better than any other, traces the consequences of humanism's continued and intensified reverence for and attachment to Latin.

Joseph, John E. *Limiting the Arbitrary: Linguistic Naturalism and its Opposites in Plato's* Cratylus *and in Modern Theories of Language*. Amsterdam: John Benjamins, 2000. Useful for its discussion of the symmetry question within modern linguistic theory.

Law, Vivien. *History of Linguistics in Europe from Plato to 1600*. New York: Cambridge University Press, 2003. The best book on this subject, containing good discussions of the symmetry question in the ancient world.

Robinson, Douglas. "Linguistics and Language." *The Johns Hopkins Guide to Theory and Criticism*. Ed. Michael Groden, Martin Kreiswirth, and Imre Szeman. Baltimore: Johns Hopkins University Press, 2005. http://litguide.press.jhu.edu. A penetrating survey of various traditions of language study, their connections, and failures of connection with traditions of literary criticism.

2

Two Famous Asymmetrists

When Plato took up the question of symmetry directly, in his dialogue *Cratylus,* he knew that he was stepping into an ongoing, high-stakes discussion. He knew that it was Heraclitus, the celebrated pre-Socratic philosopher of change, who first proposed an educative relationship between words and the things they named. Heraclitus, the philosopher who famously proclaimed that a person cannot step into the same river twice, was impressed with what he regarded as the relative stability of language. In his view, external features of the world existed in such a rapid state of flux that words about them, because they changed more slowly than other things, were capable of retaining important truths now lost to direct observation (Poster 15–17). The Stoic philosophers, however, wrote more extensively on the subject (though much of this writing is now lost), and to Plato they presented a more powerful and disturbing argument. The Stoics maintained that the forms and categories of language, in spite of all kinds of surface evidence to the contrary, existed continuously in basic symmetry with the forms of the world. They must in fact do so, the Stoics argued, or we would not be able to know anything about the world or do anything useful in it.

In ancient philosophy, the symmetry question was also linked to another question specifically about language, the so-called analogy-anomaly question. Here, we deal with the fact that the surface of every language, like the surface of the world itself, is full of irregularities. Why do we have "bring," "brought," "has brought," rather than "bring," "bringed," "has bringed," or "bring," "brang," and "has brung"? To some thinkers, such facts were, in themselves, evidence enough that language was an irregular (and therefore probably unreliable) instrument. This is the anomaly position. To the analogists, however, this view seemed as superficial as the evidence on which it was based. Apparent anomalies were either the surface manifestations of a deeper system of order (roughly akin to the deep structures of modern linguistics), or they were corrupted versions of a previously existing order.

The analogy-anomaly question runs parallel to the symmetry question, and ancient treatments of it tended to provide further support for symmetry. Nobody expects the existing, outward form of the word *duck* to be like a duck or expects an active sentence to always signify action. Language's reference is not to *things*, in the sense of objects or events, but to the (truer, more stable) *ideas* of things. If you look deep enough, or go back far enough, you will likely find the connection. "Likely," however, turns out to be a big word in that sentence. The explanation seems very reasonable, but it can be exceedingly difficult to demonstrate consistently. And this is why in all ages the case for symmetry has come forward more as an article of conviction and belief than as a statement of fact.

In the ancient discussion, the need to keep the faith might have seemed especially strong, because the issue of language connected to two important philosophical issues. The first, as already noted, was the epistemology question: Are there stable, knowable realities out there? How can we know them? And how can we communicate reliably what we know? If something is being claimed in language, is there anything in language itself that authenticates or discredits the claim?

The second, related issue is more specifically about human institutions—government, religion, the law—and that is the ancient debate of nature versus convention: Allowing for all sorts of surface differences (everybody knows the constitution of Sparta is different from that of Athens), do such institutions derive from a natural order of things, and are they therefore subject to universal laws? Or do they exist by convention—by agreements among humans at different times and places, under different circumstances. If the latter is true, then they are not accountable to universal principles, since none are better or truer than another, except as a matter of practical working.

How do questions about the regularity and symmetry of language relate to all of this? First of all, human institutions are language-saturated. They are conducted in language, and in an important sense (a literal one, in fact, in the case of constitutions and laws) constructed by language. If language has no special hold on the truth or rightness of things, it can then be asked, how can the institutions constructed by it? More ominously: If language itself is saturated with prejudice and error, then what are the prospects for these language-saturated institutions? Furthermore, language itself is an institution. Does language in some sense derive from nature, reflecting the laws and principles of a permanent reality? Or is it something that human beings invented as their way of communicating? Are there natural principles that govern (or should govern) its use? And do these have anything to do with the way language represents (or should represent) reality?

Plato and the Sophists

This brings us to rhetoric—the ancient practice and teaching of public discourse. And here we come to a quarrel that Plato himself instigated with the teachers of rhetoric in his days, known as sophists. The study of this quarrel is wonderfully instructive and complex, and its fundamental issues enter into discussions and controversies about the teaching of rhetoric and composition today (see Crowley; Scenters-Zapico; and Schiappa). Many of the actual writings of the ancient sophists are fragmentary or lost entirely; and there is a great deal of controversy about the value and even the content, in some cases, of sophistic teaching. (Much of what we know is from Plato himself, who may have distorted it in the process of opposing it.) Rather than attempting to contribute any new interpretation of the debate, I will give only a thumbnail sketch, concentrating on how it relates to the symmetry question.

In modern times, we have come to expect that a controversy about language arts will take the form of a debate about what works. We want everyone to read, write, and speak better. We want to achieve these things, but why are we not doing so? When we criticize a form of literacy education, our basic argument will be that it does not work or that it won't work. The ancient debate had quite a different shape, however. Plato's quarrel with the sophists began with the assumption, and indeed the observation, that the sophistic program was working—was working too well, in fact, and was about to destroy the Athenian state. All of the language-saturated institutions were, in Plato's view, being poisoned by a corrupted form of public discourse openly advocated by its most successful teachers.

The sophists advertised that they could ensure the success of young men about to enter public life by teaching them the skill most needed in their world—making speeches in public, primarily in courts of law, in legislative assemblies, and in public ceremonies. They did this by studying successful speeches and then, in the succinct phrase of James Murphy, "adducing useful precepts for the conduct of future discourse" (*A Synoptic History* 1). In time, the sophists accumulated a substantial body of precepts for each of the basic venues mentioned above, in five key areas: the conceptual or argumentative strategy of a speech (the art of invention, or in Greek "heuresis," the "finding" of a subject matter); the organizational plan of a speech (arrangement or disposition); the verbal strategy or style of a speech—effective selections of words, phrases, levels of diction, and figures of speech; the forceful and effective delivery of a speech; and a set of techniques for remembering the speech to be delivered. There were no doubt many varieties of approach, but two things in particular, fairly or unfairly, came to be regarded as hallmarks of sophistic teaching: a bold, unapologetic concentration on winning arguments rather than using language to discover and communicate truth; and a heavy emphasis on verbal strategy, or style—language in the primary sense. And both of these for the primary purpose of achieving personal success.

There exists everywhere a popular, visceral distrust of style over substance, contempt for slick manipulation over elemental sincerity. It was natural, therefore, that sophism would acquire something of an unsavory reputation, some of it no doubt unfair and ill-informed. However, Plato's objection to sophism went well beyond such commonplace distrust. Plato believed that sophism was based on and promoted a bad epistemology, was on the wrong side of the nature versus convention debate, and held a view of the symmetry question that placed excessive faith in the rightness and goodness of language itself. Most alarming to Plato was the claim of some sophists that a focus on acquiring sophistication in language would lead not only to success in speechmaking but also to a kind of wisdom.

An individual familiar with the practicalities of teaching speech or composition to young people might wonder out loud whether this is the sort of thing that really has power to pull down a republic. Many Athenians listening in on this debate undoubtedly did just that, and people in actual power are the sort to sneer at such a proposition. At all times it is worth keeping a measure of the distance between the practical and theoretical ends of an educational practice. Nevertheless, both Plato and the sophists knew that the stakes were higher than who would get the teaching contracts, and the claim about wisdom was more than just a bit of bravado or overblown advertising.

The question is always worth asking—especially in a time when so many teachers so often experience a sense of failure in what they are doing—the way Plato asked it: What if everything we are doing were completely successful? Would we be achieving for individuals and for society what we really want to achieve? The name "sophist" does mean "wise man," and although many sophists were undoubtedly content to attend to the practicalities of speechmaking, quite a few were serious philosophers in their own right. They had good reasons for including an overview of politics, law, and ethics (the basic subjects, after all, of speechmaking) in their teaching. And these views, like those of Plato's mentor Socrates, often constituted a serious challenge to the conventional thinking of their day. This is why Plato took them head on, in dialogues named after them: Protagoras, Gorgias, Hippias, and Prodicus.

All of the above is a frightfully compact summary of some well-known issues in the history of ancient rhetoric. Here is where we come to some of the surprises. A completely innocent observer, I should think, would expect the symmetrist—that is, the individual who posits a certain rightness about language—to be on the nature side of the nature versus convention debate, and also to be an optimist and a realist on the epistemological question. After all, if there is a stable order of nature, a coherent and well-constructed world out there, and if our minds and our language are part of that creation and participate in its essential features of design, then we should be in pretty good shape.

Does this sound like Plato? It is not. Although he is a realist on the epistemological question, he is *not* a symmetrist. He is firm on the question of whether there is a coherent reality outside of language, but he is very skeptical about the "power of language" to grasp it. In fact, it was only the Stoics who held tenaciously, even somewhat desperately, to both realism and symmetry. The interesting thing about the sophists, by contrast, is that they combined a belief in language with lack of belief in firm realities outside it. They combined linguistic symmetry with epistemological relativism and skepticism. This is what Plato considered a danger to society: For though language is not very good at grasping reality, it does have the power to charm, beguile, and persuade large audiences.

The sharpest edged, if not really the most formidable, of Plato's opponents was the sophist Gorgias, who combined a belief in the social power of language with a disbelief in its power to know anything, proclaiming famously and outrageously: "Nothing exists; if it did exist, we could not know it; and even if we could know it, we could not communicate it." We can, however, charm, beguile, persuade, and electrify audiences, and that is the juice that runs the world. It is altogether possible that Gorgias's famous saying is one of those flamboyant overstatements designed more to stir up reflection than to proclaim a serious position. A tamer and more careful restatement, if one may dare stand in for such a powerful orator, might go like this: "I'm not saying that there aren't real things out there, only that our institutions aren't universal, unchanging substances. We're always reshaping them in the here and now. I'm not saying that we can't know anything, only that we can't absolutely know anything, especially in human affairs. The most important thing is that knowledge is not always the issue. We're always having to decide what to do, what course is likely to be most successful, what to love and cling to and what to discard. These are matters about which we often have the least firm knowledge, and so knowledge plays only a minor role in the process. And besides, we shouldn't be so afraid of enchantment. It's lovely and it's fun. See my beautiful and playful little treatise, 'Encomium to Helen.'" Plato is not enchanted by this smooth talk, however, and he retorts as follows (my words again): "Gorgias talks about fun while the republic can hardly govern itself and is caught up in a tragically destructive war. The state is not about fun. As I recall, you're not really a citizen of Athens, are you, Gorgias? And trials for treason, such as the one that unjustly condemned to death my mentor Socrates, they're not about fun either. Truth is the issue, and eloquence is the problem. Look around you."

More of a challenge than Gorgias, in any case, and in its way more troubling, was a main line of sophism represented by Protagoras and Prodicus. These sophists did embrace symmetry, and they did so in a rather compelling way. There was a connection between language and the world, these teachers proclaimed, and those who were most adept at finding it would become both successful and wise in the process. These sophists offered an education based in language (a literary humanism), one that focused on procedures for finding the right words for things, claiming that language, cultivated in the proper ways, did have a hold on the truth—or such truth as we can have.

This formulation was more of a challenge for Plato because, in contrast to the provocations of Gorgias, it seemed attractive, sensible, and practical. It is in fact a kind of literary humanism that did survive and which many of us would like to endorse and to practice—it is possible that Plato himself would have liked to. In fact, many scholars believe that his writings on rhetoric and poetry, especially the beautiful dialogue *Phaedrus,* constituted a challenge to his own students to produce a philosophically defensible humanism, one that would have the power to reform as well as promote success in public discourse. Plato's student Aristotle was probably taking on just that challenge in his magnificent works on *Rhetoric* and *Poetics.*

Whatever constituted Plato's true feelings or hopes about rhetoric and poetry, however, the philosophical problems were substantial. While symmetry at some level would seem to be necessary for us to be able to know and communicate anything, there are two huge problems with it: first, it is virtually impossible to demonstrate, either practically or philosophically; and second, its natural and inevitable bedfellows are skepticism and relativism. Why? Because, strictly from the standpoint of what words and sentences refer to, the discrepancies, misalignments, and discontinuities between language and anything else are too numerous to ignore. The common language is manifestly soaked with error and prejudice, and although there would be no science of linguistics as such for about twenty-four centuries, intelligent individuals could observe that language was its own system, not just a subcategory or offshoot of some other, such as logic. And so, unless you wanted to claim that there is some sort of lost language that we need to recover, or some new philosophical language that we need to construct (and these are both positions that have been taken in the history of our subject) then language's real connection would have to be not to things but to the consciousness of things—to states of reality that are subjective and interior. And such things are notoriously unreliable and disreputable.

Plato takes up the symmetry question directly in his dialogue *Cratylus,* where the eponymous character returns from instruction by sophists. Cratylus has been persuaded that there must be an essential connection between words and things. If language is our basic instrument for discovering and communicating reality and if that instrument has no essential connection to reality, then what can we do? Socrates concludes, after a long and painstaking inquiry, that we cannot demonstrate any essential connection between words and things, or words and ideas either. The good news, however, is that this isn't necessary, because the mind has the capacity to apprehend reality directly. The mind does require training to do this, but it isn't a linguistic training that it requires. Listening to language doesn't really do you much good at all.

Now this is an interesting conclusion, and perhaps a liberation from terminal subjectivity. But even more interesting are the considerable energies that Socrates expends in exploring that other possibility, that is about possible forms of symmetry. In contrast with the way the conversation goes in some of the other dialogues—most especially the *Gorgias*—Socrates does not just set the opposition up to be denigrated. He engages in a real dialogue with his interlocutors. He really is intent, one feels, on carrying Cratylus's investigation as far as it will go.

Although some scholars have concluded that Plato's purpose here is to defend a symmetrist position, or at least to argue the urgent need for one (Genette 25–26; Krapp 130), modern historians of linguistics have demonstrated fairly conclusively that Plato is a confirmed asymmetrist. Nevertheless, the impression is inescapable that there is a stirring intellectual drama going on here. And while Plato directs us safely toward asymmetry, Socrates and the other characters do dramatize a deep fascination—again I defer to Gerard Genette's term "enchantment"—with that other thing, symmetry.

Many philosophers have considered the *Cratylus* as a kind of prolegomenon to Aristotle's massive works on logic and the principles of thought. The operating assumption of these works is that language is conventional and arbitrary but that categories of thought—what Socrates in the *Cratylus* terms "direct impressions of the soul"—are not. These impressions, not language, are our access to reality. However, if *Cratylus* is such a stalking horse, it is certainly a fanciful and deeply ambivalent one. The general case in favor of asymmetry, as I pointed out above, is not that difficult to make. What Socrates's basic excitement is about—the major thing that requires explaining—is that some words do reflect reality, some logoi, instances and acts of language, do penetrate. In these extraordinary cases, language, as Samuel Taylor Coleridge's wonderful formulation would state over two thousand years later, "partakes of the Reality which it renders intelligible" (*Statesman's Manual* 30).

To explain this mystery, Socrates engages in a bit of on the spot mythologizing: each language must have originally had a name giver. The character Cratylus gets very excited at this point and suggests that the name giver surely would have been a god, but Socrates lets it go. The important thing is that the name giver must have gotten some things right and some things wrong, and we can do likewise. Vivien Law, in her *History of Linguistics in Europe from Plato to 1600*, sums it up very succinctly:

> the fact that some words do appear to reflect reality overtly has an important implication: it suggests that it is possible to gain accurate knowledge of reality without using words. So we should not despair. Since the name-giver was able to perceive reality directly, so can we. Therefore, we should concentrate on getting to know reality directly, without bothering with inferior imitations—words. (23)

Plato, Vivien Law concludes, is now free to investigate other sources of knowledge, having dismissed as only partially true the idea that "language has truth encoded in its very words." And so, "Language no longer interests him" (23). That is certainly a just conclusion, and we will see another version of it in St. Augustine. However, the qualification, "only partially true," has to be one of the largest qualifications in the history of qualifications, since the entire argument hinges on it. We should keep in mind that there is another, poetic side of Plato, which comes out in such dialogues as *Phaedrus;* and that image of the name giver, who might have been a god, like the deep-running desire for that other thing, stays in the mind.

Saint Augustine and the Word of God

Aurelius Augustine, the powerful and influential theologian, controversialist, spiritualist, and church leader of Christianity in the late Roman Empire, began his professional life as a teacher of rhetoric. Latin had become the language of public life in lands under the control of Rome—Augustine was from a province of northern Africa, and he wrote in Latin. However, the "marriage to Latin," with its implications of the superiority and even holiness of the Latin language, had not yet taken place. From the evidence of an early textbook, *De Dialectica*, now attributed to him, he does seem to have started off a symmetrist. If so, the position is not in that work stated very passionately, and it would not have attracted much notice. In that little book, Augustine would have been taken as following that mild form of symmetry that persisted as a legacy of the sophistic tradition, and which had been tamed, qualified, and civilized in the great rhetorical works of Cicero and Quintilian. The symmetry question really began to excite him after his conversion to Christianity. It was then that he gave up teaching rhetoric, and in a startling passage from his autobiography that echoes Saint Paul, considered himself no longer a "salesman of words" (*Confessions* 9.2.2).

It's an unfortunate accident of history that Saint Augustine did not know the text of Plato's *Cratylus* when he composed his own very extensive reflections on the nature of linguistic signs. If he had, he surely would have had to do something with that character of Socrates's invention, the name giver. Such a figure would require more than passing reference from the man who was convinced that God created the universe through the Word, who was in the beginning with Him, and who sent the Word—the logos, Jesus Christ—as the historically decisive revelation to humankind (John, I). Surely enough, though, Augustine would have dismissed as a relic of paganism Cratylus's suggestion that the name giver was a god. If there was a name giver, it would have to be Adam, who in the book of Genesis was given the role of naming the animals.

However, that would not necessarily spoil the case for symmetry. After all, Augustine might have recognized him as the prelapsarian Adam, in command of a not yet fallen language. This might have been the Adam who would recall, as John Milton wrote twelve hundred years later, that he named the animals "as they passed, and understood / Their nature, with such knowledge God endued / My sudden apprehension" (*Paradise Lost* VIII, 352–54). Under such circumstances we might envision Augustine as the symmetrist par excellence, for whom the glory of God is revealed in all his creation, especially in the human mind and language. But in fact it is not so. Augustine remained a temperamental symmetrist all his life, but he did explicitly renounce symmetry in his theological works. Augustine taught that words are not natural signs but human inventions, and they have their meanings purely by agreement among their users, not on account of any connection to what they signify.

Of course, it could conceivably have been otherwise. Augustine was a fierce believer in original sin. The Fall led to the corruption of all earthly things, certainly including human speech. There is also the story of the Tower of Babel, recorded in the book of Genesis, in which the original language of mankind was dispersed into a confusion of tongues. Reflection on these possibilities might have sent Augustine on a search for the original, pure language, as it has sent others in the history of our subject (see Eco). However, it did not do so. Augustine did not believe in an Edenic perfect language (Lombardi 29). Communication before the Fall would have been direct, without the aid of language at all. In Augustine's view, language was something constructed by humans after the Fall. And so it is not simply a fallen language that we, the sons and daughters of Adam, speak, nor is it simply the fragment of some purer thing that existed before Babel.

On the ancient debate between nature and convention, Augustine's position was clearly what might be called Christian conventionalism. In this view, there exists a clear distinction between natural institutions (that is, things created by God) and human institutions (things created by humans and existing only by agreements among themselves). In Augustine's scheme of things, language (unlike the heavens, mathematics, or astonishingly, even rhetoric) is a human institution, and there is no connection between any of its parts and the rest of creation. For Augustine, even more so and more literally than for Samuel Johnson, words are completely the "daughters of earth," and not at all the "sons of heaven" (7).

By the way, individuals are not required to have a particular religious position in order to have a position on this question. It can be argued (and has been done convincingly by modern linguists) that language is a "natural institution" because a detailed capacity for it—what has been called "universal grammar"—exists as part of the structure of every human being's brain. The point is worth emphasizing here, because Augustine the fifth-century religionist comes across as much more modern than one might expect. One reason is that for Augustine the consequences of asymmetry are potentially more disturbing than they are for Plato and Aristotle.

Plato may have a lingering enchantment with symmetry, but he is willing to give it up for philosophical reasons. In fact, he needs language off center stage, because he has two more powerful players waiting in the wings: reason (the unaided apprehension of truth) and logic (a system for testing, refining, and proving what reason apprehends). Language's proper role is to be the transmitter of what reason discovers and logic approves. But for Augustine, reason and logic are not very reliable. They can be useful at times but they are fallen, along with every other human capability, and it is a mistake to place too much confidence in them. Augustine's ultimate solution, of course, is that the only thing in which we can have real confidence is the Word of God.

What is modern sounding about this very old-fashioned discourse is that Augustine's very distrust of reason and logic is shared by a strong segment of modern philosophy since the eighteenth century. Quite a few poets, philosophers, and literary humanists of the romantic period (think back to Coleridge) have not been troubled by losing confidence in reason. They too have had something else waiting in the wings: a powerful faith in language and imagination. But what happens if we have neither? The rather desolate landscape of a human society without much confidence in either reason or language is one that Augustine shares with some of the most notorious asymmetrists of the modern age, Jacques Derrida and Jacques Lacan.

Another way in which Augustine commands special attention is that he is virtually the only premodern thinker to use that very modern terminology of signs and referents (Todorov, "The Birth of Western Semiotics"). Augustine first develops such a terminology in the dialogue entitled *De Magistro*—the master, or teacher. This is a treatise that he later said (in the *Confessions*) was based on an actual dialogue with his son Adeodatus. In the dialogue, the youthful Adeodatus plays a role similar to that of Cratylus—that is, the character who wants very badly for there to be a natural connection between words and things. But Augustine, his father and teacher, talks him out of this. After a long and playfully tedious discussion—for which he apologizes more than once—Augustine arrives at a paradox: You cannot know anything except through words, but the most that words can do for you is to remind you of something you already know. And so, how—beyond simple objects that somebody can point to as they are named—can you come to know anything that you didn't already know?

We may be reminded at this point of a wonderful speculation by Plato, in the dialogue entitled *Meno*. He concludes there that all significant knowing, beyond things that can be simply pointed to, is in fact a remembering, of things preexisting in the mind but obscured by such distractions as being born. The example he puts forward is the Pythagorean theorem, which he "teaches" on the spot to an attendant servant boy who has had no introduction whatever to mathematics. But Augustine would dismiss all of this as a pagan superstition. The point that he wants to drive home to Adeodatus is that the only way you can know anything important is through the assistance of an inner teacher—the magister—who is Christ.

In his *Retractions,* Augustine said that his purpose in *De Magistro* was not really to erect a comprehensive theory of language but to demonstrate that our most important knowledge comes from revelation, not from reason. It is important to keep in mind that he never departed from this distrust in reason, for it is possible to see in some of his later writings a movement toward symmetry. In the treatise *On the Trinity,* Augustine engages in a powerful set of speculations on that most fascinating of concepts, logos—in Augustine's Latin, verbum. There are three important meanings packed into it. In its most literal sense, of course, logos means a word, a separate and delimited set of sounds pointing to something; but more commonly in traditional usage, it means a saying or an act of speaking. For Augustine and for Christians, it means more: a specific fund of speech, the Word of God as recorded in the Bible. And finally, it also names the second person of the Christian Trinity, Jesus Christ, the Word of God.

What is the logic behind the connection of Jesus to the Word? This is a difficult question that most commentators, both secular and religious, tend to avoid. Here is a partial answer: Keep in mind that speaking is acting, and acting is speaking. Language performs actions even as it "says" things about the world. Actions send messages, even as they do their work in the world. When you say to your partner that the garbage can is full, you are probably reminding (instructing?) him or her to take the garbage out. When you bring your friend a present, you may be saying that you love this person, or perhaps that you are sorry for acting so bitter about the garbage. To Jewish and Christian believers, when God said, "Let there be light," he was most definitely doing something: He was creating the world with words. In *The Rhetoric of Religion,* Kenneth Burke points out that Babylonian, Egyptian, and Indian cosmologies also employ the "divine word" as an agent of creation (11).

But the divine word also takes the form of action. To Christian believers, when God sent his son, he was speaking—sending a definitive message to the world—in the Biblical phrase, "the word made flesh" (see Lombardi 41–43). Questions of belief aside, this ancient complexity of the term logos captures a powerful insight—the interconnection of speaking and acting. This interconnection has become one of the ripest topics in all of modern linguistics and language philosophy.

Augustine was interested in the connections among all these meanings of logos, but neither he nor Christianity invented the complexity. The term logos packed in a number of significant meanings before Christianity added even more. In Greek philosophy it became synonymous with reason, connected with the Stoic conviction that the symmetry of language resides in its connection to the ideas of things, not the things themselves. In Greek rhetoric, logos refers specifically to the appeal to reason, as opposed to the appeal to emotion (pathos), or to the character of the speaker (ethos) in persuading an audience. It was in the Jewish and Christian religions, however, that the term acquired a mystical significance. Since logos was God's way of creating the world, then the Word must contain powerful insights about the world; and there you have it: symmetry.

For Christians there was even more, of course. Since the Son of God was the logos, who was with God at the beginning, it was also through the Son that the world was created: "In the beginning was the Word, and the Word was with God, and the Word was God. The same was in the beginning with God. All things were made by him; and without him was not any thing made that was made" (John I, 1–3). It would be possible to conclude that language is definitely worth listening to, something that contains the deepest religious truth. Indeed, serious thinkers in modern times have felt, without necessarily endorsing any specific religious belief, that the concept of logos in the traditions of Judaism and Christianity possesses a significant wisdom about language (Burke, *Rhetoric of Religion*; Frye). However, we should not get excited just yet. The difficulty with attributing this specific version of symmetry to Augustine is that, in the orthodox view that he helped to establish, it was not language itself but God's specific revelatory acts, both speaking and acting, that were generally taken to have this kind of shimmering significance. And this was the case not only in mainline Christian theology but also in the Jewish cabala, an interpretive tradition that took as its project the unraveling of spiritual secrets, not in language per se but in God's language, in the ways specific Hebrew words and even letters were combined in the Torah.

What makes Augustine's speculations in *On the Trinity* seem intriguingly contemporary is the terminology he develops in his analysis of the connections among the three forms of logos: logos as an act of speech, logos as the Word of God (scripture), and logos as Jesus Christ. In explaining how we are able to receive wisdom from scripture, Augustine makes a distinction between "outer word," ("vox") and "inner word" ("verbum"); and these are terms that remind us distinctly of the modern linguistic distinction between surface structure (the outer syntactic form of sentences) and deep structure (the conceptual underlay to which they are systematically connected).

In Augustine's view, the outer word does not give you knowledge of things, but instead directs you to the inner word, Jesus Christ. This presence, or teacher, will reveal to you to the scripture's true significance. This is one of the theoretical bases of the allegorical interpretation of scripture, which prevailed in medieval times. The allegorical or spiritual (inner) meaning of a text—a bright and shining revelation from God—is more important than its literal, historical (outer) meaning, which may appear strange and incomprehensible.

What's fascinating about Augustine's interpretation of logos is that it appears to acknowledge the possibility of symmetry, and it is certainly an optimistic revision of the rather bleak view of human language in *De Magistro*. Taken as a explanation, or even as an allegory, of what happens when we talk or listen, this view looks compatible with the Stoic belief that language's natural connection is not to things but to concepts. It might also be seen as a precursor to the linguistic notion of universal grammar, that magisterial inner wiring that is distinctively human.

Nevertheless, there is no hard evidence that Augustine's rather pessimistic view of the human condition underwent any revision at all. The concept of verbum or word in *On the Trinity* is quite compatible with that of the inner teacher in *De Magistro*. And Augustine did in his later treatise *On Christian Doctrine* hold explicitly to the view of language as a human institution, whose signs are arbitrary and conventional. In this case, as with Plato, both language and rhetoric are the carriers of truths derived elsewhere, and they should be disciplined to that task.

Some of the truths that language carries, however, are of the most extraordinary kind. They are to be found in God's word—inspired writings. And here is the basis for what might be termed, paradoxically, an Augustinian literary humanism. We find it in the way that multiple meanings unfold from the Word of God. A central question in this inquiry has been whether the process described in *On the Trinity* is meant to account for logos—all speech—or logos the Word of God, specifically holy scripture; and there are, we must admit, very substantial indications that the latter is the case. For Augustine, as for Plato, ordinary language lacks referential power. Its grasp of the world around it is very tenuous; however, this is a proposition that cuts both ways. If language lacks a firm grasp on the world, then the world also lacks a firm grasp on language, and language is not tied simply to its referential function. By insisting on the arbitrary and conventional nature of literal reference, Augustine is doing more than emphasizing the poverty and fallen state of human speech. He is clearing a path for its freedom. Without the kind of referential confinement that symmetry would imply (either to earthly things or to mere human thoughts) language is free to be the instrument of higher things—nothing less, in fact, than the carrier and expositor of logos. This will certainly be an arduous thing to understand, may in fact require considerable linguistic ability and training. It may occasionally require ways of talking and speaking that are considerably out of the ordinary.

Lovers of language and rhetoric are by no means out of work. Augustine did not, like other early Christian fathers, reject rhetoric as an unnecessary relic of the pagan past. Nor did he spurn other forms of secular learning and literature. In the treatise *On Christian Doctrine*, he preserves a respectable place, if not a starring role, for language and rhetoric. And there may be more: revelation has taken place not only in singular events but also through the medium of language, in the Word of God. In its journey through the prism of ordinary, asymmetrical language, logos takes on unusual forms and bright, scary colors that symmetry can neither grasp nor express.

The rhetoric inherited from Rome shored up and augmented such symmetries as existed. It intended to promote a discourse that was as close to the truth as possible: correct, clear, and appropriate to the scene and the subject. In this tradition the main purpose of *figurative* language—later referred to as "colors"—was to add a sense of dignity. This was the classical theory of style in a nutshell, as Augustine knew it. But scripture seemed far otherwise—in fact, an embarrassment to some, though not to the converted Augustine. In apparent violation of the canons of rhetoric, scripture seemed full of obscurities, inexplicable happenings and sayings, indecorous language, and inscrutable symbols. Here is something of immense interest to literary humanists: What is true of the Bible in this respect is also true of much of the world's great imaginative literature. Both can be frighteningly indecorous and implausible at times, and both are shot through with meanings beneath and beyond the surface.

We are back to a central question, which has its analogue in theology. It is no accident that one of the great controversies of the Christian church has been the question of how open or closed, public or personal is the fund and process of revelation. This is essentially the question of whether logos is confined to scripture and its central revelatory events or whether it is present in individual lives, history, and inspired literature. Religious scholars have found the seeds of powerful arguments for both sides in Augustine's works.

Clearly, Augustine regards the Bible as the primary inspired literature—not just ordinary speech but a special privileged speech, the Word of God. Moreover, there is not much doubt that he would be quick to endorse a teaching based on authoritative interpretations of scripture over any other source of inspiration. In one of his sermons he endorses emphatically "the true, the right Catholic faith, gathered not by the opinion of private judgment, but by the witness of the Scriptures, not subject to the fluctuations of heretical rashness, but grounded upon Apostolic truth..." (*Sermons* 34). Nevertheless, it is also clear that Augustine saw in his own life a continuous and progressive pattern of revelation, and that is why he wrote what is the Western world's first autobiography, *Confessions*. You don't have to believe in its religion to know that it is a wonderful book. What is immediately obvious about Augustine's autobiographical writing, in Latin or in translation, is that it is charged with a copious, exuberant, playful, and mind-stretching rhetoric. Its rhetoric is to some degree the rhetoric that Augustine learned from the so-called late sophistic side of classical rhetoric, which promoted dazzling verbal display over the more dignified and content-oriented Ciceronian program of clarity and decorum. But one can also see a language that has gone to logos and has come back with bright, shining colors. Language is asymmetrical, but it can be symmetrized, or re-symmetrized, in its contact with truth.

This review of ancient asymmetry yields some fascinating insights that serve as a foundation for further exploration of the symmetry question and its relations to literary humanism. By looking at figures such as Plato, the sophists, and Augustine, we realize that asymmetry is not the exclusive preserve of modern linguistics or of postmodern literary theory. Furthermore, interesting and powerful ways of teaching the use of language can flow from either side of the symmetry question. Symmetry may venerate great literature as something that recovers and exploits the deep connections of language to experience. Asymmetry, by contrast, may adore the discourse that powerful inspiration shapes to beautiful and extraordinary forms. What nearly all writers—and not just literary artists—will agree is that beautiful and revelatory things sometimes happen in the *process* of making discourse. The truly interesting questions for literary humanism are functional: What assists that process? And what gets in the way? Outlooks that are philosophically opposed may be functionally reciprocal.

Literary humanists are motivated by the love of language and its works, valuing those uses of language that do not merely encode but enact—and discover by enacting—the meanings they convey. We know, moreover, that language arts are connected to the intellectual growth of individuals and to the health and sanity of society. Literary humanists are not warm to the message that language is its own system, closed off from the things that matter. But this feeling does not have to imply automatic rejection or acceptance of any particular theory of language. The important thing is to listen carefully.

Asymmetry is not such a bad thing. It does not mean the alienation of language from experience (as "arbitrariness," the term most often used by linguists, has sometimes implied) but rather the freedom of specific forms from specific references and the possibility of new meanings. Functionally, the phenomenon of asymmetry exists in fruitful correlation with symmetry, both in the linguistic system and in the best individual expression and literary performance. Ultimately, it is valuable to explore ways in which language is *free from*, as well as *engaged in*, significance.

Symmetry, clearly the more enchanting of the two propositions, has always been more difficult to prove, and also the most vulnerable to error. It has nearly always been mistaken, for instance, to think that mastery of particular linguistic forms (such as the different sentence types or complex syntactic structures) will lead to other, "higher" kinds of mastery. We must, however, keep asking significant questions: What are the true, vital ways in which language participates in the world, and what does it discover by enacting its meanings? How can we energize the language arts with the knowledge of these things? It is true that the formal study of language, like all science, is primarily about mechanism. However, the science of language was born out of the desire to understand more deeply the meaning as well as the mechanism of language, and linguistics has found some interesting new ways of doing that by forging new links with cultural criticism.

Suggested Reading

Barney, Rachel. *Names and Nature in Plato's Cratylus*. New York: Routledge, 2001. This study makes better sense than any other of Socrates's apparent ambivalence about the symmetry of linguistic forms. Barney suggests that Socrates's conventionalism is about verbal forms or designations, whereas his continuing excitement is about the process of naming in language.

Derrida, Jacques. *Of Grammatology*. Trans. Gaytria Spivak. 2nd ed. Baltimore: Johns Hopkins University Press, 1976. Among all of Derrida's writing, this work contains his most explicit statements about the impossibilities of reference; the things which language attempts to name "have always already escaped, have never existed." Language is caught up in an infinite chain of substitute references, and thus meaning is always endlessly postponed or deferred.

Lacan, Jacques. "The Instance of the Letter in the Unconscious, or Reason Since Freud." *Ecrits: The First Complete Edition in English*. Trans. Bruce Fink. New York: W. W. Norton, 2007. 412–44. After Derrida, Lacan is probably the second most famous asymmetrist of the modern period. This essay contains his influential reflections on the principle, extrapolated from Saussure, that "no signification can be sustained except by reference to another signification" (415).

Lombardi, Elena. *The Syntax of Desire: Language and Love in Augustine, The Modistae, Dante*. Toronto: University of Toronto Press, 2007. Lombardi's chapter on "Augustine: The Syntax of the Word" (22–76) makes interesting observations on the various senses of "verbum," as Augustine would have known and used it.

Markus, R. A. "St. Augustine on Signs." *Phronesis* 2 (1957): 60–83. Rpt. in *Augustine: A Collection of Critical Essays*. Ed. R. A. Markus. Garden City: Anchor, 1972. 61–91. This remains the best single analysis of Augustine's theory of language.

Ringer, Jeffrey. "Faith and Language: Walter Hilton, St. Augustine, and Poststructural Semiotics." *Christianity and Literature* 53 (2003): 3–18. This provocative essay draws parallels between Augustine's asymmetrism and that of the modern post-structuralists Derrida and Lacan.

Schiappa, Edward. *Protagoras and Logos: A Study in Greek Philosophy and Rhetoric*. Columbia: University of South Carolina Press, 1991. This is one of the best expositions of the sophistic position on language and rhetoric in the ancient world.

3

Six Claims of Symmetry

A literature student's frustration and disappointment with English linguistics very often begins with the first chapter of the linguistics textbook, which typically opens with a discussion of the linguistic sign or symbol. The crucial, distinguishing feature of the linguistic symbol as opposed to natural or animal signs, the text reads, is its arbitrariness—its lack of a formal connection to (or resemblance to) the thing it signifies. This is commonly put forward as a first principle of linguistics and a pervasive feature of language itself. There is nothing controversial about it. At the simplest level, there is nothing in the word "tree" that resembles a tree or expresses the character of a tree. This apartness from the thing signified, we are informed, is displayed at all levels of organization—phonetic, morphological, syntactic—and the progression never seems to stop.

Arbitrariness is exciting to the linguist. It is precisely this freedom from bondage to things (or to ideas for that matter) that makes possible the infinite use of finite means uniquely characteristic of human language. It also makes language an independent field of study, not a subcategory of some other field such as logic or psychology. To the student of literature, however, the celebration of arbitrariness can be dissonant, because it seems to go against one of literature's first principles. What excites the student of literature about the literary symbol is what excited S. T. Coleridge: it "partakes of the Reality which it renders intelligible" (*Statesman's Manual* 30). It is its simultaneous involvement in, enactment of, and revelation about experience. The linguistic symbol, by contrast, is presented to us as a serviceable throwaway, a mere designator, a "counter," as the seventeenth-century philosopher Thomas Hobbes put it (29). It is neither involved in what it signifies nor particularly revelatory about it.

This particular problem might well be addressed by a more expansive and insightful presentation on the part of the linguistics textbook writer. Of course, the textbook might concede that language in artistic use does participate quite deeply in the experience it signifies, and the student might realize that star player the literary symbol has to be supported by a stage, crew, and a cast of thousands (that is, words), only a few of which can be particularly significant. But these stipulations would not address the frightening apartness of language when considered objectively as a system of signifiers.

Many textbooks also begin in a more expansive way, calling attention to language's centrality to every form of human endeavor, implying that to know a good deal about language is to know a good deal about human life and culture. The text will quickly plunge, however, into the miraculously intricate system of language itself, very much its own thing, marvelously efficient, and marvelously free. The perceptive student may conclude one of two things: either that language has no secrets to reveal, except about itself; or that if it does provide broader insights, these revelations only come after a much deeper study than this introductory approach will ever acknowledge. The student may also be disappointed to learn that there are very few interventions of a strictly linguistic sort that will improve writing or speaking. Linguists are generally skeptical about such things and even opposed to them.

This is not just a problem of textbooks, or even of particular methods, or language philosophies. It is a problem of language itself. It is true that modern linguistics has often allied itself with a philosophy of mechanism or behaviorism that limits its gaze to forms and processes only. There does exist, meanwhile, a more expansive tradition of philosophical semantics, much more congenial to the interests of literary humanists, and represented most notably in the twentieth century by Kenneth Burke. This tradition has not been very interested in the plumbing and wiring of language, however, or in the standard fare of linguistics. It has gone in a different direction, attempting to fathom the meanings of symbolism in culture and in the individual psyche (see Robinson). However, this very division is symptomatic of the broader condition: One side is often factually solid but not very illuminating, and the other side is often intellectually stimulating but very speculative. Moreover, the problem is not simply a modern one. In the history of speculation and inquiry about language, the strong intuition of symmetry and the desire to make something of it have run up against the formidable barricades of asymmetry. It is fruitful to consider the many conspicuous claims and counterclaims not as arguments for one side or the other but rather as the reciprocal components of any language-saturated activity.

Asymmetry is not simply a special disappointment to the lover of literature; it is counterintuitive, even for individuals who are not symmetrists of the first order. Even granting that the knowledge of things is separate from their articulation, and even realizing that most of what we normally say is a kind of pointing to something else, most of us do experience a feeling of rightness in the presence of something said or written well. The author has discovered or happened upon just the right words, just the right form for expressing something. This is what English teachers love, and this love motivates them to help others accomplish it. It's not surprising, therefore, that symmetry has been the default position of common sense as well as a motivating hypothesis of most literary humanism. Asymmetry has most often emerged as a corrective.

Claim 1: The Symmetry of Sounds

Some proponents of symmetry have argued that the sounds of language, although time has wrought distortions in many of them, imitate sounds in the world. The sounds of language can also convey the quality of such nonauditory phenomena as hardness, softness, speed, and thickness. They also project—purely as sound—such basic human responses as anger, affection, hostility, and surprise. This is true not only of the external sounds themselves but also of the actions of human speech organs that produce them (the pursing of lips, the gritting of teeth, and so forth). There is much to be learned in studying these things in the older forms of words. One of the purposes of poetry is to restore or replicate the primal connection of the sounds of language to experience.

Commentary

It's not surprising that this proposition of symmetry is perhaps the most basic yet, at the same time, most easily disappointed expectation about language's relation to the world. It is a basic claim because language is an auditory medium, and it is the most easily disappointed because the narrow selection of sounds employed by any human language (usually placed at between forty and sixty sounds) stands in obvious and stark contrast to the immense matter outside of language. This claim of symmetry is also the first possibility that Socrates mentions in the *Cratylus*, and it is also swiftly refuted.

Although the sound-sense correlation has always been fertile ground for poets and discussions of poetry, most poets view their work as the artful crafting of resources on the surface rather than the recovery of a deep underground repository of meaning. No broader literary humanism has ever been extrapolated from it. We should not just dismiss it out of hand, however. Like most intuitions of symmetry, it is based on *something*, and understanding that something can help us understand other claims as well.

Beyond the exceedingly limited words that directly imitate sounds in any language, some basis does exist for a more generalized sound symbolism. Given an either-or selection, for instance, everyone would choose "oom" for roundness and softness and "teek" for sharpness and narrowness. But the range of such sound-sense connections is actually very limited, and they usually go unnoticed except where authors make deliberate attempts (as in poetry) to coordinate them with specific tones of voice, situations, and meanings. Gerard Genette has collected some interesting historical attempts to locate broader systems of sound symbolism, such as the following:

shr—contraction
gr—rough, hard
sw—slight lateral movement
cl—adherence, retention
str—(initial) force or strength
thr—violent movement
wr—twisting
br—breach, splitting apart

This is an abbreviated version of an inventory of initial consonant clusters by the Englishman John Wallis in 1653 (cited in Genette 37–38). Although these sound-sense correlations are initially intriguing, it quickly becomes apparent that they are based more on their association with selected words (shrink, growl, swish, and so forth) than on any consideration of the sound qualities themselves. Alternate words with no such semantic connections (shrine, greet, sweet, and so forth) readily come to mind; and the game is lost completely if you carry it to different languages.

Another interesting fact noted by Genette plays into our discussion: As an English Protestant, Wallis was sympathetic to the Puritan campaign to break free from any allegiance to or dependence on the Latin Bible, commentaries, or the theology of the Roman Catholic Church. A broader purpose of his treatise, *Gramatica Linguae Anglicanae* (written in Latin, primarily for foreigners) was to demonstrate the greater expressiveness of English, a vernacular language, over Latin. Naturally, the particular sound-sense correlations in his scheme work better for English, and an unsympathetic paraphrase of Wallis's argument might go like this: "For a speaker of English, there is something more natural and true-sounding about the way words sound in English. Here are some clusters of auditory association that contribute to that sense."

This unfriendly paraphrase leads to another fascinating point: the feeling of comfortable naturalness is actually likely to persist only so long as we do not notice correlations of sound and sense, and that means there should not be too many of them. When we hear a lot of them, we do notice them, and then we recognize the poetic device of onomatopoeia. And then, suddenly, things are not natural at all. This is an important point, because it illustrates an essential principle of the symmetry debate: In all our speaking and writing, symmetry and asymmetry constitute a double desire and a double need. While we do want language to connect to the world, most of the time we want the *forms* of language, particularly the sounds of language, to be out of the way. A language too full of sound-sense correlations would lose the transparency and flexibility required to convey messages clearly and efficiently. A language required to have sound-sense correlations would be too large to be manageable (in its attempt to cover everything) or too small to be useful. Language would quickly expand beyond the number of forms that humans could remember; or it would shrink below the range of things that humans need to talk about.

If the case for the symmetry of sounds is so easily dismantled from the standpoint of reasoned observation, why does the symmetry of sound and sense remain such a strong intuition? Must there exist such an unbridgeable divide between the conclusions of science and the feelings and prejudices of humans? Textbooks in linguistics very often imply such a divide. My thesis, to the contrary, is that while specific claims of symmetry are often incorrect, the intuition of symmetry is never simply wrong. In this case, there are two considerations that not merely explain but, to some extent, validate the intuition of symmetry.

First, as recent work in anthropology has uncovered, there does exist a rather firm substrate (albeit a narrow one) of sound symbolism that may cut across the world's languages (see Nuckolls). Second, as is apparent from this work, a good deal of what is called (or perceived as) sound symbolism is based on something other than strict correlations of form and meaning. The phenomenon of magnitude sound symbolism is a case in point. This refers to the various raisings, lowerings, and in-between modulations of voice that convey a great deal of meaning in actual oral performance. Some of this symbolism may be universal (anger, for instance), while a good deal will differ from culture to culture. The important thing is that with such phenomena as magnitude, we experience a transition from linguistic form to performance in language. As with all transitions from one serious thing to another, it's difficult to locate the exact line of demarcation. The critic Julia Kristeva notes approvingly that for primitive peoples language "is not conceived as a mental elsewhere, or as an abstract thought process. It participates as a cosmic element of the body and nature, and is joined with the motor force of the body and nature" (*Language—The Unknown* 50). Whether or not such a primitive view can be validated, it does capture an insight too often lost to linguistics in the tradition of Saussure, which the modern field of pragmatics has attempted to recapture: that is the transitional zone between language as mental system and language as social performance. The feeling of rightness that we feel about language is substantially derived from the successful performance of actions and meanings in language, either spontaneously enacted in speech situations, artfully dramatized in ritual and dramatic art, or scripted and simulated in writing.

With the transition from linguistic form to linguistic performance, we come to a crucial point where our regret for an imagined lost symmetry of forms can be shed. We can in fact begin to celebrate the possibilities of asymmetry. With the sounds of language in particular, there is a process of change and forgetting, which over long periods of time obliterates associations that may have once existed. A language that is (mostly) free of such elemental connections to the world is a language that is out of the way, allowing humans to carry out both their social and intrapersonal business. It is a language that can be even more expressive, at particular moments, of such things as elemental sincerity. With respect to sounds or sound combinations and particular meanings, the achievements of poets are more often constructions rather than recoveries of sound and sense. And these constructions are made possible by the freedom and adaptability of linguistic forms, not their fixed relation to meanings.

It does remain true, of course, that the love of good writing tends toward the love of the perfect way of saying things—just the right correlation of form and meaning. However, we must also reserve an equal amount of appreciation for new and surprising ways of saying things. The experience of comfort and rediscovery that we get from symmetry is challenged and sometimes bested by the startling new discoveries that we get from asymmetry. There do exist in any language community a fund of expected correlations of form and meaning, not just in sound but at all levels of structure. Some of these correlations are grounded in natural connection. Most, however, are primarily shaped through custom and usage over time, and as human customs, usages, and practices they can be shed and, in some cases, even shattered altogether. Good writing knows how to respect and to exploit these connections, when the time is right, but also how to do something new, and occasionally how to shatter them.

Claim 2: The Symmetry of Words

Although most of the sounds of words in a language do not directly correlate to their meanings, symmetrists will argue that there still exists a certain logic about words, giving them a recoverable "when-you-think-about-it" connection to the things or experiences they signify. Studying words, especially their original meanings, can lead to greater knowledge of things as well as to more precise and varied usage. Finding the right words for things—a process aided by knowledge of their histories—can create a more exact and a more persuasive discourse.

Commentary

This is a much more defensible position than the attempt to connect sounds to the world. It appears to be so reasonable and circumspect that it would seem pedantic to object. It is a stance that acknowledges that most words derive not directly from experience but from other words. This process of derivation takes place through multiple activities—compounding, borrowing, functional or semantic shifts from existing forms, and so on. As a consequence, laying aside the mystery of how languages originated (and how certain things were named in the first place), we can usually uncover how a particular entity received its name. The reason for its name is usually *not* arbitrary (although it may seem fanciful after centuries of social and historical change); and its uncovering is often instructive. Here is a classic example: The word "bedlam" is a phonological reduction of "Bethlehem." In fifteenth-century London, the old priory of Saint Mary of Bethlehem was converted into a hospital for the mentally deranged. Subsequently, "Bethlehem" or "bedlam" came to be used for any scene of disorder, uproar, or confusion.

All of this is true enough. It is a good reason why asymmetry is a better term than arbitrariness for the loose, rather than one-to-one, association of linguistic forms and meanings. It is also the reason why a good unabridged dictionary should be close at hand to any educated person. A salient question for literary humanism, though, lies in the distinction that we saw in the dialogue *Cratylus*, where Socrates insists that there is an important difference between whether things are well-named (in most cases, yes) and whether they are significant (usually, no). In this distinction we find the symmetry question laid bare: do names tell us very much about the deep meanings or essential nature of things? Socrates's answer is, not very often and not to any great degree. Think about "bedlam." Does knowing its derivation tell you very much, either psychologically about mental illness, or sociologically about states of disorder and confusion?

What etymologists have to acknowledge is that names are usually based on an external characteristic of the thing being named, and languages are quite haphazard and promiscuous in selecting the particular characteristic on which a name will be based. In some cases it may be the color of a thing, in others its height, in others speed or function, and so on. Even in such transparent processes as compounding, the selection and semantic ordering of terms seems to depend less on an exact logic than on the linguistic resources conveniently at hand. Consider the different logical relationships between the base elements in the following compounds:

floppy disk   disk that is floppy
book bag   bag for carrying books

winepress	device for extracting juice from grapes
steakhouse	"house" (eating establishment) specializing in steaks
storehouse	"house" (building) where goods are stored
flophouse	"house" (hotel) where one can "flop" (hobo slang for "lie down," to sleep); cheap hotel of disrepute

What is fascinating is that we process these types of relationships, even though the form is exactly the same, with no conscious effort and usually without even any conscious awareness of the compound status of the words. In Genette's terms, we accept them as single "designations" rather than significations or expressions of particular meanings (Genette 16–17). In most cases, we can be thankful that this extra load of meaning is out of the way. It's significant that many words that now present themselves to us as singular units were originally compounds. Their exterior forms have been obscured by the process of phonological reduction or simple forgetting. Here is a famous example that illustrates both processes: The form "-wich" in the name "Greenwich" is a now forgotten term for "town." Hence the name "Greenwich Village" is, strictly speaking, redundant.

It is important not to confuse expressiveness with accuracy. It is certainly true that some words designate particular things more accurately than other, related ones. There is a difference, for instance, between an "accident" and a "mistake." If you look up the etymologies of these words, you will find a logic behind the different meanings of these words. However, even when they are being most careful about it, writers and speakers are not aware of, nor do they care about, the etymological background of these terms. What they care about is the difference of meaning itself, to which the etymology will only sometimes provide an accurate clue. If you are dealing with individuals who persistently portray their "mistakes" as "accidents," you may have to read out the dictionary definitions to them, but the etymologies are not going to help much unless they are trained philologists. Most of the time, bringing in the etymologies would be considered a distraction, a pedantic one at that.

This case parallels that of the potential symmetries of sound. We need insignificance as much as we need significance in order to accomplish very much with language. Too many terms vying for attention in a discourse would be like several instruments contending for the lead in a concerto at the same time. Once we develop a taste for asymmetry in words (which is really a taste for freedom of choice in speaking and writing), it is easier to identify the benefits. As a cardinal instance, it is readily apparent that words need to be able to assume multiple meanings and uses. No individual's active vocabulary can be more than a small fraction of the recorded words of a language, and the core vocabulary of any language will contain an even smaller fraction, consisting of words that are recycled into multiple senses. Consider the words "have," "thing," "do," and "take," each of which functions as a kind of stand-in, playing all sorts of impromptu roles in the rush of spontaneous conversation. Moreover, language needs this flexibility over periods of time as well as in given moments of history to account for new experiences, while remaining learnable and shareable between generations.

The process of semantic change, which has sometimes been lamented by literary humanists because it obscures the meanings of older texts, must in this light be considered to have its considerable benefits as well. Semantic change works together with phonetic change to create a process of forgetting that is both useful and necessary. In its simplest and most transparent application, semantic change is that process that makes a word like "car" adaptable to new technologies, so that what used to mean a horse-drawn wagon now means a motorized vehicle. The same process frees the word "go" from "riding on a horse"—this was its specific meaning—to any kind of moving about. It is well-known by etymologists that the term "fee" long ago had something to do with cattle, while the term "villain" long ago had something to do with agricultural labor. However, both of these terms have long ago been liberated from these associations. It is true enough that the etymologies of such terms reveal interesting bits of social history; but no one would seriously propose that there are lasting, subconscious implications of bovinity or agricultural labor lurking in our ordinary uses of these words.

Points well taken, but here comes a question exactly parallel to the one that arose regarding sound symbolism: if these etymologies are of such little actual significance to usage, why are literary humanists, poets, and word lovers of all sorts so taken with them? This interest is more than antiquarian curiosity, and something aside also from scholarly interest in the history of the language as spoken. It stems from a broader intuition of symmetry that is true, arising in the presence of words exactly and creatively chosen and used to make a difference in the world. As with the symmetry of sounds, the interest lies in the realm of successful performance more than of formal properties. Literary humanists are legitimately devoted to the love and encouragement of this performance, and clearly this performance should not be grounded solely upon etymology.

Claim 3: The Symmetry of Grammar

Allowing for surface anomalies and exceptions, symmetrists have argued that the structures and operations of grammar offer reliable connections to fundamental structures and operations of thought, to larger units of discourse, and perhaps to reality itself. Therefore, the study of grammar and the production of sophisticated grammatical structures leads to greater sophistication of thought and skill in composition.

Commentary

One of the most interesting things about this claim is its modernity. Grammar in its ancient meaning of "skill in letters" has always been foundational in the sense of providing the basics of reading and writing. However, in ancient teaching there is virtually no mention of grammar as something that contributes directly to the development of thinking or learning ability. In both Greek and Roman schooling, when grammar went beyond the function of imparting basic literacy and good usage, it involved the reading of literature. For Roman students, this could mean literature in Greek, and consequently the extensive study of grammar was already associated with learning a foreign tongue. Grammar books were written primarily to assist in the reading and translation of literature, or as in the case of the Roman grammarian Varro, as theoretical works.

The next fourteen centuries of European history would experience the ascendancy of Latin. In the Middle Ages, grammar became the first stage of the trivium, the elementary series of grammar, logic, and rhetoric; but the term grammatica was virtually synonymous with teaching and learning the universal second language, Latin. Nowhere in either ancient or medieval schooling are there examples of systematic training in the grammar (sentence structure) of one's native language as a mental discipline. Nor do we find claims or suggestions of a strong association between correct speaking and writing and correct thinking.

On the side of philosophical speculation there were, to be sure, efforts in medieval thought to elevate grammar to a philosophical subject. The so-called modistae grammarians of twelfth-century France attempted to link grammatical categories (such as noun, verb, nominative, accusative, and so on) with Aristotelian categories of being (such as substance, quality, action, and so on). These grammarians, however, were not very interested in teaching grammar in the modern sense. They were chiefly interested in the philosophical and theological implications of the subject.

In any case, there were major obstacles from the outset. It was in fact at the level of grammar that discrepancies between language and thought had always been the most immediate causes of doubts about symmetry. The basic grammatical categories, while easy to identify formally, are maddeningly difficult to pin down conceptually. Nouns, for instance, are supposed to name persons, places, or things. But what really are such "things" as a "bath," "sorrow," "immediacy," a "project," a "mistake," a "program," or indeed a "language"? The word "thing" itself is shockingly omnivorous—look in any unabridged dictionary. The best we can do is to say that nouns are the names of "all sorts of things." More accurately, we can say that language is capable of treating multiple categories (actual things, actions, qualities, quantities, relations, and so forth) as if they were things, by making them the subjects of sentences or the objects of verbs.

We have a similar problem with verbs. Verbs are supposed to name actions or states. However, consider the verbs "require," "know," "insist," "foresee," and "fear." Dictionaries and traditional books of grammar will label all of these verbs as active and transitive. However, put these verbs in sentences and ask yourself: What is being done and by whom? Who is receiving the action, and what is really being received?

What is true of parts of speech is also abundantly true of grammatical constructions: They are asymmetrical with conceptual categories. One of the best examples is that of the genitive, labeled possessive in most English school grammars. Such constructions are expressed in English either with the apostrophe *s* construction (as in, Jack's friend) or with the "of"-construction (as in, a friend of Jack). The following are all genitive constructions:

Shakespeare's plays

Shakespeare's worldview

Shakespeare's style

Shakespeare's death

Shakespeare's sexual orientation

Shakespeare's ignorance of mathematics

Shakespeare's popularity

Shakespeare's condemnation by the Puritans

Shakespeare's portrait by Holbein

Shakespeare's portrait of Richard III

Shakespeare's toothbrush

Each of the above constructions expresses a different logical and existential relationship involving Shakespeare. However, it is easy to see that only the last one has anything to do with "possession" in the ordinary sense. The older term "genitive" captures more broadly the sense of origination in a number of these constructions, but that term does not really come close to comprehending all of them. All the examples demonstrate a pervasive fact about grammar: Its surfaces mask multiple relationships of meaning. This is what is maddening about attempts to teach children (or anyone else) a simple, basic grammar.

The appropriate conclusion from all of this is not that language itself is deficient or unreliable in expressing these relationships. Rather, it is the opposite. Children actually "know" very well the structures that are so maddeningly difficult to teach them. Under most circumstances we get along just fine without any special marking of those various differences in meaning. This is probably another of those cases where we really want the forms of language to be out of the way, and grammar is wonderfully accommodating to that desire.

My conclusion in these reflections matches that of virtually all educational research: ultimately, studying the grammatical structures of your own language will not, in any special way, generate clear thinking (Weaver 7–13). The discipline that might do so would be logic, or dialectic. The founder of this discipline, Aristotle, based it (probably too confidently) on the premise that although the structures of language are inconsistent and not directly reflective of logical categories, they are good enough for conveying our thoughts. Why would Aristotle come to this conclusion? Because both the "mental experiences" and the realities behind them "are the same for all" (*De Interpretatione* 16a). The key to clear thinking, therefore, is to learn methods of interpretation that will carry you beyond grammar. For hundreds of years, a standard list of categories, originally posited by Aristotle, served as the bulwark of logical training:

substance (horse, man)
quantity (6 feet tall, a quart)
quality (brown, mercy)
relation (larger than, opposition)
place (in the stable, London)
time (for three days, a year)
position (seated, chairperson)

possession or "habitude" (wearing a robe, attire)

action (eats, a bath)

passion or "being affected or acted upon" (is beaten, resentment)

These ten categories may be taken as representing either the basic types of reality we use language to describe, or our basic ways of conceptualizing reality through language. Note that in every case the category of thought or experience can be expressed by a noun, as indicated by the second example in parentheses.

A search for "natural" grammatical correlates of the categories might indeed yield some regular expectations (noun = substance, verb = action, adjective = quality, time = adverb, and so on). However, with the exception of the lead category of substance (all the others are considered accidents or possible predicates of substance), the conventional pairings would have to be considered heuristic only, with multiple forms of language easily capable of representing each category. Note that nouns such as "bath" and "program" are not substances but actions; nouns like "sorrow" and "mistake" are passions; and another noun, "immediacy," is actually a time. Note also that each of the categories could be represented by a sentence as well as a particular part of speech or structure.

We now come once again to the noun "language," which stands as a reminder that no complex subject matter can be comprehended under any single category of thought. Language may legitimately be considered as a thing (a set of structures), though not a tangible one, as an action (a set of behaviors), or as a habitude (part of the neurological wiring of a human being). Different theories of language, or branches of language study, have indeed been based on these categorical placements. This may stand as a warning of sorts. In any discussion of complex topics, one must be wary of the tendency toward reification, speaking of abstract concepts as material, concrete things. A purpose of logic is to correct ordinary language in this way—to motivate us toward more accurate and rigorous ways of conceiving things.

Some linguists might object that a low estimate of the correlation between grammar and reasoning is based upon an oversimplified understanding of them both. It can be easily recognized, for instance, that "bath" is not a basic noun but is derived from the verb "to bathe"; and the deeper workings of grammar recognize its verb-like qualities by restricting it to certain verbal corners. For instance, "He didn't take a bath before the party" is a perfectly normal sentence. But "bath" is never allowed in such sentences as "He didn't bring a bath to the party" (except humorously, or perhaps in a poem). Aristotle's confidence about our ability to see through grammatical structures to the universal structures of thought behind them could be restated (and has been stated by modern grammarians) as optimism about the way language functions below the surface.

Undoubtedly, the classical demarcations of language and logic are oversimplified, and many wise thinkers and teachers have known this without being able to say exactly how. Modern philosophers of language have indeed found new ways of listening to language that reveal a much smarter instrument than traditional grammars allowed. On the one hand, it is intriguing, for instance, to think that such verb-like nouns (and noun-like verbs) as "love" might have a deep grammar capable of saying something interesting about the thing itself as well as our language. On the other hand, it should be acknowledged that this revised understanding about language and logic brings with it a revised understanding of what grammar is. In this conception, grammar is not something that has to be taught to individuals but something that the speakers of a language already know. (Nobody has to teach us not to say, "He brought a bath to the party.") Even if what formerly appeared primarily as a network of asymmetries now can be understood as a rich interplay between symmetries and asymmetries, it does not necessarily follow that formalizing or intensifying the native speaker's already intuitive grammatical knowledge will practically strengthen this interplay.

There is another problem with assuming that an individual's grammatical knowledge will improve thinking: Even if grammar and logic do intersect at some fascinating places, these may not be those places where logic is needed most, which is for analyzing concepts and propositions and finding and testing arguments. The vogue of "transformational sentence-combining" as a language pedagogy in the 1980's was based at least partially on the premise that the operations of transformational syntax more closely approximated the processes of thinking than previous grammars. However, such a direct connection was never claimed by grammarians themselves, and claims for the pedagogy were careful never to step beyond a vaguely stated hope for a kind of "conceptual growth" (see Mellon; O'Hare).

How did grammar get to be so necessary? If the classical estimation of the grammar-logic correlation was so low, and if contemporary linguistics has not provided a new rationale for linking them pedagogically, where did this new idea about the correlations of grammar and clear thinking come from? Certainly, it can be traced back to the enormous prestige of Latin in the medieval and Renaissance periods, and Latin's virtual identification with the study of grammar. But more tellingly, it came from the new practice, in the eighteenth century and later, of replacing (in some cases supplementing) Latin grammar with grammar in the vernacular. Along with this shift in practice came a radical shift in purpose: From teaching reading and writing in a second language to the hope of teaching improved reading and writing in the language already known.

This shift in practice and purpose stood at the end of the hegemony of Latin and at the beginning of new economic need and new educational resolve—to extend the benefits of literacy to a much broader range of citizens than had ever received them. The purpose was necessary and laudable, but the shift to studying vernacular grammar involved a major mistake in an area of language that had never before received or required much scrutiny. From the standpoint of producing and understanding discourse in one's native language, neither parts of speech, nor inflections, nor even sentences are the basic components of the process. The basic components of discourse are not sentences but rather speech acts that take the outward form of sentences. From the standpoint of translating Latin—primarily a written language that few individuals could learn except through studying formally its grammar and vocabulary—it makes sense to use one's formal knowledge of those outward structures to get at the meaning of the speech acts underneath. However, this is not a process that can lead to improved writing or reading ability in the language one already knows. In fact, it is certain to be both boring and debilitating.

The new teaching of vernacular grammar was based additionally on four principal assumptions. First, it was assumed that the vernaculars were both grammatically looser than and conceptually inferior to Latin, and therefore should be improved by the imposition of a more Latinate structure. Furthermore, the old linguistic rigors of teaching Latin (notoriously accompanied by whippings) were thought to be conducive to intellectual growth and rectitude, and they should be replicated as much as possible by new rigors in the vernacular. It was also assumed that most individuals (especially those bred outside of educated households) had an imperfect knowledge of their own language, and therefore needed to formally learn the grammar of their language in order to use it well. Finally, many thought that errors and infelicities of usage and style (such things as double negatives and split infinitives) were signs and sources of conceptual degradation. All of these assumptions have been proven wrong, both by the formal study of language and by the history of teaching grammar itself.

Why then have these assumptions been so persistent? Perhaps, it is partly because a valid intuition of symmetry persists against the formal evidence, but literary humanists have never known exactly where symmetry exists or quite what to do with it. In educational settings there is a natural and institutionalized drift toward formalism—a concentration on things that can be readily marked, tagged, taught, and tested in a systematic way. But language needs the freedom and flexibility that belong to asymmetry in order to adapt its finite resources to multiple situations and new experiences. Every form must be adaptable to some new purposes; and so symmetry will beat its wings and fly away from anything that attains the status of a regular form. As an educational practice, formalism is the attempt to enhance language and reasoning ability through the cultivation of specific forms of discourse. But formalism always leads to frustration. We know that there is a correlation between verbal ability and reasoning ability, and we look for ways of enhancing the correlation. Unfortunately for formalism, correlation is not cause, and as regards the rules of school grammar, there don't exist many correlations either.

Claim 4: The Symmetry of "Diagrammatic Iconicity"

This is a term borrowed from the American philosopher Charles Sanders Peirce, who defined the "diagram" in language as "an arrangement of signs, none of which necessarily resembles its reference, but whose relationships to each other mirror the relationships of their referents" (Nänny 197). The basic observation and subsequent claim is that in all of the world's languages, once past the level of sounds and surface grammatical relations, there is actually quite a bit of parallelism between forms of language and the various semantic relations being communicated. The simplest example is Caesar's famous "Veni, vidi, vici," in which the arrangement of words parallels a sequence of action.

Language is a sequential medium—at every level, one part follows another until the communication is finished—and the way things are ordered usually parallels the semantic relationship of the parts. This is true of the order of words in sentences, the order of sentences in paragraphs, and the order of paragraphs in larger discourses. One image, action, or idea will usually follow another in a recognizable spatial, narrative, or logical progression. Here is certainly a kind of symmetry.

In "Veni, vidi, vici," the progression of ideas is both causal and temporal. The structural linguist Roman Jakobson discovers another sort in sentences like, "The President and the Secretary of State attended the meeting." In this sentence you can see that the order of names mirrors political rank ("Quest" 350). Such orderings form icons of the matters being discussed, providing a kind of word-order symmetry that lies on top of a (mostly arbitrary) phonetic base. Jakobson points out examples that go down to the level of inflectional sequencing as well. In languages that have comparative and superlative forms of adjectives (high, higher, highest), the latter cases are always formed by adding syllables, never by subtracting them. Many languages form the plural of nouns by adding a syllable, while no languages subtract a syllable ("Quest" 352). By and large, however, the case for diagrammatic iconicity rests upon observations of sequencing at the sentence level or higher. This case is summed up succinctly by the American linguist Dwight Bolinger: "Arbitrary and conventional is a fitting description of distinctive sounds, less so of words, even less of sentences, and beyond that scarcely fits at all. The larger the scope, the looser and less arbitrary the structure" (18).

Commentary

The claim of iconicity makes a great deal of practical sense, and it serves as a useful corrective to the linguistic overemphasis of the concept of arbitrariness. It also helps to explain why asymmetry is something of a counterintuitive idea. We normally expect some kind of matchup between linguistic and real-world sequences, and discourses are usually easier to assimilate when these matchups occur. Indeed, we experience a special satisfaction when the matches are highlighted or intensified. "Veni, vidi, vici" is especially memorable because the iconic sequencing is very compact, and also because it is intensified by alliteration of the first syllables and by repetition of the *i* inflections at the end.

The problem with diagrammatic iconicity as an argument for symmetry is this: Having acknowledged its presence and its occasional beauties, we also have to acknowledge that diagrammatic iconicity remains more of an option and a potentiality in language than a natural condition. In many cases at the sentence level, the sequencing of items is more conventional than natural. And in many cases, a satisfying and reinforcing sequence is more the result of art than nature. Given the naturalness of temporal sequencing, it is rather remarkable that we so readily process sequences of a different sort. In English, for every sentence, "I selected a belt and then tried on some shoes," there is an alternate rendering that reverses the order, "I tried on some shoes after selecting a belt." We cannot say that one of these is more natural or more English than the other.

In negative sentences, should the "not" particle come before the verb? A modern speaker of English might think so, but a fifteenth-century speaker would not have thought so, nor would a modern speaker of German. Should objects come after verbs and subjects before them? It seems natural in modern English, but many languages allow—in certain instances require—different orderings. Moreover, the passive voice in English provides a perfectly acceptable reverse ordering: "A perfectly acceptable reverse ordering of subject-verb-object is provided by the passive voice." However, can it really be perfectly acceptable when everyone is familiar with the "rule" that admonishes overuse of the passive voice? As every teacher of composition knows, this is a principle of readability, not a rule of language, and the rule would not be so often repeated in style manuals if there was not a strong "natural" tendency toward the passive.

Mention of the term "readability" brings up another issue with regard to diagrammatic iconicity: It is more characteristic of written language than of speech. The problem with Bolinger's assertion above is that language in its natural, spoken state is not only a sequential medium, but it is also a fading mechanism. The more we say, the more we lose track of what has come before, most particularly the form of what has come before. The more likely, therefore, will it be that what comes next will not follow, either logically or formally, what has come before. This has in fact long been a central preoccupation of the art of written composition—the problem of coherence. Those extended discourses that follow a satisfying, logical sequence are more often than not the products of careful revision, often with the assistance of teachers or sympathetic editors. Even narrative sequences have to be carefully attended to. And as every lover of fiction knows, the possibilities of alternate sequencing constitute an important part of the craft. Diagrammatic iconicity is best understood as a possibility of language, particularly a possibility of carefully crafted written discourse. It should not be considered as a condition of language itself.

Claim 5: The Symmetry of Language and Culture

Many scholars have believed that the languages of different cultures and nationalities either possess or develop, over very long periods of time, features in their various systems (phonology, morphology, syntax, vocabulary, and so on) that correlate with national, ethnic, or cultural characteristics.

These features may in turn enable, channel, or limit further development. In this view, the historical study and reconstruction of these languages not only provides access to the literature of earlier ages but also offers clues about the mind-set and cultural development of ancient peoples. In consequence, the historical study of national languages may go hand in hand with the study of national literatures, in understanding and celebrating a national heritage.

Commentary

It should be noted at the outset that this is not a claim of symmetry in the strict sense, for the claim is not about the relation of language generally to structures of reality, but about the relation of specific languages (or language groups) to the cultural forms that are expressed in those languages. The most visible and intensively studied of these cultural forms have been mythologies and systems of religion. The relationship of language and culture has been one of the animating principles behind the massive amount of scholarship in comparative linguistics, which was originally known as comparative philology. Much of this work was accomplished in the nineteenth century, primarily in Germany, England, and France. Leaders in the field were responsible for transforming the study of language into a science.

The term comparative philology was most often used by these scholars, because the work of linguistic description and theory went hand in hand with the collection of ancient texts, mythology, and folklore. Intense interest in the correlation of ancient cultures and languages was there from the beginning. The first breakthrough came from the discovery that ancient Sanskrit bore a distinct relationship to ancient Western languages, such as Greek. These languages must have had a common ancestor, in spite of their seemingly vast differences, and what separated them was centuries of isolated linguistic change. In wake of the prodigious scholarly efforts that followed this discovery, it came to be understood for the first time that "families" of languages existed in "genetic" relationship to one another, and that the differences among them were explainable in light of systematic and universal laws of linguistic change. Also, for the first time, scholars developed ways of reconstructing the older, unrecorded forms of languages. This was accomplished partially from fragments of old manuscripts and chiefly from a set of procedures that came to be known as the comparative method, which uses the laws of linguistic change to work backwards, as it were, from the evidence provided by existing cognate languages.

For many scholars, these discoveries in themselves were sufficiently exciting to justify committing whole careers to their study. For others, however, there was an even greater excitement: If languages as disparate as Sanskrit and Greek existed in a state of systematic kinship, with ancestors in common, then the disparate mythological and religious systems recorded in them might also possess similar relations. If there existed universal principles explaining the relationship and development of languages, these principles might also exist for systems of mythology and religion. Just as importantly, language was not merely the medium in which these systems were conveyed. Language was the primary material out of which these systems had developed. Most mythological deities, for instance, get their names and their characters from the names of natural phenomena (thunder, rain, the planets, and so forth) that stood as mysteries to ancient peoples.

Such considerations as these gave the study of language a new importance. Europeans in the nineteenth century were facing enormous challenges to traditional religious belief, both from science and from the sheer diversity of peoples. At its most ambitious, the project of comparative philology became the attempt to demonstrate the kinship of the world's religions. They might accomplish this, it was hoped, by tracing the common origins and subsequent diaspora of such beliefs through a process analogous to and influenced by the development of languages.

These hopes were never quite realized, but the comparativists did establish that the study of cultures and the study of languages were essential to each other and not simply for the purposes of communication and translation. During the course of the nineteenth century, they developed comparative philology into a science as ambitious and as systematic as biology and geology, and in the process they helped to create respect and admiration for a new kind of intellectual sage, a person learned in languages, history, and human culture, wise about human character and the affairs of nations (see Holloway).

Even as this science was leading the way toward a new and loftier notion of symmetry, however, it was developing methods and principles that would push it in an entirely different direction. The rigid, empirical attention to phonetics demanded by the comparative method was leading inevitably toward an understanding of language as its own separate system, subject to its own internal laws. A language might reflect national character (a troublingly elusive term) in the history of key vocabulary; however, at the level of phonetic and morphological change (which was understood to be primary), it had to be seen as running a historical course that had little or nothing to do with that character. Except in some isolated corners, the scientific and descriptive impulse won the day over speculation about world religions, basically because it was more productive and less open to bitter controversy.

As it turned out, scientifically verifiable insights about the history of culture and religion were fewer than many had expected in the early decades of the project. In his autobiography written late in life, the German/English philologist Max Müller could pronounce confidently the belief that "language—our own inherited language—exercises the most powerful influence on our reason and our will." Müller goes on to speculate that "A Greek speaking Greek and a Roman speaking Latin would certainly have been very different beings from the Romance and French descendents of a Horace or a Ciccro, and this simply on account of the language which they had to speak" (*My Autobiography* 31). Müller, however, like most of the best comparativists, was a very careful scholar, and he shied away from generalizations, particularly of the sort that attributed superiority or greater advancement of one people over another on the basis of linguistic differences (Joseph 120–21). The great bulk of his life's work actually consisted of the sorting and translation of ancient Sanskrit texts. He was honored by the people of India as well as the Western world for this work.

A famous speculation that Müller did attempt concerned the earlier development of monotheism among speakers of Semitic languages. This development stands in stark contrast to the polytheistic mythologies of all the members of the Indo-European group, most notably Hindu, Greek, and Germanic. The cause for this Müller related to a condition mentioned earlier, namely that the names for the gods and goddesses of mythology are almost always related to natural forces and phenomena—for instance sky (Zeus) and sun (Apollo). Among all primitive peoples, the most spectacular of such phenomena are associated with the spirit world, as are the words that name them. However, the ancient branches of Indo-European languages underwent a much faster rate of change, Müller speculated. This obscured the relation of the names to specific natural phenomena, leaving a cast of gods and goddesses, even after the forces of nature that they had once named were understood in a more down-to-earth way.

The Semitic languages, by contrast, were comparatively stable and slow in their rate of change; and as a consequence (in Müller's explanation), their speakers came more quickly to the realization that these were simply the names of natural objects. In time, of course, the supernatural associations with nature faded, and so did the overtones of divinity associated with the names. With this move accomplished, the Semitic peoples were then freer to move to the next "higher" step in the development of religion: the location of the transcendent (whose apprehension is universal) in a single force behind all of nature (see "Semitic Monotheism"). Müller's explanation is far less objectionable than some of the racial theories circulating in his own day, but it is, after all, only a speculation. He received a great deal of criticism for it, and he was much more cautious in nearly all of his other work.

Ultimately, the contributions of comparative linguistics turned out to be much greater in the description and history of languages themselves than in the illumination of culture. In neither its nineteenth- nor its twentieth-century versions has the linguistic relativity hypothesis, as it has come to be called, produced very much in the way of specific, verifiable correlations between language and culture. The more sophisticated forms of the hypothesis by the American linguists Edward Sapir and Benjamin Lee Whorf are very carefully qualified and generalized. They should not be confused with the rash and unsupportable speculation that connects alleged national or ethnic attributes to formal features of language. In one of the more notorious of these, Germans are said to exhibit a greater penchant for abstract philosophizing because their philosophical vocabulary consists almost entirely of compounds from native base terms, while the corresponding Anglo-American vocabulary is chiefly borrowed from Latin or constructed from Latin roots.

Neither Sapir nor Whorf would endorse that short-lived and now discredited strain of German linguistics, which in the 1930's and 1940's supported the Nazi ideology by extolling the superiority of Aryan languages and the cultures they produced (see Hutton). Edward Sapir's view is essentially a very careful restatement of Müller's view. Sapir speculates that language is a "prepared road or groove" of thought, and that "thought arises as a refined interpretation of its [language's] content" (15); however, Sapir is very cautious about details, especially comparative ones. Benjamin Lee Whorf's more ambitiously stated view, that the particular internal structures of languages create a predisposition to see the world in different ways, has been much debated, without certain conclusion.

Two important things stand out in the aftermath of these debates. No version of the linguistic relativity hypothesis has engendered significant specific research that links features of language to features of culture, and twentieth-century research in linguistics has come to emphasize the sameness of languages' internal structures more than their differences. Consequently, while the relativity hypothesis is still recounted and debated in popular books about language, discussions in serious scholarly literature range from cautious to dismissive (Lee 180–221). Nevertheless, the development of comparative linguistics in the nineteenth century did alter the relationship of language study to the newly developing forms of literary humanism in the vernacular.

Partly under the influence of nationalism, Europeans were for the first time formally studying, in school and university settings, their national literatures. In the beginning, this study primarily concentrated on the medieval and Renaissance periods of literary history. The science of philology validated this study, added prestige to it, and assisted it practically by providing materials and methods for interpreting and, in some cases, reconstructing texts in older forms of the language. The earliest English professors were both philologists and literary scholars. Most had at least enough linguistic training to read texts in Old English, to understand scientifically the evolution of English into its modern state, and to comprehend the cognate relationships of European languages. As the study of literature began to encompass more recent periods, however, the connection between philology and literature was bound to weaken. Meanwhile, lower forms of schooling were hardly affected by the new linguistics, and the project of teaching school children to write and speak effectively proceeded with outmoded methods and materials transferred to the vernacular from the old Latin grammar schools.

Claim 6: The Symmetry of Language and Imagination

In eighteenth- and nineteenth-century speculations about the relationships between language, the human mind, and emotions, language was understood as a creation of the imagination, and its direct connections, its symmetries, were not to things in the external world but to internal states of feeling and consciousness. In the words of the romantic poet Percy Bysshe Shelley, language is "a more direct representation of the actions and passions of our internal being . . . and is more plastic and obedient to the control of that faculty of which it is the creation" (*Defence of Poetry* 678). This claim of symmetry is not unrelated to comparativist views about the relationships of language and culture; however, it represents a strong interiorization and personalization of those views.

Arguably, the highest and most exalted use of language is poetry, which in Shelley's famous phrase, "lifts the veil from the hidden beauty of the world" (681). It stands to reason, therefore, that the expressive use of language, without too much regard to issues of usage or integrity of reference, will lead to self-discovery and personal growth. Imaginative expressions of various kinds, including unshaped dreams and fantasies, unlock secrets of the inner life, providing a knowledge of human experience that cannot be found anywhere else.

Commentary

This is a view of language and discourse that has come to be known as "romantic" or "expressivist" (see Fulkerson). Although it is clearly associated with nineteenth-century reactions against Enlightenment rationalism, it is interesting that more sedate versions of it were actually put forward by Enlightenment thinkers. There were in fact both symmetrists and asymmetrists in the field. What they were all seeking was a rational and psychological explanation of the origin and character of human language—something to replace the old mythological view found in the Bible (Aarsleff 13–18).

The Biblical account of Babel appeared to endorse what might be called a lost symmetrism, in which a single original language was dispersed into hundreds of corrupted ones. What bothered Enlightenment scholars was not the specific position of lost symmetrism but rather the nonrational character of the Biblical explanation. And the shift to rational explanation opened the door to other viewpoints, most notably a new form of rational asymmetrism.

The view expressed by Shelley constitutes a considerable upgrading of language's possibilities from most traditional views. However, it is also considerably more optimistic than the most prominent Enlightenment position, to which it is consciously opposed. That is the rational asymmetrism associated with science and most forcefully articulated by the English philosopher John Locke. In this view the origins of thought lie in the primary sensations of sight, touch, and sound, to which the nomenclature of language bears only a conventional relationship. Concepts or ideas are formed from complex amalgamations of and generalizations from these sensations. Furthermore, the names of various concepts and ideas are derived, for the most part, from the names of physical acts or sensations. For example, the word "attention" is derived from the Latin *ad* and *tendere*, meaning "to lean toward," constituting a metaphorical extension of that physical act.

Both on account of its highly conventional nature and its embeddedness in common emotion and prejudice, language is in Locke's view a weak instrument for philosophical or scientific work. It should be disciplined, consequently, by the methodologies of science. These methodologies accomplish two things: they narrowly restrict the meanings of words to precise designations in a particular discourse; and they restrict them also to referents—things on the outside—that can be precisely observed and measured. Ordinary language was considered in some quarters so unsuitable to such a task that it should be replaced altogether, hence several attempts to create new "philosophical languages" that did not bear the stain of common usage (Eco; Aarsleff). It should be noted that restoring symmetry was not the aim of such projects. The new philosophical languages attempted by John Wilkins, an English clergyman and author of *An Essay towards a Real Character and a Philosophical Language,* and others might be more consistent and more directly referential than natural languages, but they would not necessarily be more symmetrical. The natural tendency of words in a real language is to take on additional meanings, and therefore more ambiguity. The makers of philosophical languages took on the project of replacing words with symbols that stood directly and unambiguously, though still conventionally, for things outside of language. In fact, the more conventional the better, since the new symbols (and in some cases, diacritics) would not be made ambiguous by prior associations from real usage.

The philosophical language project did not succeed. In fact, it was satirized and scorned by such hardheaded thinkers as Jonathan Swift, who in the third book of *Gulliver's Travels* depicts the over-intellectualized citizens of Laputa as going so far as to attempt to replace words with the actual things they represent. Swift and others, even some of the strongest advocates of science and the new spirit of reason, such as the German philosophers Gottfried Leibniz and Emmanuel Kant, held the (basically Aristotelian) view that, when used carefully and properly, natural language was for most purposes good enough and certainly more flexible and expressive than any artificial replacement could be.

However, the controversy that had taken place in the previous century did perhaps have a clarifying effect for thinkers such as Shelley, who perceived for language and literature a role far greater than "good enough." What Shelley and other thinkers of the romantic school believed was that the true source of "rightness" in language beautifully and successfully used—and the real reason to pay attention to it—lay not in its referential but in its expressive and imaginative power. The symmetry of language was neither its natural connection to external reality nor its connection to the structures of reasoning and logic, but to truths and imaginative resources that lay deep within the human psyche. This imaginative truth and power was accessible through language. It was expressed, and would continue to be expressed, through great works of imaginative literature, including the classics of the literary canon, the works of Homer, Virgil, Dante, Shakespeare, and, somewhat alarmingly to traditional religionists, the Bible.

The looseness and subjectivity of such views about language are notorious. A reader coming to them for the first time could well anticipate that they would turn out to be even lighter on specifics (much lighter in fact) than those of the comparativists discussed in the previous section. This criticism is a just one, as is the question of just how one person's imaginative expression is to be validated over another's. However, these views should not be dismissed lightly. The absence of proof is not the same as the absence of a just line of reasoning. The great insight of the romantics, expressed notably in such works as Shelley's *Defence of Poetry* and Samuel Taylor Coleridge's *Biographia Literaria,* is that all uses of language, even (and sometimes especially) under humble circumstances, contain an element of imaginative exploration. In fact, it could be claimed that this is one of the most basic and important functions of language.

Precisely because the external resources of language (sounds, words, grammatical structures, and so forth) are finite and limited, we are always stretching them to new use and new expression, primarily through the "natural" linguistic process of metaphorical extension. A term that previously applied to one thing or set of things is now extended to apply to some new thing. This is the power of the human imagination, and it has not just an expressive and decorative function but an exploratory and enlightening function as well. It constitutes a linguistic technique for bridging the gap between known and unknown territories—things for which you already have words, and things for which you do not.

The romantics were able to see quite plainly that the functions of reason and logic, to which thinkers of the previous century had given so much attention, are not especially exploratory. They do not primarily produce new insights but, instead, put them to the test of rational consistency and validity. All the great ideas and perceptions, we are now in a position to see, have been leaps of the imagination, the works of language carrying understanding where it had not been before. And of course, this works for personal insight as well, ever the haunt of poets.

The great importance of the romantic philosophy is that, while conceding most of the external forms of asymmetry we have discussed, it still put forward boldly, for the first time since the sophists of ancient Greece, an outlook that gave language a purchase on reality. In this view, there exists a labor of insight, wisdom, and personal integration, for which the basic tools are language and the work of the imagination.

This was a motivating body of theory behind a brilliant output of romantic literature in the early nineteenth century. Along with the work of the comparativists, it added prestige to the emerging study of vernacular literature. It also enhanced the general opinion of imaginative literature itself at a time when European civilization was beginning to promote and experience literacy among all classes. Interestingly, it also proved to be an impetus to the study of regional dialects among common people, for there too lay the works and processes of the imagination.

Why? It was not merely that the language of common people was more direct and down to earth than educated speech. The romantic view was that this language was also, in its way, more creative and poetic, and its very limitation makes it so. Such a language is even more finite of resources than that of sophisticated peoples, and the smaller reserve of "ready-made" words and phrases calls into play much sooner the process of metaphoric extension. The result is a more figurative and more participatory form of speech, and along with it a way of viewing the world that is more full of wonder and fresh revelation.

What is now considered true of the romanticized common folk will also be considered true of children, one of whom Wordsworth addressed in his famous "Immortality Ode" as "Thou best philosopher"! Here is a more commonplace example: lacking a sophisticated understanding of weather, a child will ask, "Where is the wind when it is not blowing?" In doing so, the child animates and personifies the wind in a manner that is similar to what we see in myth and folklore, and also in great epic poetry, such as *The Odyssey*. The mature educated speech of civilized people, by contrast, can be derogated as a blanket of asymmetry over the senses—in fact, a large store of old metaphors now deadened by the processes of change, custom of usage, and specialization of usage. The purpose of poetry, in the romantic view, is to re-symmetrize language to the inner life, restore its direct and participatory link to perception and feeling, and restore wonder to the world.

It is also interesting that, though their fundamental sensibilities and lines of inquiry tended in opposite directions, the romantics and the comparative linguists managed to share some basic ideas about language and peoples. As already noted, the comparativists were of a much more empirical and scientific bent, and for the most part they stuck to their factual, descriptive labors. However, they did not strongly attack, and in some cases they held implicitly, the romantic view of language.

From the standpoint of education, perhaps the most fascinating question to ask about the romantic revolution is why it did not spawn a new program of native-language teaching, focused on the imaginative and expressive use of language as an organ of exploration, self-discovery, and personal growth. In the early twenty-first century, the project of "expressive writing" has become so widespread at all levels, both as an end in itself and as preparatory to more formal and transactional practice, that it may be useful to pause over this question. One answer is surely that English—either as composition or literature—did not exist as a school subject, certainly not in the comprehensive form we see today. The marriage to Latin came undone only slowly, over a period of two centuries, and even as it did so, the methods of teaching Latin carried over for a long time into the practice of teaching English.

An additional matter of importance is that educators of the eighteenth and nineteenth centuries began to take on a new and ambitious project that turned in a different direction altogether. This was the task of imparting "correctness" and social acceptability to whole classes of individuals who had never before received such attention. The goal was to provide access to economic opportunities being created by the industrial revolution, and this tended to create a division between practical training and belles lettres. Romanticism articulated its position in such a way as to cut itself off from the world of work, creating a division with which literary humanists still wrestle, between literary culture and the newly developing civilization of science, industry, commerce, and mass communication.

Furthermore, and quite simply, the discipline of written composition did not exist in the romantic period. There is something about the potential for exploration, self-discovery, and personal growth that is uniquely the province of written monologue. There are many wonderful examples to demonstrate that individuals of previous centuries understood and exploited this potential. It was not until the twentieth century, however, that scholars began to study the cognitive and operational basis of this potential, to harness it in school settings, and to coordinate it with the broader purpose of producing a successful public discourse. Nevertheless, the job of coordinating these things is not always so easy, and sometimes the temptation to give up the effort is very strong. We still need to know more about, and we will never completely solve, the problem of how the interior and the exterior, the symmetrical and asymmtretical, struggle against, play against, and (when things are going well) cooperate with each other in human language.

Suggested Reading

Bolinger, Dwight. *Language: The Loaded Weapon.* London: Longman, 1980. Bolinger is a linguist who rejects the trademark asymmetrism of twentieth-century descriptive linguistics and emphasizes the expressive potential of linguistic structures in actual use.

Burrow, John. "The Uses of Philology in Victorian England." *Ideas and Institutions of Victorian Britain.* Ed. R. Robson. London, 1967. 180–204. This outstanding essay chronicles the role of comparative philology in the competition among belief systems and scientific theories in the nineteenth century—most notably Darwinism.

Jakobson, Roman. "Quest for the Essence of Language." *Selected Writings II: Word and Language.* The Hague: Mouton, 1971. 345–59. This landmark essay represents an attempt by one of the great structuralists to come to terms with the prospect of symmetry.

Lee, Benjamin. *Talking Heads: Language, Metalanguage, and the Semiotics of Subjectivity.* Durham: Duke University Press, 1997. Lee's chapter, "The Semiotic Mediation of Language and Thought" (180–221), contains one of the clearest and best informed summaries of ideas about the relativity hypothesis, as articulated by its major scholarly proponents: Boas, Sapir, and Whorf. Lee then proceeds to conduct some grammatical analyses to demonstrate some ways in which the hypothesis may or may not be justified.

Nänny, Max. "Iconicity in Literature." *Word and Image* 2 (1986): 199–208. One of the best short explanations of the potential for diagrammatic iconicity.

Nuckolls, Janis B. "The Case for Sound Symbolism." *Annual Review of Anthropology* 28 (1999): 225–52 Acknowledging that "arbitrariness" is necessarily the dominant linguistic position, Nuckolls reviews a good deal of the research and criticism, making the case for a substrate of sound symbolism in all languages.

4

Reading the World
Structural Analogy

Beyond our most elemental responses and biological functions, there is no human acting, thinking, understanding, or organizing separate from language. Our talking and writing are not simply called in to represent things; they actually make, perform, and enact them. To use the language of modern discourse theorists, language is constitutive as well as communicative of consciousness and culture. The meaningful connection of language to the world comes not through individual forms or structures, which are for the most part asymmetrical, but through internal processes and features of design. There are few problems of human culture and understanding that do not have an analogue in the process and design of language. Consequently, there may be ways of learning from language that provide a greater understanding of these problems.

These are some of the views about language that lie at the heart of the argument for structural analogy and its claims of symmetry. Clearly, structural analogy incorporates insights from a number of modern language philosophies, and experienced readers will recognize an element of structuralism, a heterogeneous set of theories which share the principle that "cultural forms, belief systems and 'discourses' of every kind can best be understood by analogy with language" (Norris 855). Structural analogy also owes something to British ordinary language philosophy, which spawned what has come to be known as the linguistic turn in modern philosophy (see Rorty). Among its most influential practitioners were the Austrian-born British philosopher Ludwig Wittgenstein and the British language philosopher J. L. Austin. The most ambitious and audacious claim of ordinary language philosophy is that many of the traditional problems of philosophy are essentially questions about how to use words. The more modest and demonstrable sort of claim is that every serious investigation ought to begin with an analysis of language. This claim presupposes a connection between linguistic structures and conceptual problems, so that by seriously examining language we have a chance of looking "not merely at words . . . but also at the realities we use the words to talk about: We are using a sharpened awareness of words to sharpen our perception of . . . the phenomena" (*Philosophical Papers* 182).

Structural analogy also owes a good deal to American pragmatism, fathered by the great nineteenth-century philosopher and psychologist William James, but represented most notably in recent decades by the American philosopher Richard Rorty. Although pragmatists would affirm the constitutive nature of language, they would be troubled by the notion of symmetry being used here. To say that language in some way mirrors realities or structures of reality outside of language is to imply that such realities exist, and most modern pragmatists have concluded that they do not. Closer to the view being presented here is the work of the great American literary and cultural critic Kenneth Burke, who spent a lifetime exploring analogies between the designs and processes of discourse and the structures of human and social problems. In fact, several passages in Burke's work *The Rhetoric of Religion* are highly influential to the arguments being presented, even evoking the term structural analogy itself. Finally, elements of the structural analogy view are embodied or implied in some of the traditions of ancient rhetoric, specifically in the writings of Cicero, and it was in recognition of the insights within that tradition that scholars like Burke sought to revive and draw attention to them.

The Form/Meaning Analogy

To some readers, structural analogy may seem nearly as amorphous as Percy Bysshe Shelley's claim in the previous chapter about language and imagination. The superiority of structural analogy over that claim, however, is precisely its greater specificity. I want to look, therefore, at some specific examples of just what it means to say that there exist human problems that have analogues in structures or processes of language.

An initial example can be drawn from the most obvious and pervasive feature of linguistic organization: the pairing of forms to meanings. At every level, from a simple cry, to a sentence, to a play or novel, we encounter a form or structure on the one side, and a meaning on the other side. Modern transformational grammarians have shown that the relationships among such pairings are much more intricate and systematic than traditional accounts of structure were able to demonstrate. It is well-known that a single, basic message or deep structure can transform into at least three different surface structures—active, passive, and it-cleft—creating different points of contextual emphasis:

Active   Lapcore developed the first laptop computers.

Passive   The first laptop computers were developed by Lapcore.

It-cleft   It was Lapcore that developed the first laptop computers.

At more complex and extended levels of discourse, the choices among transformations may be more difficult and the implications more treacherous. The pairing of form to meaning is sometimes successful and sometimes not. Sometimes we find just the right way of saying things; sometimes we do not say what we mean at all; we anger or alienate the persons we are talking to; they go out and do things we did not want them to do.

The "analogy" in structural analogy is to something in human culture, broadly speaking—in this case to the dichotomy of design and purpose. The basic form/meaning, structure/message feature spreads out into—"predicts," we might say—quite a few of those instances in which we perceive harmonies or disharmonies between design and purpose in human organization. Here, I am talking about the way things are organized, on the one side, and the messages they are supposed to send (or the goals they are supposed to reach) on the other side. Here are some things that are often heard:

"This campaign is all show and no substance."

"The whole event was wonderfully designed to give you a feeling of safety."

"They had a good idea, but the indoor setting just destroyed it."

Whenever we say things like this, we are "reading" events as if they were discourses, and of course, in some ways, they are. Having understood this, the leap is not a large one to a claim for literary humanism: when you introduce sophistication to the structural and /message-oriented dimensions of language and discourse, you are producing sophistication in reading the world and conducting its business. This example above is useful not only for its clarity but also for its suggestion of a generally embraceable literary humanism that seeks to prepare individuals for an essential function of leadership: the ability to read situations in the language-saturated (and language-constituted) institutions of society; and, in addition, the ability to design good things that will send good messages and accomplish good in the world.

The One and the Many

The form/meaning, design/purpose analogy is such an important one that it can be designated as a pilot analogy. In Plato's dialogue entitled *Philebus* we encounter an intriguing rendition of another pilot analogy through a dramatized discussion of the philosophical problem of the one and the many. An explanation of this philosophical problem can best be provided by considering this question: Is there a single abstract reality, mercy, that covers and informs all the various ways that humans express and show mercy? In the midst of the dialogue, Socrates remarks, without explanation, that the problem of "the one and the many" is something built into the very nature of sentences: "as the result of the sentences we utter; in every single sentence ever uttered, in the past and in the present, there it is" (*Philebus* 15d–e). Plato's claim is that the larger philosophical question has an analogue in the structure of sentences; the implication of that claim, of course, is that we can understand the universe better by peering into the structure of language.

Moving forward to the twentieth century, Kenneth Burke speculates very much along the same lines in *The Rhetoric of Religion,* proposing that the human yearning for transcendence is also something that has its origin in the structure of sentences. It is an appetite that is stimulated by the way we grasp a nonmaterial and unified meaning above and apart from what a finite sentence is—a string of material sounds in time. In Burke's own complex phrasing, the material/transcendent pairing comes about because of "the distinction between the unfolding of a sentence through the materiality of its parts and the unitary non-material essence or meaning of the sentence" (*Rhetoric of Religion* 3). In this same passage, Burke points out that Saint Augustine makes the same speculation. At this point, the reader should recall that both Plato and Augustine were confirmed philosophical asymmetrists, in the strict sense of the term; however, they were both fascinated by some of the possibilities of symmetry, making them appear to be temperamental symmetrists. Perhaps a better way of saying this is that Plato and Augustine were poets and visionaries as well as philosophers, and the same can be said of Kenneth Burke.

A conspicuous feature of all the examples of structural analogy presented so far is that they involve a binary pairing of some sort: form/meaning, one/many, finite/infinite. This suggests the possibility of any number of additional examples. However, it first calls for a brief explanation of how these binaries are related to linguistic structure, which will in turn help to explain one of the principal contributions of structuralism as a linguistic and philosophical movement.

It is noteworthy that structuralism's founder, the Swiss linguist Ferdinand de Saussure, coined the very term "arbitrariness of the sign," establishing with that phrase the fiercely asymmetrist doctrine that the meanings of linguistic forms (sounds, words, and sentences) are based not on their relationships to things outside of language but on their structural relationships to other forms. Paradoxically, at the same time Saussure's work laid the foundations for what would become the primary tool of what could be termed an analogical symmetry—the principle of binary opposition, where those relationships of structure that are essential to conveying meaning in language often take the form of binaries: this/that or yes/no contrasts between pairs of formal elements.

The most unambiguous example of such structuring in language is in the sound system, where the most important things about individual sounds is not (as we have clearly seen) their linkage to meaning but their "structural" relationships—that is, their relationships of contrast with other sounds. A contrastive pair in English is *t* / *d*. They are sounds that are produced in a similar way (they are both stop sounds), in a similar part of the mouth (they are both made by touching the tongue against the alveolar ridge), and sometimes they even come very close to one another in actual sound—notice that the *t* in "writer" sounds much like a *d*. However, the important thing about the pair is the way they contrast with one another at strategic places to signal differences of meaning, as in the pairs tin and din and fat and fad.

Such relationships of sound are termed phonemic in structural grammars. However, phonemics is just the beginning of it. Instances of binary opposition are ubiquitous at all levels—so pervasively, in fact, that they constitute a pattern in the way we interpret (or read) our experience. Think of such commonplace dichotomies as action versus contemplation, outer-versus inner-directed personalities, spiritual versus material, literal versus figurative. The symmetrist of structural analogy is eager to point out that this tendency toward binary conceptualization is an outgrowth of language itself. Such a person is also motivated to listen to language for specific analogies to particular lines of thinking or patterns of understanding.

Another pilot analogy can be found in what might be considered a tamer, more down-to-earth version of Burke's speculation about transcendence: the sequence/pattern analogy. Unlike painting, sculpture, or photography, language is a fundamentally linear and temporal medium. Every linguistic thing—from individual sounds, to words and parts of words, to phrases, sentences, paragraphs, and upwards to term papers and heroic epics—occurs in sequence, one thing after another in time. The all-pervasive and inalterable movement at all levels is one-item-following-another, with previous items fading out of the very limited aural space in which acts of language occur, just as new items come into our awareness. These new items then fade out themselves, behind the inexorable march of additional new sounds, words, and sentences.

Speaking is the one, true medium in which you cannot do two things at once. In music, miraculously, we can hear multiple "voices" in a polyphonic composition, but the situation closes in radically when words are added. We can successfully hear two spoken things at once in a choral composition, but what we are almost always hearing is two very simple, formulaic phrases for which we have been well prepared in advance—and even then, with one of them given a bit of lead time. It's true that the medium of writing, and even more the medium of internet presentation, broaden considerably that space of material realization, making several things happen at once by exploiting the visual sense. In addition, with their multiple possibilities of formatting, both writing and pixilated discourse present visual indications of pattern that speaking simply cannot accomplish without visual aids. It should be noted that writing also *takes away* the visual aids of body language and accompanying action that occur in any real time and space communication.

The remarkable and miraculous thing, of course, is the emergence of pattern out of this linear flow. In our primary acts of communicating with each other, we "build in" (on the speaking side) and intuit (on the hearing side) a shaping of all those things coming after one another, imparting to them coherence so that the act of saying is not just a succession of things but also a single thing that means and accomplishes something. This is a pattern in which all of those things continue to exist separately but relate to each other in nonlinear ways—some subordinated to others, and some existing in recognizable tensions or pairings with each other. At the plainest and most obvious level, this could be the relation of subjects to predicates in sentences: one materially follows the other but we understand a different kind of relationship (one of the various things that a subject-predicate pairing can mean). Moving several stages higher in the chain of discourse, we might perceive a causal relationship between one action in a story and the action that directly follows it, or we might perceive both of these actions to be the effects of some previously narrated cause.

In ordinary conversation, and in simple written or email communications, we accomplish all of this, amazingly, with very little conscious effort. In oral settings, of course, we use body movements to create a visual pattern that cuts across the linearity of words. In writing and on the internet, we have other resources. As discourses get longer and more complex, the roles of planning and signaling (on the production side) and conscious interpretation (on the receiving end) do become more conscious and even laborious. When we are writing, we find ourselves wanting to say several things at once, but we have to submit to the discipline of linearity. When we are reading, we often find ourselves asking, "I wonder where the author is going with this?"

The remarkable thing, however, is the role of intuition, improvisation, and gradual discovery on both sides of the equation. Most of us do not consciously "know" where a sentence is going when we start it. Billy Collins's poem, "Winter Syntax," expresses the journey of a sentence quite remarkably:

> A sentence starts out like a lone traveler
> heading into a blizzard at midnight,
> tilting into the wind, one arm shielding his face,
> the tails of his thin coat flapping behind him.
>
> . . . .
>
> At dawn he will spot the vine of smoke
> rising from your chimney, and when he stands
> before you shivering, draped in sparkling frost,
> a smile will appear in the beard of icicles,
> and the man will express a complete thought.   (1–4, 23–27)

And how often are we surprised by what we said, and by what we accomplished? And how often does a friend or loved one actually finish the sentence for us, intuiting its purpose well in advance, sometimes even before we do? Most students of language understand that such things could not transpire in the absence of unheard and unseen deep structures—not only of sentences but also of larger units of discourse. How often do we hear authors confess that they did not know where a novel was going until they actually got into the process of composing? Or that a planned direction changed unexpectedly? And yet, the thing that emerged was miraculously coherent, hanging together, displaying a recognizable and even pleasing structure and pattern.

Many patterns, of course, are not as beautiful and creative as Collins's poem. Many are entirely set and formulaic, the extreme example being the bureaucratic, institutional "form": the application form, the purchase order, the notice of separation, the death certificate, and so forth. We know "the whole thing" as soon as we see it. However, the role of intuition, improvisation, and unfolding discovery remains potent in our most interesting discourses, especially that of story, where a seemingly random string of events will suddenly reveal its participation in an archaic deep structure or archetype, such as the myth of the eternal return. Interestingly, some of the most satisfying and moving of these are the ones that we experience as a gradually unfolding surprise. By contrast, some of the least satisfying, we feel, were planned or known in advance.

The element of structural analogy comes in when we move from patterns of discourse to patterns of life. Some individuals do not know where they are headed at first, but end up discovering or settling into something quite recognizable with their lives. Others think they know where they are headed, but they keep having to revise and start their lives over. A few others do everything they can to make sure the pattern of life is set and does not change—rather like that death certificate mentioned above. All of this suggests a broadly embraceable literary humanism aimed at reading, interpreting, articulating, and revising the pattern of individual lives, of institutions, and of nations.

The spectrum of individual lives we just noted—from being completely in the dark to being absolutely sure about where one is going—calls into view another design feature of language: wherever there are binary oppositions, there are also elements of a continuum. At every level we can observe in language, those binary oppositions of form are always "filled in" and connected by a succession of forms in between. Here is the structural principle: wherever there are opposite poles of form, there exists a graduating series of forms in between them.

Looking down into the plumbing and wiring of the sound system, we can readily observe this feature, again, in the contrasting pair of the phonemes *t* and *d,* which represent opposite poles of "voicing": The phoneme *t* is unvoiced, with the stream of air slipping up from the lungs without disturbing the fleshy bands of the larynx. The binary phoneme *d* is voiced, as its air comes forward through an ordeal of vibration in the larynx, creating the phenomenon of voice. In between these two poles, however, there exists in actual speech a succession of partially voiced versions (allophones) of *t* and *d*. Interestingly, in a rather remarkable demonstration of asymmetry, a number of these versions continue to count as the one, while actually displaying more the physical characteristics of the other. The *t* in most American pronunciations of "liter" is physically and tonally closer to the *d* in "leader," while continuing to be counted systematically as *t*. (This is partially evidenced by the slightly tenser version of *i* in the word "liter" just preceding.) These variations of form do not matter in one sense, but they do have their situational places on the continuum. The *d*-sounding version of *t,* for instance, is the one that typically occurs in the middle of a sequence between vowel sounds.

Here is another example from grammar books that teach us to recognize a hard-and-fast distinction between transitive and intransitive verbs; however, consider the following:

Jack is dying.

Jack is sleeping.

Jack is exercising.

Jack is smoking. (In the sense of "consuming tobacco products.")

Jack is undergoing surgery.

Jack is taking a nap.

Jack is reading a book.

Jack is driving a car.

The first and the last of these sentences are definitely intransitive and transitive, respectively, while everything else is actually in between. "Exercising" definitely has an intransitive form, even though the meaning is ambiguous: he is not doing anything to anybody, but on the other hand, he is exercising his own body. "Smoking" is not really a conceptual or deep structure transitive at all: something has been deleted, namely a cigarette, cigar, or pipe. "Undergoing surgery," although it has transitive form, is certainly less transitive than "exercising." Move on down the list: Jack is reading the book, to be sure, but is he really doing anything to it? Affecting it in any way? Or is it Jack who is being affected?

From here, with the continuum analogy and with others we have discussed, the march upward through forms of discourse, and then outward into patterns of life, human organization, and culture, becomes an interesting and instructive one to trace. It starts with sounds and ends with lives. At every level the strategy is to ask: What are the opposite poles of possibility here? And what are some plausible points of continuum in between?

In those language-saturated institutions that are most important to us, action in the world is never far from or separate from making discourse about it. A case in point: after you have used language to discover the opposing poles and also the continuum of possibility for solving a particular problem, you will still need to communicate your position. How should you do this? Look again at the continuum of possibilities: Perhaps you should make your argument, perhaps you should tell your story, or perhaps you should do something in between.

The Dangers and Shortcomings of Structural Analogy

There is much to be excited about when considering the possibilities of structural analogy, but like any form of symmetrism it possesses dangers and limitations. The first and most obvious deficiency with structural analogy is a flaw inherent in all analogies: they break down at some point. With structural analogy, the place beyond that point is the place of asymmetry—a root difference between the signifier and the signified. This fissure will never go away.

The continuum analogy just discussed is a classic case in point. If you look carefully at the pairs presented below, you will quickly conclude that not all the things that our language classifies as opposites are opposites in the same way; nor are many of them really logical, deep-structural, or real-world opposites:

black / white
heads / tails
buying / selling
paper / plastic
capitalism / socialism
standing / sitting

In many cases, politically as well as dialectically, the search for positions in-between will be a futile exercise. There may be moments in the political or moral realm in which there simply is not a viable middle ground, even though language allows us and may even prompt us to articulate one.

A strong case can be made, as a matter of fact, that a weakness of that mainline tradition of rhetorical humanism emanating from Greece and Rome was precisely its tendency to accept commonplace formulations and the promptings of ordinary language. This tradition tends to promote and to celebrate a go-along, get-along character type—one whose unwavering impulse is to gravitate toward middle positions, rather than to embrace an extreme when it is necessary. The situation may even call for rejecting altogether the preexisting binary formulation, searching for a different way of thinking about the problem altogether (R. Weaver 75). And where are we supposed to get the intellectual and moral stuffing for such a move?

Plato disdained the character of the language-confident rhetorician precisely because the rhetorician lacked this stuffing. He mistrusted the language-confident approach of the sophists because he saw in it the corruption of the state, and also because he was confident of a Truth that ordinary language could not reach. Saint Augustine, our other fierce asymmetrist, came to a relatively low opinion of language because he also had come to believe in a higher truth, a Word so powerful and so beyond the mark of both language and science that it could yank mere human discourses into strange forms, sometimes out of the very moorings of human intelligibility.

Not all critiques of structural analogy come from the same place, however. Its weaknesses and dangers have been pointed out by individuals of widely different philosophical and political leanings: by ancient conservatives, such as Plato and Saint Augustine, both devoted to a higher truth; but also by postmodern, post-structuralist thinkers, anxious about the contingency and impermanence of all truth. From this latter perspective, any sort of confidence in analogical relations between linguistic structures and structures outside of language is misplaced, because those latter structures cannot really be said to exist. Another critique is less metaphysical and more political, arguing that the common language and its structures are too often complicit in "truthifying" (reifying) what may no longer be true (or was never true) and justifying what may be no longer just (or was never just).

Overall, the weakness of structural analogy may be summed up as follows:

Like all forms of symmetry, structural analogy is seen by many to be too optimistic about the relationship of language to the world. Furthermore, the view presented by structural analogy is more dangerous than most, the argument will go, because (unlike the symmetry of sounds, for instance) it aims at broad and comprehensive understandings of human culture. This broad overconfidence can lead to a characteristically "humanist" downgrading and neglect of expert knowledge, from special disciplines whose methods and procedures are designed first and foremost to improve upon ordinary ways of conceptualizing and talking about things. Resorting to analogy is too often driven by ignorance and the absence of an exact, scientific vocabulary for describing things.

Another danger—one to which teachers of writing have been particularly at risk—is that of too readily assuming that lower levels of structure in discourse are microcosms of higher levels. We see this most readily in the belief that, because there are analogies of organization between the two, concentration on the sentence or the paragraph will lead to skill and sophistication in producing whole essays. Such a view actually constitutes a reversion back to that old and untenable form of symmetry that equates and locks in specific forms to specific meanings and purposes. It has been rightly criticized as analogous to the proposition that if you inflate a tire long enough, you will end up with a car.

Finally, recalling the continuum analogy and the language-directed search for middle positions, a weakness of structural analogy is its suggestion of a necessity to accept, work within, and look for satisfying compromises within existing structures—most notoriously, existing relations of class, race, gender, and sexual preference. It is true that, in order to speak and listen at all, you are required to accept the structures of language—its preexisting categories, binary oppositions, and the stages in between—however, you are not necessarily required to accept the structures of your culture as the necessary confines of thinking, behaving, or ordering lives. It may be necessary, and it may make you happier, to think and perhaps live entirely outside of those structures. The established forms and structures of language and discourse can have a limiting and blinding as well as an exploratory and enlightening function.

A thoughtful response to these criticisms can be divided into two sides, the practical and the theoretical. On the practical side, after we have acknowledged that all analogies eventually break down, we can also recognize that many of them do go far enough, and last long enough, to be provocative and instructive. This is particularly true in relation to the language-saturated arenas of art, society, and human relations. Structural analogies may not (and perhaps should not) provide or substitute for philosophies of life or ultimate truth, if such a thing exists; however, they do provide windows of exploration—hints of something larger—in that ongoing process of improvisation and gradual discovery that connects the art of discourse to the art of living. And so learning from language is an honest and useful vocation.

From a theoretical perspective, all of the objections are true and warranted, but they are also (except in the most extreme and self-defeating articulations) ways of saying that wherever there is symmetry there is also asymmetry. As it turns out, this is a view that I have conceded, and indeed promoted, from the beginning. All symmetry is partial and provisional, and much of it is illusory. Every intuition or claim is subject to a correction and a counterclaim; however, that does not always invalidate the claim itself, though it will certainly put a limit on its application. Listening to and learning from language, therefore, should always include the search for both things. Ultimately, the theoretical escape from the strictures against structural analogy is to fuse together and install the complementary and divergent visions offered by symmetry and asymmetry as the reigning pilot analogy of this discourse.

Symmetry/Asymmetry as Pilot Analogy

As we have already seen, symmetry and asymmetry are not simply separate theories or ways of viewing language. They are contrasting and complementary elements—"needs," we may term them—within the system of language. They are also feelings and intuitions we have about language as we are using it. There are times when language enacts and performs its very message, and there are others when it needs to be out of the way. With symmetry, language retains its communicative power, its attachments to feeling, and its complicity in the specific actions that we are using language to perform. With asymmetry—which is specifically the asymmetry of forms—it retains flexibility, the possibility of detached reference, the ability to adapt old forms to new uses, and the ability to fashion new ones altogether.

Symmetry and asymmetry are also contrasting and complementary functions—though far less technically understood ones—in individual uses of language. There are moments in our lives (a time of intimate and heartfelt condolence, for instance) when the specific content of a message is far less important than the fact of the message and the "package" of its sending—the family of expressions, familiar sentence forms, tones of voice, accompanying gestures, touch, embrace, everything. Alternately, there are other moments when none of this matters or should matter. The information is paramount, detail is important. We want language to perform its humble duty and stay out of the way.

From this basic dichotomy, language performing and enacting its very message versus language as a dressing for deeper meaning, emerge different ideals of composition and style. An easy way to exhibit these divergent ideals is by investigating what they might identify as "the best writing":

1. The best writing conveys its message with the greatest clarity, efficiency, and readability without interference and distractions of language.
2. The best writing reveals and dramatizes the full richness and complexity of its subject, bringing the reader into an experience of discovery and appreciation.

What anyone knows who has taught and practiced writing is that these are not necessarily competing ideals. They belong to different arenas of experience and of purpose, and the world is certainly large enough to contain them both.

The two ideals have certainly competed, however, in the world of rhetoric and composition teaching, and the reasons for this are not that difficult to discern. First of all, our time is always short, and so there are always questions and conflicts about what to emphasize. Second, we are never quite sure about how learning develops, and so there are always questions about what is more "basic." Finally, we have different levels of what may be termed epistemological confidence with respect to different subjects and situations. Sometimes (as in technical communications) we are highly confident in those "already knowns" that language is supposed to convey transparently. At other times, we concentrate rightly on those processes of discourse making that we hope will assist in discovering and gaining knowledge.

Participation and Freedom

Such considerations of timeliness, discovery, and learning lead us outward from language to the world. And so what is the analogy to? The cultural and intellectual counterparts of symmetry and asymmetry—the interpretive poles that they anticipate and extend toward in our lives—are participation and freedom. As a very plain example, we can point out that in any family or close-knit social situation an individual will characteristically struggle between two desires: the natural desire to belong and be part of the group, and the desire to stand apart, to attempt new things and create new associations.

The same pattern holds, of course, for the place of the individual in any sort of human organization. Some individuals are "wholly into it," we observe; they represent the institution and dramatize its values. At the same time, others are more "balanced" in their approach; others are anxiously conflicted and in a state of transition; others may be fighting for their freedom; and still others have already planned their escape. Once this pattern of involvement and detachment, the simultaneous longing for participation and freedom, is put forward in a simple outline, we may be prepared to plot its presence in all sorts of individual, organizational, and social relations.

For literary humanists, the more familiar ground is the representation of these relations in literature. Consequently, we might expect the symmetry/asymmetry analogy to be useful in understanding works of literature themselves. For the adventurous analogist, however, this suggestion will go beyond the observation that participation/freedom is a ubiquitous theme in literature, and a pattern to listen for in any complex literary work. A familiar, structuralist strategy involves listening for those elements of form (character, setting, opposition, symbol, analogy, and so forth) that the author has employed in special ways within the discursive system or "language" of the literary artwork. We use this strategy, for example, when we point out that the forest in Nathaniel Hawthorne's story "Young Goodman Brown" is not at all a realistic depiction of a New England rural setting. It exists, rather, in a contrastive (or binary) relation to the village, and this pair in turn relates to other pairs representing conflicts and states of mind in the main character.

Yet another strategy is to examine closely the ways in which established forms of discourse—from words, to story types, to such higher level, generic forms as pastoral elegy—are used in both symmetrical and asymmetrical ways. They are evoked and exploited for their conventional associations; but they are also stretched to new meanings and new purposes, giving us a renewed understanding and appreciation of things. We follow this strategy when we point out, for example, that the form or genre of the pastoral elegy in John Milton's "Lycidas" is stretched to serve an autobiographical purpose. He is participating in a particular way of doing things, for a particular purpose, but he has also broken free of that conventional purpose and moved it into new territory.

Moving outward again to the world of language-saturated practice, we find that in any particular setting there are symmetries of form and purpose—established genres, ways of doing things. In "real life" every person and every organization will have different messages to send as well as different things to be accomplished—either by full, conventional participation, by experimentation, by startling modifications, or outright declarations of freedom. A good deal of this directly involves the framing of discourse. The language arts can be useful preparation for that, of course, and, if imaginatively organized, for a good deal beyond.

Suggested Reading

Burke, Kenneth. *The Rhetoric of Religion.* Boston: Beacon Press, 1961. This is one of Kenneth Burke's most interesting works, attempting to trace the etiology of key religious concepts to human ways of producing and language. Not unaware of the meanings packed into the concept of logos, Burke rather audaciously proposes a new discipline of "logology," devoted to exploring implications of ultimate value in language and the uses of language.

Crusius, Timothy. *Kenneth Burke and the Conversation After Philosophy.* Carbondale: Southern Illinois University Press, 1999. Among the many studies of Kenneth Burke's theory and criticism, this book provides the best explanation, I believe, of Burke's affinity to the linguistic turn of pragmatist language philosophy.

Maddox, Kristy. "Finding Comedy in Theology: A Hopeful Supplement to Kenneth Burke's Logology." *Philosophy and Rhetoric* (2006): 208–32. An excellent demonstration of the continuing relevance of Burke's *Rhetoric of Religion,* both to rhetoric and to religious studies. Offering some corrections to Burke from the perspective of womanist theology, Maddox nevertheless admires the way Burke has shown "how the cycle of order, which culminates in atonement by sacrifice, is fundamental not only to the Christian religion but also to human language systems" (209).

Rorty, Richard, ed. *The Linguistic Turn: Recent Essays in Philosophical Method.* Chicago: University of Chicago Press, 1967. This landmark collection of essays by British and American philosophers constitutes an excellent introduction to the reasons why, and the methods by which, traditional philosophical problems can be illuminated by the analysis of language.

Vendler, Zeno. *Linguistics in Philosophy.* Ithaca: Cornell University Press, 1967. Although its conclusions are limited and modest, this is one of the most skillful attempts that I have seen to coordinate detailed grammatical analysis with conceptual analysis. The emphasis is less on making breakthroughs in the latter than in demonstrating how language "knows" conceptual subtleties through rules of grammatical context restriction.

5

Creating the World
The Performative Principle

> In this beginning, O God, hast thou made heaven and
> earth, namely in thy Word, in thy Son, in thy Power,
> in thy Wisdom, in thy Truth; after a wonderful manner
> speaking, and after a wonderful manner making.
> —*Saint Augustine, Confessions, XI, ix*   (Watts trans. 2:227–28)

While investigating Saint Augustine's view of language in chapter two, I suggested that Judaism and early Christianity captured intriguing insights about language in the following ideas: that God created the world through speech; that the Word was with God in the beginning; that without the Word "was not anything made that was made" (John, I. 3); and that the sending of the Word into the world constituted an important message (gospel) about the coming of the kingdom of God.

These ideas have been the subjects of endless theological discussion in Western civilization. What is linguistically interesting about them is their implicit understanding that there exists a reciprocity of saying and doing, of conceptualizing and enacting, and of expressing and creating reality with words. These traditions appear to understand that in our use of language we are not merely saying things but also doing and making things; and through our actions, conversely, we are also saying things to those who witness them.

Saint Augustine makes a valiant attempt to understand this reciprocity in his treatise *On the Trinity*; however, he restricts his treatment to God's language, the Holy Scripture, not human speech, in which Augustine has very little confidence. As a consequence, the reciprocity of saying and doing is basically put forward as part of a great mystery, like the mystery of the Trinity itself. And a mystery it remained, in both theology and philosophy, in those few cases where it was acknowledged at all. The Enlightenment poet and philosopher Johann Wolfgang von Goethe took a stab at it in his great poetic drama *Faust*. Here, in a famous passage Doctor Faust meditates on the meaning of that mysterious term logos, from the beginning of John's gospel:

> "In the beginning was the Word"—thus runs the text.
> Who helps me on? Already I'm perplexed!
> I cannot grant the word such sovereign merit,
> I must translate it in a different way
> If I'm indeed illuminated by the Spirit.
> . . . .
> The spirit speaks! And lo, the way is freed,
> I calmly write: "In the beginning was the Deed"!
>
> (*Faust* I, 1224–37, Arndt trans.)

What makes this passage such a tour de force is that Dr. Faust ends his meditation by confidently translating "the word" as its opposite, "the deed." The impiety—spiritual rebellion, even—of this idea lies not merely in Faust's refusal to recognize the Son as logos but also in a broader implication: the Word is the act of creation, and not just God's creation but the poet's as well. (Keep in mind that Faust is the man who sold his soul to the devil, in pursuit of knowledge and power past mere human capacity.) And so in Goethe's rendering, the reciprocity of saying and doing is now stolen from the heavens and humanized into the mystery of poetic creation.

Like most modern literary humanists, I am a worshiper at the alter of poetry. However, I consider it no act of impiety to point out that the air of mystery surrounding the reciprocity of saying and doing derives, at least in part, from a defect in the tradition of Western language philosophy. Unfortunately, from ancient times into the twentieth century, the Western tradition of language philosophy has worked from within a paradigm that obscures the notion of reciprocity altogether. This is the paradigm of linguistic form as the signifier of things outside of language. Additionally, as we have already seen, most philosophical discussions within the signifier paradigm have focused on a single question: language's adequacy to perform its role of signifying. If structures of language (the ancient question goes) do not match in some way the structures of things outside of language, how can we adequately know or communicate knowledge about these things? Modern language philosophy and linguistics have found ways to break out of the signifier paradigm—chiefly through what has become known as the performative principle.

The Theory of Speech Acts

If we step back for a moment from the epistemological questions that have preoccupied philosophers, we can observe that a good deal of what drives the fascination with symmetry—the analogy of language to the world—is aesthetic. The mirror-imaging—observed, felt, or imagined—between language and the objects of its attention is a source of intense pleasure and satisfaction for the listeners and readers of linguistic performance. And this pleasure coincides with the strong feeling that language is not merely signifying or representing things but also dramatizing and participating in them.

The problem is that the case for symmetry is practically always vulnerable to a rather damaging rational and scientific critique, and Augustine even manages to put forth a theological critique. Moreover, as it turns out, asymmetry—that other side of the coin—is a good thing. The condition of asymmetry, as we have seen, is also a condition of freedom. The forms of language are not locked into corresponding values and experiences; they are free to discover and embrace new things. The French literary theorist Gerard Genette, at the end of his exhaustive study *Mimologics*, is quick to concede that mimology (Genette's term for symmetry) remains at best a kind of "enchantment," though a lovely and persistent one. As a consequence, it appears that if we want to account for the feeling of participation, rather than simply to dismiss it as an illusion, we will need to reach beyond the signifier paradigm altogether. We will need to find a rational way of recapturing the old wisdom of the Word as creator of the world.

Fortunately, such a way lies close at hand, in the branch of language philosophy known as speech-act theory. First developed in the mid-twentieth century by the British philosopher J. L. Austin, speech-act theory is the founding body of principle and description behind the field of pragmatics, the branch of linguistics that studies how language operates in situational contexts. Speech-act theory has had a widespread influence on a variety of other fields as well, including epistemology, ethics, rhetoric, literature, and literacy studies (see Searle; Pratt; Fish; Culler; Beale; and Olson). The great American critic and philosopher Kenneth Burke should also be mentioned at this point. While making only scant reference to the actual terminology or linguistics of speech-acts, Burke (in such works as *The Rhetoric of Religion, A Grammar of Motives, A Rhetoric of Motives,* and *Language as Symbolic Action*) pursues a parallel line of insight and is involved in precisely the same project: that of reclaiming the study of language from exile in the land of asymmetry, and reconnecting it to significant action in the world.

The central insight of speech-act theory, first put forward by Austin in a charmingly titled series of lectures, *How To Do Things With Words,* is that sentences do not merely say things, they also do things. In fact, the basic unit of human speech is not the sentence at all, as traditionally understood, but what may be termed the act of speech—something that may or may not coincide grammatically with the sentence. The initial proof of this lies in the existence of an entire class of sentence nuclei—that is, simple predicates—known as performatives. These are verbs that do not really say or claim things at all; they perform actions. They include such verbs as "pronounce," "dub," "sentence," "apologize," and "submit," as used in the following sentences:

> I pronounce you man and wife.
>
> I dub you knight.
>
> I sentence you to death by hanging.
>
> I apologize for what I said (or did).
>
> I hereby submit this application.

A basic characteristic of speech acts such as these is that they are neither true nor false but rather successful or unsuccessful, workable or not, according to the circumstances and behavior of the participants. You might question the wisdom, appropriateness, or even the legitimacy of the marriage or the death sentence, but you would not claim either to be true or false. Similarly, you might doubt the sincerity of your friend's apology, or even consider it unacceptable, but your response would not be to say, "I disagree," or "That's not true." The apology is something your friend is doing rather than asserting or claiming. Conversely, the pronouncement of marriage will be valid or successful not on the basis of its conformity to facts or of valid reasoning (the couple really do love each other; it makes sense for them to get married) but on the basis of certain socially determined qualifying conditions: the couple are legally eligible; the individual making the pronouncement is actually empowered to do so, and so forth.

The apology is a trickier matter—there is in fact an enormous literature on the subject but it leads us to a different kind of "success condition" (see Meier). So, I ask you to think of apologies focused upon minor incidents—the kind that friends and coworkers deliver to each other all the time in the course or normal interactions:

> I'm sorry I broke your pencil!
> Sorry to be a bit late with this.
> I realize I shouldn't have said those things.

The purpose of such a speech act is to restore a certain equilibrium to the relationship, and in general, we can say that it will be "successful" not on the basis of its conformity to the facts of the matter (whether your friend really was at fault in the matter; whether she really does believe she owes you an apology, and so on) but on its being delivered and put together in "the right way" ("It wasn't what she said; it was the way she said it"). The right way, as it turns out, might include a variety of factors, including the following:

> It was performed in an appropriate setting (either just the two of you or in the company of others, as appropriate).
>
> It was performed with a tone of voice and a choice of words that convey an appropriate level of sincerity, with an "explanation" (not necessarily a true one) that matches in weight and gravity the level of the offense.
>
> It was performed with appropriate accompanying gestures and body language, leading into handshakes, pats, perhaps even hugs and kisses.

Significantly, the entire event (the verbal apology, its surrounding conditions, and behaviors) is an action, embedded in and continuous with broader actions. We can also say without cynicism or deprecation that it is a kind of performance. Its language participates in, even constructs, the reality it names. This does not mean, of course, that there are not real things out there. The discourse does not make that pencil or undo the breaking of it. It does, however, preserve or restore a state of personal equilibrium with its audience, and that is the social reality that it creates. In this respect it is like the language of public ritual and of literature, also discourses that are more performance than statement. We do need to make a hasty concession at this point: in such discourses, there is of course a "truth of the matter" that has to be taken into account. This truth, however, may not always be a complete truth or a literal truth. The success of the discourse will depend less upon strict fidelity of reference than upon its well-constructedness, its apt response to preexisting conventions, and its winning engagement of an audience.

So striking is the difference between performative and nonperformative verbs that Austin, early in his lectures, asks us to consider the proposition that human discourse is made up of two fundamentally different kinds of speech acts: performatives, whose purpose is primarily to commit actions; and constatives, whose primary purpose is to make statements (1–12). He then outlines the surprisingly varied kinds of actions that language can perform. On the one hand, such acts as apologizing, for instance, assuring, thanking, warning, or scolding are labeled "behabitives"—that is, speech acts that adjust or create relationships (160–61). On the other hand, such acts as finding someone innocent or guilty, assigning grades, delivering sentences, or calling penalties in a football game are "verdictives"—that is, speech acts that formally decide matters (153–55). Austin adds several more such categories, with enough examples in each to convince us that a substantial portion of our regular discourse consists as much of performing actions as of making statements—of constructing certain realities with language as well as describing certain realities outside of language.

As Austin's discussion unfolds, however, a fact emerges that will not surprise anyone who has been considering the symmetry question: the particular category or character of a speech act may or may not be directly signaled by the choice of verb. In some limited cases of legal or official discourse, it is true, a specific performative verb is required in order to foreclose any possibility of ambiguity. Consider the following examples:

I *pronounce* you man and wife.

The defendant is *hereby sentenced* to death by hanging.

However, in most instances, the particular character of a statement—is it constative or performative, or what kind of performative?—usually has to be determined from the verbal and situational context. A good example is the statement, "He's only ten years old." If you think about it, you will realize that such an utterance like this is never a simple statement of fact. Depending on the context, it might be an act of congratulation, or of apology, perhaps even a warning. Here, as elsewhere, we find a limited circle of direct correspondence between form and meaning (represented by official or ritual words) encompassed by a much broader area of disconnection, ambiguity, and indeterminacy.

So great is this area of indeterminacy, in fact, that later in his own exposition Austin is led to discard the constative/performative distinction in a strict sense. Every utterance, after all, whether overtly or distinctly performative or not, has a certain performative character. Even statements that simply state or record information, after all, are engaged in the acts of stating or recording. And even the strictly referential discourses of science and scholarship characteristically do their work through such purely discursive acts as claiming, substantiating, proposing, analyzing, concluding, and so on.

Conversely, even such overtly performative utterances as "I pronounce you man and wife," and "Off with her head!" have some constative or referential character. Without this content they would be nonsensical. Just as importantly for the present discussion, neither of the statements above can actually consummate their actions. Just as words are inevitably involved in actions, there is a level at which they are irretrievably cut off from them. In this particular dimension, as well as in the broader consideration of symmetry and asymmetry, participation and nonparticipation remain entwined in one another. The paradox of saying and doing does not go away.

Performatives and Performance

Austin's next step in *How To Do Things With Words* is to replace the constative/performative distinction with a threefold analysis now familiar in the field of pragmatics: the theory of locutionary, illocutionary, and perlocutionary acts. In this more capacious view, every act of speech is seen to have three dimensions of meaning at once: what it says (locutionary), what it does (illocutionary), and how it affects (or is intended to affect) an audience (perlocutionary). Thus, when in a particular circumstance Jack's father says, "I do want you to wash the car," he is at one level making reference to specific individuals, things, and operations (locutionary); he is actually, however, giving an order (illocutionary); and he is in effect clarifying the issue of who is in charge (perlocutionary). All of that constitutes the total meaning of his statement.

This comprehensive view of meaning helps us to understand that differences and even failures of interpretation often have less to do with what a speaker was saying than with what the speaker was doing by saying it, or what she was hoping to accomplish through saying it. How often do we find ourselves backtracking or clarifying with statements such as, "I certainly was not recommending that you buy a new wardrobe!" or "I didn't mean for you to take it as a criticism"? A rule of thumb for understanding any discourse, large or small, is to get a grip on at least two things: What is it saying? And what is it doing?

For those of us who spend a good deal of our time interpreting texts, this theory stands as a sharp reminder that there is always a great deal more to be done than to understand what the words of a text mean, what its sentences say, or even how its parts fit together into a coherent whole. In order to get at those broader elements of significance (What is it doing? What is it accomplishing with its audience?), we need to understand its contexts, and this may require a great deal of historical and cultural understanding.

Austin may have created a slight distortion by casting his broader theory as a rejection of the constative/performative distinction. Although the trio of locutionary, illocutionary, and perlocutionary acts certainly delivers a more comprehensive understanding of meaning in discourse, and although the constative/performative distinction can never be absolute, there are still some verbs that are more recognizably performative than others (compare "warn," "object," and "appeal" with "ride," "dig," and "fall"). In addition, what is true of verbs is also true of whole speech acts. Such statements as "Let there be light!" or "Off with her head!" are unambiguously actions, standing out as more performative in character than such statements as "God created the world in six days" or "The queen ordered Alice's beheading." These are unambiguously about matters outside the language that conveys them.

It is not surprising, therefore, that some linguists have retained the constative/performative distinction for some descriptive purposes, and there exists some speculation that sentences contain underlying or deep structure performatives (see Lakoff). Just as importantly for our purposes, there are clearly some extended discourses and kinds of discourse that are more important for the social acts they perform than for the things they say. Think of eulogies, welcoming speeches, and the like. How rare is the graduation speech that, in addition to praising, congratulating, exhorting, entertaining, and in other ways gracing the occasion with the already familiar, actually makes an important statement or argument (Beale, "Rhetorical Performative Discourse")?

In addition, there are some discourses that have a primary character as performances rather than as direct statements or arguments about reality. We are now of course in the realm of literary art. Significantly, we are also into the realm where elements of language (sounds, words, sentences, and larger units of discourse) have precisely that participatory character that symmetrists have sought to explain and understand. A traditional way of understanding this is to say that art is an imitation or representation—a re-presenting or reenacting—of reality rather than a statement about it or a description of it. It is less traditional to think of art as actually creating reality; however, the notion is not far-fetched if you consider that "reality" consists as much in the relations among things as in the things themselves. These relations exist as common understandings, and these in turn are influenced, even created, by statements—by discourse. Shelley's famous statement in *A Defence of Poetry* that "poets are the unacknowledged legislators of the world," though it remains extravagant, begins to be understandable in linguistic terms (701).

Have we gone too far in equating the performative principle in language (the doing, making, or carrying out of something) with performance in the sense of showing, enactment, or public exhibition? Austin did not do so, and most of the linguists who adapted his insights have not done so either. Nevertheless, we must proceed with caution. We have already recognized that the command, "Off with her head!" does not in itself dramatize or "perform" the execution. Such recognition does remind us of an inevitable disjunction between commands and carrying those commands through (lucky for Alice!). However, even caution can be taken too far. This sort of "realism" also runs the risk of associating the notion of action too thoroughly with end results. The ordering of Alice's beheading is after all a significant social event in itself. If it were accomplished, the queen would certainly be considered more guilty than the poor minions who carried it out; and significantly at this moment, we see that the queen's act is "performed" with great dramatic flair. It is in fact an action, a demonstration, and an enactment all at once.

The vital connection of the performative principle to public exhibition or enactment can be most readily witnessed in the civic, scholastic, and ecclesiastical rituals that punctuate significant moments in the life of a community. Such events are focused upon performative speech acts (congratulating, conferring, celebrating, consoling, bequeathing, beseeching, and so on). They are accomplished through ritualized dramatic enactments, and they are accompanied by elaborate costuming, pageantry, music, and other artistic performances. These rituals are sometimes cynically dismissed as "not where the real action is," and they do characteristically exist in tension with "what is going on in the real world." However, they are significant actions in themselves as well as performances. They do count for something.

From the connection of performatives to ritual performance, we can carry the connection forward logically to literature. We can see the connection not merely in the dramatic and artistic character of most rituals, but also in the special character of literary language, even when it is transferred to the printed page for individual readers, freed specifically from communal ritual. Historically, we know that much of our literature has its origins in civic and religious festival (which in traditional societies are one and the same). The most notable example of this is the Greek drama, which began as an actual performance of the annual festival of Dionysus, and in its later, more mature expression came simply to accompany that festival. Centuries later, after the art of drama had been lost to Europeans of the Middle Ages, it reemerged out of the liturgical practices of the medieval church.

Literature performs reality. For this reason the more important connection of the performative to literary performance lies in the use of language to enact and to construct worlds of meaning. As we have just noted, this is most conspicuously true in the drama, where dialogue and simulated, symbolic, somewhat ritualized action intermingle to compose scenes of human life that are far more concentrated and charged with significance than most of what we experience in our daily lives. It is also true of lyric poetry. Here, even when they are not combining words with musical performance, poets mine language for those elements of phonological and diagrammatic iconicity that can be brought to bear upon expression. More importantly, I think, they use words to create scenes of dramatic interaction that we may not have witnessed before.

Perhaps even more importantly still, poets are able to discover forms of metaphorical and symbolic representation that go beyond saying things in different, arresting, or beautiful ways. Saying things beautifully is what happens, you might say, in good poetry; however, the best poetry actually discovers and enacts new ways of experiencing the world—and therefore creates new kinds of social realities. Up to this point, nothing has been said about prose narrative, where the role of specific acts of language is less direct and less conspicuous. However, the principle in fiction is the same as in other forms of literature. The prose narrative performs and enacts a vision of human life, and out of this performance, in the best instances, comes a new way of experiencing the world.

With the performative principle, we discover a way of accounting for the powerful experience of participation—that is, of language's participation in the reality it names—without upsetting or contradicting the well established counterprinciple that there is very little one-to-one correspondence of form to meaning. We do not have to upend what we have repeatedly discovered, that with respect to reference and even to expression the forms of language are largely asymmetrical. At the same time, we discover that saying and referring are only half of the story: in addition to talking about things, we are using language to perform a multitude of social acts, creating the very social realities we are talking about.

Is everything we say, then, a performance? Certainly it would be monstrous to think so, if we are thinking of performance as a contrivance, a manipulation of events. However, we do have to recognize, as actors, poets, and rhetoricians always have, that there is a continuum of performance in all of our saying and doing, from the "natural" and least formal utterances to those highly planned, structured, and scripted events that we recognize as rituals and works of art. And with this recognition we are back to the point of reciprocity: we use words to perform actions, and we use actions to send messages, both as individuals in intimate settings and as communities on a grand scale.

Contemplation versus Action

In chapter three, the concept of the pilot analogy was introduced as a significant structural property of language that "predicts" or has an analogue in a problem of human culture. The cultural analogue of the saying/doing binary is contemplation versus action. The discussion of the performative principle has shown the reciprocity of saying and doing in all our uses of language. At the same time, we can identify different specializations of language use that favor either contemplation or action. In such discourses as contracts, constitutions, and public rhetoric, we see in varying degrees a leaning toward action; conversely in such discourses as scientific descriptions, theoretical and historical discussions, we see an orientation toward pure saying, or contemplation. Just as importantly, we encounter in some discourses (substantially on the "saying" side) a use of language that is primarily and intentionally transparent, "out of the way"; and on the other side, in varying degrees, a use of language that is deliberately, sometimes extravagantly, performative and participatory.

In literary art we have the intriguing spectacle of a discourse whose orientation is not toward action (unless considered, as in the drama, a simulated action) but whose language is fully performative and participatory. Intriguing, yes, but not contradictory to the basic point here, because we have to remember that art is no more committed to the contemplative side of the equation, really, than to the active side. It is no more bound to the literal truth of things than to direct participation in the world's business. And it does help to keep in mind that most forms of literary art have their origins in public ritual. Literary art, then, while not a self-contradictory enterprise, is certainly a matter of endless fascination in this respect, and this is what much of literary theory, from its beginning with Aristotle's *Poetics*, has been fascinated with.

The linguistic paradox of saying versus doing anticipates the cultural paradox of contemplation versus action, a topic that has for ages engaged philosophers, theologians, mystics, and poets in a variety of cultures. Every serious human endeavor, like every speech act, has its contemplative and its active dimensions, its theoretical and its practical sides. And like human discourses, human occupations tend to specialize in one direction or another. But even such active-leaning occupations as engineering and building have their theoretical dimension (a grounding in mathematics and geometry); and even such contemplative occupations as the history and theory of discourse have practical dimensions and applications (the activities of writing, publishing, lecturing, teaching, and composing primarily instructional materials). Every practitioner of any serious art faces at every turn the opportunities and problems of balancing or combining these dimensions in creative and different ways.

The prospect becomes more fascinating, and sometimes more vexing, if we think not of occupations but of human lives, every one of which has both an active and a contemplative or reflective side, but not every one of which has found a happy coalescence of the two. In prosperous and complex civilizations such as our own (but also in simpler and poorer ones), we witness a spectrum of lives from contemplative to active. Some of these are quietly analogous to constative speech acts, while others are strenuously and ostentatiously performative. Every person's problem, of course, is in some way to accommodate both dimensions. Lives are more difficult to manage (less tightly structured and rule governed, we might say) than language, but the analogy does hold.

An especially interesting point of analogy brings us once again to the symmetry question. With forms of living, as with every aspect of language that we have examined, there exists a condition of asymmetry—a lack of one-to-one correspondence, form to meaning. For instance, the form or medium of the discussion circle, which for many people would be considered a stepping back from frenetic activity to think and reflect, might be experienced by its leader as a putting into practice of certain therapeutic or spiritual principles and precepts. And even the act of reading a book, which most people would certainly consider a contemplative activity, might by a theorist be considered the active part of her job, the necessary act of information gathering—antecedent, actually, to the contemplative act of devising and solving new problems. If you will look at the multiple uses of the word "act" in the previous sentence, you will see the analogy of act to speech act. Even the most oracular, nonperformative saying—"Absence makes the heart grow fonder"—can be under particular circumstances an act of some kind: an assurance, a warning, or a consolation.

We have identified the various relations between action and contemplation as everyone's problem. However, there can be no doubt that by its very nature the problem has always appeared more vexing to intellectuals. A commitment to understanding things theoretically, even such practical and urgent things as engineering or politics, requires a substantial stepping back from practice, both because of the need for objectivity and also because of the need for time to think—to develop generalizations, definitions, and statements of cause and effect. What the intellectual gains in general clarity of understanding, however, may be compromised by the consequent lack of familiarity with practical workings. The intellectual observer of the world may be considered by others to be hopelessly abstracted and withdrawn from "the real world."

It could be worse. Such a person might in some circumstances find the broader, contemplative vision to be positively at odds with the everyday way of seeing things and acting in the world. This has happened classically in the realm of politics, and the classic portrait of the "tragedy of the philosopher" in this realm appears in Plato's *Republic.* Here, in a famous allegory, the mass of humanity are depicted as confined to a dark cave with their heads and necks chained so that they are allowed to see only the shadows of things, being displayed by puppeteers behind them, and projected by the light of a fire onto a wall in front of them. A rare individual (the philosopher) among them escapes from the chains, and through an arduous process (the disciplines of the intellect) eventually works his way to the outside, gradually accommodating his eyes to the blinding light of the sun until he is able to see the true reality of things. Such a person, the narrator Socrates believes, would obviously be fittest to lead the mass of humankind to a better life. However, so accustomed are these people to the ways of darkness that when the philosopher returns to active life on just such a mission, the people disbelieve and distrust him, even to the point of putting him to death (*Republic* 514a–20a).

The contemplative vision is always placed steadfastly in tension with active life in Plato's philosophy. It is therefore a topic of discussion in all philosophies influenced by Plato, including much of Christianity, into modern times. So pervasive is this discussion that Plato's statement that some philosophical issues are "built into the nature of sentences" would certainly appear to apply in this case (*Philebus* 15d). There does exist in the Western tradition a rich philosophical and meditative discourse on the topic, and a tradition of poetry in which it is enacted. Here is a great example, from Shakespeare:

> Poor soul, the center of my sinful earth,
> Lord of these rebel pow'rs that thee array,
> Why dost thou pine within and suffer dearth,
> Painting thy outward walls so costly gay?
> Why so large cost, having so short a lease,
> Dost thou upon thy fading mansion spend?
> Shall worms, inheritors of this excess,
> Eat up thy charge? Is this thy body's end?
> Then, soul, live thou upon thy servant's loss,
> And let that pine to aggravate thy store;
> Buy terms divine in selling hours of dross;
> Within be fed, without be rich no more:
> So shalt thou feed on Death, that feeds on men,
> And Death once dead, there's no more dying then.
>
> (Sonnet 146)

In this famous sonnet, we have what might be considered a Christianized and personalized dramatization of Plato's cave. In this drama, it is the individual soul that is confined (thus cut off from a higher reality) in a castle or mansion (the body) and besieged and deceived, as in medieval warfare, by the rebel army of the senses and worldly enjoyments. In the narrator's rather excited and lurid exhortation to the soul—that is, in what the poem says—only an escape or release from this imprisonment (which is partly a self-imprisonment) will lead to truth and happiness. And yet, what the poem dramatizes or enacts is something rather different: not the soul's escape but rather the soul's precarious and vulnerable predicament of continuing entrapment. The narrator of the poem, observe, is not the (superior) soul speaking to the (inferior) body, but a voice superior to them both—an alter ego, let us say—speaking to a rather hapless and indecisive soul. The soul is active in this drama—just as our minds and our discourses are active in figuring out how to live—and so too is the voice that speaks so engagedly to the soul, although it claims to speak from a place of contemplation, beyond the soul.

Shakespeare's sonnet is not only a wonderful example of our civilization's continuing discourse about action and contemplation, but it also dramatizes for its readers a language, a voice, that both acts in the world and stands above that action. It is no accident that a great deal of modern philosophical discourse about the objectivity or accessibility of truth has turned upon the question of whether such a place above action and performance really exists. It is clear that language itself, with its simultaneous locutionary and illocutionary character in every instance, seems to whisper that there is such a place. Skeptics have tended to disagree with the suggestion for precisely this reason: it is something that our language prompts us to believe, they argue, but that is not true. Austin, by contrast, believed resolutely in the "value of paying close attention to ordinary language" (Pitcher 18).

So far we have established that a great deal of the human use of language is better thought of as acting or enacting rather than saying, depicting, or expressing—in fact, that all saying is a kind of doing. Austin notes that many of the things we say are not properly thought of as true or false, but rather "happy or unhappy" (25). They work or they do not work. It follows from this insight that the feeling of rightness we experience when language is successfully used derives less often from symmetry—some kind of fit between structures of language and realities outside of language—than from "happy" performance—a convergence of success conditions for particular social actions.

There is an important lesson here for those of us who teach the arts of discourse. It follows also from these insights that a successful literary humanism will concentrate more upon strategies for "happily" performing actions—actions such as persuading, dissuading, convicting, exonerating, praising, and commemorating—than upon particular patterns of language or discourse that are thought to embody right thinking. Classical rhetoricians understood this, and they oriented their teaching around performance of these very actions. It is true that successful performance in many arenas does involve a different kind of symmetry—a meeting of audience expectations, including expected forms of language and structure; in others, however, it can involve an element of surprise and disruption, as when we encounter the human soul depicted as the unhappy lord of a handsome castle, besieged by "rebel powers."

Constructing Reality

We can now take the next step, from illocution to perlocution—that is, from acting with words to accomplishing things with words. Consider the meaning of the word "fact," which derives from "factum," past participle of the Latin "facere," to do or to make. A fact is something that has been done, made, that happens, or that exists. A good deal of what happens or comes to exist in our lives together, in societies and institutions, is brought about through acts of language, and that includes an array of common understandings and behaviors—beliefs, ways of understanding and conducting ourselves, attitudes, and prejudices. Many people who teach the arts of discourse do so out of a sense of the importance of these arts to a just and peaceful world. Many of these individuals participate avidly in a broader discussion about the social construction of reality—that is, the fascinating but difficult to explain idea that many things "exist" primarily because we think they do and say they do (see Berlin; Olson; and Roberts-Miller). I am not going to undertake here anything close to a review of this discussion, but I will point out that disputes in this arena center on issues of language that are not far from questions that surround the symmetry question: whether social realities are subjective or objective; whether any distinction can be made between subjective and objective dimensions; whether the language we use to build such realities is always already contaminated by prejudices of class, race, and gender; whether there is an attainable point of reason outside of such contamination; whether language itself is primary in performing reality, or whether language is basically expressive of (and secondary to) forces that are economic or psychological; and just how wide or narrow is the domain of things that have their existence because people believe them to be so.

Most of the time when we are speaking, we are barely aware of the medium of language. Partly for that very reason, we are not conscious of the prejudices and bigotries embedded in what we say and do. That is why the "social constructedness" of certain ways of talking and acting is sometimes best observed from the vantage point of opposition. We are always more apt to notice the strangeness or the defect in someone else's way of talking, particularly when that talking is at odds with our own way of thinking or being. In our own time, we have come to recognize race, class, gender, sexual orientation, and associated divisions, hierarchies, and value systems as socially constructed realities—not natural categories but formations of common consciousness that are entrenched in our common vocabularies and ways of speaking. Consequently, many discussions of social construction derive from particular strands of cultural criticism that are designed to expose elements of social constructedness in our presuppositions about these things.

There does exist a specifically linguistic angle of vision on social construction, however, and that is worth noting here. One of its most prominent expositors is the philosopher John Searle, a student of Austin, whose early work was in the theory of speech acts. In Searle's view, articulated in such influential works as *The Construction of Social Reality, Mind, Language and Society,* and *Consciousness and Language,* social constructedness is not simply a synonym for prejudicial or subjective viewpoints. There are distinct realities that we can call social—laws, money, arrangements of property, structures of government, and so forth—and these realities have their existence by common consent. They are spoken into existence, we might say, and they continue to exist because they constitute a valid and believable speaking. Much of Searle's work is devoted to explaining how such apparently subjective realities are in fact material and objective. And much of the explanation, for Searle, comes from the performative or illocutionary character of language. "In institutional reality," Searle notes, "language is not used merely to *describe* the facts but, in an odd way, is partly *constitutive* of the facts" (*Mind, Language, and Society* 115). Language itself is acting in the material world, and the realities it creates are objective, material realities.

Quickly, however—and departing somewhat from Searle's text—we need to bring back to mind the reciprocity of saying and doing, for realities that are "objective" and "material" can remain contingent nonetheless. And this contingency can be expanded to all social constructions. If words can become actions and things, those actions and things still send messages: they retain their status as "discourses." This is quite notably the case with laws, court sentences, and punishments, as the postmodern theorist Michel Foucault has dramatically shown (see *Discipline and Punish*). The American Democrat Hubert Humphrey, in an oft-quoted speech, famously said: "There are not enough jails, not enough policemen, not enough courts to enforce a law not supported by the people" (Shapiro 376). Laws are discourses; some individuals disobey them because they do not "believe" in them.

In Searle's rather cautious and moderate social constructionism, the sphere of realities that are spoken into existence is confined to specific arrangements of institutional life. Searle does not venture very far into the realm of attitudes, beliefs, and informal social relations, and this is something of a disappointment. This view is valuable, however, for a number of reasons. First of all, it is instructive to the project of listening to and learning from language for its specifically linguistic character: it gives us specific tools for understanding how language constructs reality. In Searle's *Mind, Language, and Society*, the reader encounters a restatement and refinement of Austin's types of the performative. There are "assertives," which simply represent certain things as true. Beyond this, there are the following sorts of illocutionary forces, which we can think of as ways of acting and ways of making things come about in the world (147–51):

- There are "directives," which "cannot be true or false, but they can be obeyed, disobeyed, complied with, granted, denied."

- There are "commisives," that is commitments or promises to undertake certain actions; and these also "cannot be true or false, but they can be carried out, kept, or broken."

- There are "expressives," apologies, congratulations, welcomes, and the like, whose success, as we have seen, is dependent not upon truth but upon sincerity.

- And there are "declaratives," the Declaration of Independence, an individual's oath of membership, a resignation, whose function is "to bring about a change in the world by representing it as having been changed" (see Derrida, "Declarations of Independence," for a viewpoint contrary to Searle's).

Searle's viewpoints also provide us, in a way that other social constructionisms do not (Derrida's, for instance), with a way of understanding that such notions as "truth," and "validity" can have an "objective" standing without always depending upon strict truth of reference—that is, a close linkage between language and entities outside of language. The fact of asymmetry does not, in and of itself, doom all of our ways of representing the world to subjectivity or ideology—that is, to self-justifying distortions influenced by relationships of power and domination. We are, to be sure, led by our ways of talking about things into essentializing realities that are by their nature contingent and, quite possibly, radically imperfect. Searle's view certainly does not rule out the existence and even the exuberant profusion of such errors; however, it does preserve a place, even if a modest one, for the sensible proposition that not all of our social realities (social agreements brought about through language) are contaminated.

Searle's philosophy is also valuable because it gives us a specific way of making the connection between operations of language and works of literature—discourses that have a primary character as performances and representations of reality. If the material and objective can be nonetheless contingent, it follows that the contingent can be nonetheless real. We might term this the law of spoken realities. The performative character of literature has been noted above, in particular its historical associations with acts of public ritual. Keep in mind, additionally, that a strong function of ritual, aside from such specific acts of welcoming, commemorating, celebrating, and so on, is the reinforcement, through strong and beautiful reassertion, of beliefs and values.

Searle does retain the assertive as a kind of referential speech act requiring a "fit" of language to an exterior reality; and this does appear to bracket off assertions, beliefs, and attitudes from those illocutions that are less dependent upon such a fit than upon happy performance. However, there is a type of assertive—let us call it strong representation—that has a more performative character: it establishes something as "real" by representing it in a particularly powerful way. Adapting Searle's (and Austin's) terms, we can say that it is neither true nor false, but it can be "happily" experienced. This type of strong representation is precisely what we experience with great works of literature, and so it is not going too far to say that literature goes beyond the making of imaginary worlds, as the conventional saying goes. Literature is undoubtedly involved in the construction of reality.

A Dialogue

I would like to test the rather startling proposition that literature is involved in the construction of reality by asking you to return to the sonnet by William Shakespeare. Suppose I were to claim that Shakespeare, through his powerful and engaging representation of the soul's imprisonment in the body, that "mansion" of sensual preoccupation, had "created" a social reality—in which everyone's personal life is viewed as such an imprisonment, and everyone's life, therefore, is involved in a consequent struggle for release? This might seem unobjectionable as a casual way of talking about the poem, but nevertheless not really the case, strictly speaking. However, suppose I do want to claim that it is strictly speaking the case. In order to move us toward a reasonably acceptable view of the performative principle at work, I'd like to create a drama of my own, in which the objections of a polite but stern examiner are answered by a very conciliatory but determined defendant.

OBJECTION: Didn't the brilliant literary theorist Stanley Fish, in a famous essay entitled "How to Do Things with Austin and Searle," discredit rather a long time ago the sort of thing you're trying to do with Shakespeare's poem? I seem to remember that Fish argued persuasively: "It is simply wrong to think of an illocutionary act as producing meaning in the sense of creating it. Indeed the meaning the act produces . . . necessarily pre-exists; or to put it another way, in speech act theory, meaning is prior to utterance" (1003).

RESPONSE: You have a keen memory! I've reread Fish's essay, and I too find it persuasive. However, I'd like to point out that Fish's objection is to the idea that sentences, even poetic ones, can create new meanings, or that speech-act theory endorses such a notion. I'm not claiming this, nor am I attempting to produce a new, speech-act interpretation of the poem. I'm claiming that the poem, as a successful, composite act of discourse, creates a social reality. Does that reality need to "pre-exist"? I don't have a problem with this, but anyway, I'm sure it will come up later in our conversation.

OBJECTION: OK, I see your point. You're not attempting an application of speech-act theory but rather an extrapolation from that theory. But I'm concerned about that as well. Your leap (extrapolation, whatever) from performative to performance so as to spotlight literature seems rather loose and amateurish to me—something of a word game, in fact. Don't you think it's rather ironic that Austin specifically excluded literary discourse from the performance of actions, counting it as "parasitic" on real, normal discourse? Didn't Jacques Derrida ("Signature Event Context") question the usefulness of the whole theory for that very dismissal and exclusion?

RESPONSE: First of all, there's a "Reply to Derrida" by John Searle that explains why Austin's use of the term "parasitic" doesn't mean what Derrida took it to mean. "Pretend" might be a better term. When Rhett Butler (in the movie *Gone With the Wind*) says to Scarlett O'Hara, "Frankly, my dear, I don't give a damn," the sentence is "pretend" in the sense that it's not happening—or did not happen—in real life; it does, however, perform an action within the fictive universe of the story. But more importantly, the real "extrapolation" here is from speech acts to whole discourses, literary or nonliterary. Literary theorists have found speech-act theory useful as a way of talking about the various ways that fictive discourse is "in the world" while out of it; there exists a rich critical literature about "uses and abuses" of the theory (see Gorman; Fish; Culler). Although it is not endorsed by any of the authors we've mentioned, I think my own extrapolation, all things considered, is a rather modest one: that literary art "performs" versions of social reality (as defined by Searle in particular), and so helps to construct and sustain them.

OBJECTION: Those words again. Aren't you using the words "create" and "construct" in an odd and promiscuous way? The only thing that Shakespeare created, really, was a poem. Wouldn't it be more accurate to say that Shakespeare "expressed" or "discovered" a certain view?

RESPONSE: Yes, this usage of "create" does seem odd, if you're thinking only about the world of objects and artifacts. In that sense, it is true that all that Shakespeare created was the artifact of the poem. But I want you to keep in mind those performative speech acts we've been talking about: there are some things that are "put together," established, or constructed only with words. Not physical objects, surely, and I'll concede also that things like the Pythagorean theorem are discoveries of reality, not creations of it. But the founding fathers of America didn't just discover or express a democracy; they made one. And so if you've been accepting what I've said about performatives and the performative principle, I think you should allow me to use the words "create" and "construct" in this way.

OBJECTION: OK, I can see that contracts, constitutions, and even things like money amount to social constructions that are primarily verbal; but poetry of all things is not a contract. This poem does have lots of performatives (the imperatives "live," "buy," etc.), but they are all "pretend," that is, related to the fictional conversation inside the poem. Besides, didn't W. H. Auden say famously and persuasively that "poetry makes nothing happen: it survives / In the valley of its saying where executives / Would never want to tamper" ("In Memory of W. B. Yeats" 36–38)? I still say that what we're talking about is very compelling expression.

RESPONSE: You've got a very good point there, and I'm almost persuaded by it. There certainly is a difference between discourse that actually performs official acts (instrumental, we might call it) and discourse that doesn't (poetic and rhetorical). And, yes, there's a further difference between the rhetorical, which plays a role in causing things to happen (such as the passing of laws and the building of bridges), and the poetic, which doesn't. But still, I think we miss something important about the significance of this poem if we stop at the notion of "compelling expression." The poem does something; it makes a reality.

You've also got a good point about the fictional character of those performatives. But keep in mind the asymmetry principle. The nucleus of a discourse doesn't have to be outwardly and recognizably performative for the discourse to have a performative character. Keep in mind also the connection we've established between performative and performance. The poem is definitely a performance more than an expression, wouldn't you say?

OBJECTION: OK, it's more than expression; but I don't see how this "reality" you're talking about is really more than just a belief. And what makes the poem successful is that its fiction comes across as believable. We do rather often talk this way about successful literature, don't we? And don't we rather often say about something we don't like, that it's just not believable?

RESPONSE: Yes, we do talk this way about literature. And I'm of course ready to concede that there's a substantial referential, even informative and educational side to good literature, particularly longer works of fiction, drama, and film. Successful writers of historical fiction go to great lengths to ensure the historical accuracy of what they are representing; and part of the trick of science fiction and fantasy writing is to make it out-of-this-world and believable at the same time. But still there is more than simply believing the poem. In Shakespeare's poem, we experience the predicament of the soul as real, even if we don't any longer believe in the metaphysics or the religious system that makes the expression possible. That predicament remains real and alive.

OBJECTION: OK, I see the point, but that phrase "remains real" does you in, I think. Obviously, Shakespeare didn't invent these conceptions about the body and soul. In fact, they had existed for a very long time, and in his own time we could say that they were rather commonplace, couldn't we?

RESPONSE: I had to think a long time about this one, and I think your objection may lead to a refinement of what we're saying. It would seem, sure enough, that Shakespeare is transmitting rather than creating this reality; and that is a valid way of talking about it.

Still, I'd like to hold out for the notion that Shakespeare is re-creating rather than simply transmitting this reality. Social realities need to be re-creatable and thereby re-experienceable, in the same way that the results of scientific experiment need to be reproducible, and thereby reaffirmed. Realities that are no longer happily experienceable come across as repulsive, and they don't deserve to live. In addition, social realities do exist in competition with other possible or existing ones. For instance, a more modern voice speaking to the "soul" in Shakespeare's poem might be exhorting him or her to learn live more comfortably in that pretty-good house, perhaps take better care of it; and also do a little negotiating—make friends again with those "rebel powers," ask them in for tea. That older reality is kept alive by our "happy experience" of Shakespeare's poem.

OBJECTION: Are you saying that we can never disagree with a work of literature, or with statements in it; we can only judge it as a successful or unsuccessful performance?

RESPONSE: Not at all, and thank you for asking. Works of literature are performances, but they are also discourses, in two ways: First of all, as you know, they have statements about the world in them, and many of these statements (though not all) are put forward as true. And second, remember the reciprocity of saying and doing. Even as doings, they are sayings. And sometimes, even though they are successful works of art, they send messages that are not true, not true in every respect, or no longer true. And so the integrity of their action begins to unravel under the gaze of inspection from the outside.

This point, by the way, underscores the importance of criticism in any enlightened culture. Criticism maintains the broader balance of saying and doing, action and contemplation. We've been emphasizing the "doing" side of things, because it's the more difficult side to understand. But the saying side is equally important, and criticism is that stepping back from action that everybody needs. Everybody knows how difficult it is to have an objective view, or to open ourselves to fresh perspectives, on matters in which we ourselves are main players. In its role of performance and deep participation, art is always at risk of that same self-involvedness. It needs the counter-discourse of criticism.

OBJECTION: Yes, I'm remembering the paradox of action and contemplation. So I'm almost ready to shake hands. But one last thing: suppose I wanted to contend that some realities are deep-down permanent, and that's really what makes them "re-creatable," as you say. There is a structure of the universe and a structure of human life. The greatest works of literature rediscover and "recreate," as you say, that structure.

RESPONSE: We can still be friends, although we have a different metaphysics, and you'll be more often embarrassed than I will (I predict) when you come to acknowledge the socially constructed nature of things you once thought were foundational. Keep in mind also that it is social reality, not deep-down reality as you call it, that I have from the beginning been talking about. And lots of believers in what they consider permanent realities do work rather hard to keep them socially alive and socially viable. Why do they have to work so hard?

Suggested Reading

Austin, J. L. *How To Do Things with Words.* Cambridge: Harvard University Press, 1962. This is the initial, groundbreaking series of lectures on the theory of speech acts, which is excellent, exciting reading.

Butler, Judith. *Excitable Speech: A Politics of the Performative.* New York: Routledge, 1997. This is an interesting work of cultural criticism that applies the concept of the performative to issues of gender—that is, the gender roles that people play; not what one is but what one does by saying.

Culler, Jonathan. "Philosophy and Literature: The Fortunes of the Performative." *Poetics Today* 21 (2000): 479–502. This outstanding article reviews the vicissitudes of the concept in literary and cultural theory, including feminist and queer theory. It deals with the irony that Austin originally excluded literary discourse from the realm of performative utterance. Culler also ably discusses uses of the concept by the two deconstructionists Jacques Derrida and Paul de Man.

Derrida, Jacques. "Signature Event Context." *Glyph* 1 (1977): 172–197; and Searle, John R. "A Reply to Derrida." *Glyph* 1 (1977): 198–208. This well-known exchange, centered on speech-act theory, dramatizes the conflict between postmodern skepticism (asymmetrism) and a position of moderate realism.

Derrida, Jacques. "Declarations of Independence." *New Political Science* 15 (1986): 7–15. Read this for an interesting deconstructionist take on a classic genre of performative discourse.

Fish, Stanley E. "How to Do Things with Austin and Searle: Speech Act Theory and Literary Criticism." *MLN* 91 (1976): 983–1025. This landmark essay was the opening sally in a long-going discussion about the relevance of speech-act theory to literary criticism.

Roberts-Miller, Patricia. "Post-Contemporary Composition: Social Constructivism and Its Alternatives." *Composition Studies* 30 (2002): 1–13. This article develops an interesting perspective on how the (now decades long) discussion of social constructivism has played out among specialists in written composition.

Searle, John R. *Mind, Language and Society: Philosophy in the Real World*. New York: Basic Books, 1998. Searle's important works include the much earlier *Speech Acts*, a validation and extension of Austin's work; and (for our purposes) the more directly titled *The Social Construction of Reality*. However, *Mind, Language and Society* articulates most directly and clearly of all his works, I think, a moderate position of social construction from a linguistic point of view.

Sedgwick, Eve Kosofsky. "Queer Performativity: Henry James's The Art of the Novel." *GLQ* 1 (1993): 1–16. This is a much discussed article by a well-known cultural critic on the social construction of sexual identity.

6
Naming and Renaming the World

In John Milton's *Paradise Lost,* the character Adam describes an astonishing psychic event. Having completed the task of giving names to all the newly created animals, Adam recalls: "I named them as they passed, and understood / Their nature; with such knowledge God endued / My sudden apprehension" (VIII, 349–54). Earlier, in our investigation of Saint Augustine, this passage was introduced to illustrate a persistent view of symmetry: that names of things have a deep and permanent connection to their essential natures. As we have seen repeatedly, this view does not stand up to empirical observation or rational reflection. Nevertheless, while specific attributions of symmetry are usually mistaken, the broad intuition of symmetry is never simply wrong. I want to begin this chapter by examining a special way in which Milton was right.

Designating versus Naming

Milton speculates that Adam came to know the essential natures of the animals as he named them. Insofar as it encourages the belief that the names of things (perhaps in their original, pure form) can instruct us as to what the things are really about, this speculation is mainly erroneous. We will not learn a great deal about dogs, cats, or any other animals by contemplating their names or through researching their etymologies. About the porpoise, we may be temporarily fascinated to discover that its name is a blending of the Latin words "porcus" (pig) and "piscis" (fish), but this only tells us something about an impression the animal once made, nothing about its nature.

At this point it may be useful to clear the air once again about the function and usefulness of names and etymologies. The alert and opportunistic symmetrist might well object: What you are saying might be very true about simple names like "dog" and "cat" and even "duckbill platypus," but how about complex terms like "justice" and "courage"? In trying to understand what justice is, does it not help us to know that the term "justice" derives from the Latin root "jus," meaning law; and that in earlier usage the word also has the meanings of precision, correctness, and straightness, as in the "justification" of lines on a printed page?

The answer is, yes, it helps a great deal, as a record of how people have used this term in the past. Any serious study of an idea such as justice ought to begin with an examination of this record, and such an examination will often uncover bits of forgotten wisdom and knowledge—encapsulations of what other people have known and thought. However, the meaning of justice is not contained in its name, or in its accumulated usages. It is in fact the asymmetry of names to things that makes possible the long and varied histories of usage and semantic change that we find so interesting—not to mention the fact that the twenty-first century American idea and practice of justice may be different from (and superior or inferior to) ancient belief and practice. For individual cases of justice and for the attempt to define justice in such a way as to guide us in these individual cases, the linguistic investigation may be initially useful, but it has to be supplanted fairly quickly by investigations that are historical, empirical, and philosophical.

And so, back to Adam's animals. Having pushed back once again the hard claims of symmetry between words and things, even very complex things, I will contend that Milton knew what he was talking about—that his narrative about the first human being giving created things their first names carries an important insight. It is important to realize that Milton is not actually claiming that the names of the animals contain their essential natures. His claim is that Adam came to know their natures in the act of naming them. Here is where Milton's speculation is highly insightful: the process of naming, especially naming for the first time, is an imaginative process, a process of coming to know something. In some cases, Milton would add—most especially in God's creation of the cosmos with words—it is commensurate with the process of creation itself. This is an insight entirely compatible with our conclusion about social construction—that important realities are made by language.

Adam, of course, was highly privileged. Most of us do not get to name (or rename) the species of animals; we simply use the names that are already given. We do, however, often find ourselves searching for just the right way of saying something. Alternately, if we are thoughtful individuals with interesting experiences to share, we find ourselves searching for new ways of describing (or indeed, dramatizing) those experiences. This is especially true if we want to emphasize their special importance in a given moment. Here is an opportunity, therefore, to introduce an important difference (a binary opposition, if you will), between what I will call designation and what has already been termed naming or renaming.

When we designate a thing—an experience, a problem, a feeling, a complex entity, and so on—we scroll through an existing inventory of names, phrases, and experiences, looking for the one that best fits what we are talking about (this inventory can be on the spot memory, of course, or aids to memory, such as dictionaries, thesauruses, and the like). An educated person is often identified by her or his ability to access and use this existing storehouse—precisely, fluently, and copiously—in a variety of situations. When we name or rename a thing, we reach out for a new way of expressing it. Interestingly, when we do this, we only rarely make words entirely anew; instead, we scroll through that same inventory of existing words and phrases, attaching them this time to comparable or related things. This may be because we lack an existing designation for the thing we are discussing, or perhaps because we are less interested in designating the thing and more interested in conveying something new or special about the thing. A creative person is often identified by his or her ability to access and apply these *as ifs* ingeniously and arrestingly.

Often, we congratulate ourselves for having found the exact word for a thing, when what we have really done is to create a new word. The word as formed is not new, but we have turned it in a new direction ("turn" is the actual meaning of the word "trope," or figure of speech). I can remember, for example, a conversation in which several professors were admiringly discussing the work of another professor, who was in charge of a program designed to train and nurture aspiring poets and fiction writers. None of the terms suggested to describe his service—"custodianship," "leadership," "caretaking," and so on—seemed to capture the quality we had in mind. Then someone said, "It's really a ministry," and everyone agreed immediately that this was "the exact word," especially when it was recalled that the individual had previously been an actual minister. Of course, this term was not an exact designator at all but rather an exploratory device for better understanding or communicating what the group was thinking about. What is "exact" in such a case is not the designation but the fitness of the analogy to the specific circumstance.

At this point it may strike the reader that the word "naming" is being used as a composite term for a variety of figurative or poetic uses of language—metaphor, symbol, analogy, and the like. Why invent new terms, you might ask, for what is more commonly referred to as the difference between literal and figurative speech? We can for most purposes safely define the figurative in the same way that "naming" has been defined—as a new way or a departure from the ordinary way of representing things. In most cases, such a departure will be based upon some kind of likeness or mental connection to the thing being represented. This is textbook introduction to poetry. In the previous chapter, I asked you to examine Shakespeare's Sonnet 146 in which the soul is represented figuratively as a medieval "lord," confined to a gaily painted "mansion," and surrounded and besieged by "rebel powers." Without very much difficulty we understand the mansion to be a "figure" for the human body (on which the soul has lavished far too much attention); we understand those "rebel powers" to be both the pleasures and the perils of fleshly existence (pleasures will turn against you; focusing on material gain is a dangerous way to live).

A good deal of the pleasure as well as the intense reflection we derive from this poem is the higher degree of symmetry that is present in its language—that is, the direct and exciting fitness of language to the things being represented. The term "mansion," for instance, presents through comparison an interesting image of the human body; and this element of "secondary symmetry" (Genette 26) stirs reflection in us, even while for most of us the precise etymological connection between the word "mansion" and its literal referent, "large, grand residence" is now long lost. The figurative representation gives us fresh and stimulating symmetries, while the literal meaning has for the most part receded into asymmetry. The poet has revivified, even resymmetrized speech, we might say, so that it participates in the reality it represents; and that, many poets and literary humanists have believed (and I also believe), is a major function of poetry.

The literal/figurative opposition does serve us rather well, so one may ask what the problem is exactly. Nothing, except that we run the danger of separating the forms of speech from their purposes. In the way we have come to use these opposing terms, the "literal" is too closely tied to the referential and objective purposes of speech, while the "figurative" is linked to subjective, expressive, and decorative purposes. The literal, we suppose, is the language of science, scholarship, and the workaday world, while the figurative is the language of self-expression, beautiful crafting, and perhaps even the powerful affecting of audiences. However, as plausible as it may seem on the face of it, this is an erroneous and even dangerous set of connections. It distorts our understanding of where true expressiveness comes from, and perhaps more importantly, it misdirects our thinking about where good ideas come from. In using the literal/figurative distinction, we need to come to understand that the "literal" does not mean reference to hard fact as opposed to imagination, or even objective as opposed to subjective understanding; it does not even mean language that is not metaphorical, and the reason is that many metaphors have "died"—or at least become tamed—and receded themselves into the literal (see Davidson). The literal is perhaps best understood as designative as opposed to new-naming language.

One way of clarifying our thinking about the literal/figurative distinction is to come to an awareness of how thoroughly saturated with metaphor much of our everyday, designative discourse actually is. In their intelligent and remarkably readable book *Metaphors We Live By*, George Lakoff and Mark Johnson put to rest in short order any illusion that our speech can refer directly to such concepts as time, love, mind, ideas, or communication. These are complex, nonphysical matters, and in our regular talk and writing we always name them by analogy to something else—almost always to something more material and physical. One of Lakoff and Johnson's best and earliest examples is the concept of time, which very often is talked about as if it were money—apparent in such expressions as "spending time," "saving time," "investing time," "wasting time," and so on (7–8). Everyday thinking about concepts and ideas is loose and inexact, precisely because it is loaded with such unconscious metaphors.

Lakoff and Johnson point out that we are not merely using metaphors when we think we are referring directly to things, but also that our thinking about important concepts tends to be dominated by "systematic" metaphors: time as money, the mind as a machine, and theories as buildings. Their work is directed toward questions of whether and how we can escape the entrapments of such systematic metaphors, or alternately, verify their usefulness and validity. These are interesting questions; however, I want to stay focused on that all-important process of new naming. Whereas Lakoff and Johnson are interested in unconscious uses of figurative language that direct thought into familiar patterns, I want to focus on a conscious process that can produce new and original thinking.

From Saint Augustine to Lakoff and Johnson and beyond, philosophers and linguists have wrestled with the question of reference. It is a necessary question to ask about acts of speech; however, the status of this question diminishes if we think not of individual speech acts but of larger discourses. As we have seen in previous chapters, referring is never a larger purpose of discourse, and it is better not to think of it as a purpose of discourse at all. Every discourse of any complexity, from a conversation across the dinner table to a large book, is a combination of saying, acting, forming, performing, exploring, and discovering; and the purpose in every case is not to refer to things but to perform acts, to achieve a variety of social and cultural ends. They are mostly familiar ones, to be sure, but they are functions rather than pointings to. In fulfilling any and all of these functions, we have recourse to both the already named and to the process of new naming.

Many of the most heartfelt "expressions" (of sorrow, pity, joy, and commiseration) you have uttered or heard may have contained no figurative language at all. The memory bank of the already named may have served quite well for such purposes, and the stress of circumstances may have prevented very much in the way of additional linguistic exertion. A similar condition holds for works of literary art. While poetry is, to be sure, the primary haunt of figurative language, many poems and certainly most works of fiction achieve their purposes with ordinary speech. In such cases it is the situations and incidents designated by language, not the language itself, that are significant. Moreover, we often find the literal and the figurative coming together in unexpected ways. Consider the poem entitled "Pastoral," by the American poet William Carlos Williams:

> When I was younger
> it was plain to me
> I must make something of myself.
> Older now
> I walk the back streets
> admiring the houses

>   of the very poor:
>   roof out of line with sides
>   the yards cluttered
>   with old chicken wire, ashes,
>   furniture gone wrong;
>   the fences and outhouses
>   built of barrel-staves
>   and parts of boxes, all,
>   if am fortunate,
>   smeared a bluish green
>   that properly weathered
>   pleases me best
>   of all colors.
>   No one
>   will believe this
>   of vast importance to the nation.   (*Collected Poems* 1:64)

In this poem, Williams has deliberately chosen from a fund of ordinary, unadorned, and conspicuously literal words and phrases. The resulting expression, however, is far from ordinary. What is surprising and arresting about the poem is not its overturning of regular speech but its overturning of regular viewpoints. What happens in the process is a re-enlivening of regular speech. The ramshackle habitations of the poor are presented as objects of serious reflection and even of beauty to a mature man, as opposed to the not any longer impressive ambitions of his youth. And there is, of course, a singular element of figuration in the poem: the title "Pastoral" is used ironically, and irony is a figure of speech, the one in which there is a strong difference between what is expected by the reader and what is actually delivered. Pastoral is that genre of poetry in which we expect to witness idealized portraits of country life (not realistic descriptions of urban decay), expressed in a highly figured language, "poetic" in the conventional sense. Under the circumstances, we might venture to say that Williams's plain speech becomes in its totality an image, both of the scene he is describing and the thought he is expressing. Here is another example of participation—of symmetry in the midst of asymmetry.

As Williams's poem demonstrates, the revivifying of language that we associate with good poetry can take place through a strong representation of the world in ordinary speech. At the same time, as a good deal of not very interesting poetry demonstrates, overtly figurative language often fails to meet this goal, and in fact it tires out fairly quickly. Such figurative expressions as "light at the end of the tunnel" or "take with a grain of salt" have a way of passing rather quickly over into the land of the already named, in effect, the realm of the literal. They are just regular, clichéd expressions. They belong in the dictionary, that great repository of dead metaphors, buried in such words as "acumen," "agony," "ambition," "anecdote," "arrive," "assassin," and so on through the letter *A* and then down the alphabet (I'll spare you the etymologies of all but the last of these words: "assassin" derives its name from the Arabic word "hashshashin"—hashish; during the eleventh-century period of the Crusades, a secret sect of hashish users became notorious for their undercover killings of European crusaders). What is really figurative, if we insist on calling it that, about "real" figurative language is the element of new naming, the search for the "as if," and along with it an exploration and discovery of new experience.

As a teacher of literature, I like this recasting of the literal/figurative distinction into the alternative of designating/naming, because it helps me to explain a part of the great importance of poetry. Poetry's ability to name and rename the world makes it not just a clever or beautiful way of expressing things but also an important form of knowledge. It takes ordinary language into areas where it has not been before. Obviously, in adopting this alternative terminology I have been engaging in an act of renaming of my own—for a scholarly and not a poetic purpose. A good part of the reason for doing so, in fact, has been to reclaim this creative and exploratory function of language for ordinary speech and for specialized uses of language other than the poetic.

In all of our speaking and writing, beyond the most formalized and formulaic, we are engaged in some combination of designating and naming—of scrolling through an existing store of forms and phrases for the one that fits, and alternately, of pushing that existing store into what is new territory. Both of these processes are exploratory, and it is not just the one that produces figurative language that is creative. Indeed, the designating process itself—that scrolling through the existing lexicon for just the right word or expression to describe a thing—can be an exploratory and revelatory process, especially for an educated and thoughtful person. Such a person's education has equipped them with a large storehouse of words and phrases, a memory of how wise and thoughtful people have used this storehouse, and also with the skill of scrolling itself. For such a person, the process of finding the right word for a thing is also, to paraphrase Milton, a process of discovering its nature. That said, we have to acknowledge that there is something especially exciting and revelatory about the process of new naming. Poetry is the special preserve of this process; however, another part of poetry's importance is that this preserve is also the training ground for a much broader range of discourse and discovery.

Langue and Parole

Here is a possible snippet of ordinary conversation, out of which we can easily pull the designative and the naming components: "At this point I was in such a state of confusion about my life that—I don't know, it was like a siege and a betrayal—it was like I was trapped in my own house, and all the things I'd loved and counted on were out there aiming guns at me." You may recognize this as a colloquial paraphrase of Shakespeare's Sonnet 146. The speaker, in a momentary "loss for words" about a particular state of feeling, gives to it a provisional name by comparing it to a feeling of being under siege. Despite their importance to specific moments of expression, most individual acts of naming such as this are of little consequence to the permanent lexicon. They emerge spontaneously under the stress of circumstance, and although they may persist in private memory, they have no effect on the language as a whole. Other acts of naming, however, hope to achieve, and do in fact achieve, an honored place in the common vocabulary. From Shakespeare we have such phrases as "a pound of flesh," "rotten in the state of Denmark," and "the sound and the fury." But also from the worlds of scholarship, investigation, and even politics we have such naming and renaming as "Oedipus complex," "dialectical materialism," "fear and trembling," "Murphy's Law," "The Laffer Curve," and "sunset law."

In addition, there is a process of social aggregation in which certain expressions or extensions of existing meanings catch on in a small community, spread to larger and larger ones, and then into the common storehouse. This is one of the ways in which a language grows and changes over time. What is commissioned at first as a metaphor, "the spur of the moment" for instance, is eventually decommissioned, so to speak, and sent over to the storehouse of the designative. While it sits there, people forget its "as if" derivation from the actual spurring of a horse. There it loses its metaphoric, dramatizing power and becomes a designator. From the standpoint of vocabulary and phraseology, the history of a language is largely a history of such commissionings, decommissionings, and occasional recommissionings. Henry David Thoreau performed just such an act of recommissioning, revitalizing the "spur of the moment" cliché as he wrote: "Let the spurs of countless moments goad us incessantly into life. I feel the spur of the moment thrust deep into my side. The present is an inexorable rider" (*Winter* 255).

The process characterized as designating, naming, and renaming from a common existing storehouse is consistent with the distinction that the Swiss linguist Ferdinand de Saussure added permanently to our scholarly discourse about language: the distinction between langue and parole, first introduced in his landmark study, *Course in General Linguistics*. Langue in Saussure's usage is the existing system of the language—an intricately coordinated and unified network of phonological, morphological, and syntactic rules plus a vocabulary—that exists basically in peoples' heads. Langue is a composite psychological entity that is prior to parole, the individual act of speech that a person makes in an actual historical circumstance. The single most remarkable thing about language, in Saussure's view, is the wholeness, stability, and complete consistency of langue, the underlying system—the software, we might say—shared by all speakers of the language, at any given moment. And this system, in Saussure's view, is the primary thing that the linguist should study.

One does not have to agree with Saussure's rigid cordoning off of the software from its actual uses to grasp from his distinction an important point regarding symmetry. In all our talking, we do draw upon an existing fund of phonological and syntactic as well as lexical and semantic forms. We use these forms with varying amounts of freedom—very little on the phonological side, and a lot, comparatively, with words and phrases. We exercise this freedom to create discourses in which language does participate in the acts it performs and the realities it names. If you recall the performative principle, you will observe that this freedom makes possible new actions and new social realities as well as new namings (and therefore new understandings) of the world. And this very freedom is dependent upon a high degree of looseness, arbitrariness—asymmetry—at every level, between the existing forms and meanings of language.

A more pointed and more satisfying discussion than Saussure gives us of the new-naming phenomenon can be found in the Danish linguist Otto Jespersen's *Mankind, Nation, and Individual from a Linguistic Point of View*. Not completely satisfied with Saussure's dismissal of parole as unsystematic and ephemeral, Jespersen suggests that any comprehensive understanding of the larger phenomenon of language has to include both langue and parole. Jespersen portrays the interaction between the two as "a constant struggle going on between the speech of individuals and the organized language which never satisfies the whole body" (12). Keep in mind that in trying to understand this relationship between individual usage and the underlying system (which Jespersen is metaphorizing as a kind of struggle) we are talking about a phenomenon that cannot be quite designated—that is, divided into operational components and described literally. We can only try out alternate as ifs. Jespersen strikes another comparison that is more violent in its connotations: "In the regular siege-war, which 'speech' makes upon language, the former always succeeds in getting a few soldiers admitted into the fortress" (12).

In his more capacious adaptation of Saussure's terminology, Jespersen goes even so far as to suggest a division of labor between the opposing forces of langue and parole: langue "satisfies the craving for the communication and understanding of thoughts," while parole or "speech . . . stands at the service of actual life; what it would express is feeling, desire, action" (12). This statement is both elegant and satisfying because it comprehends the role of language in performing actions and dramatizing experience, as well as its role in making statements. In a follow-up formulation, Jespersen improves further upon Saussure's thought by distinguishing between "the word," a "potential linguistic action . . . as it lies unused in the brain or as it stands in a dictionary," and the "word pronounced," an "actual linguistic action" in the world (20). A great deal of language theory in recent decades (see Harris, for instance) has been aimed at tearing down Saussure's wall between langue and parole. Few have done so quite as effectively as did Jespersen in the 1920's, but this is not to say that Jespersen has the last word.

Jespersen's division of labor between understanding and feeling is worrisome. It conforms to a conventional division between poetic and scientific discourse, and it runs a danger that we have identified—of tying figurative language or new naming to the expressive as opposed to the cognitive, epistemic, knowledge-making functions of language. As is evident from the discussion going on at this very moment, a good deal of the back-and-forth that takes place in scholarly exploration takes the form of debates about what to call—how to name—the phenomena that we are studying. And these debates are obviously about more than the question of which terms from the common vocabulary work best. If this were the case, the whole business could be decided by a lexicographer!

In serious attempts to understand the world, the debates are not really about what words (designations) to use but about what renamings—

what as-ifs, stretchings, and reappropriations of existing vocabulary—best capture, apply to, indeed reenact in language, the experience we are attempting to understand. This is why an individual attempting to explore a new subject, or to explore a subject in a new way, will so often find herself or himself inventing new terms or using old terms in new ways. For the bleary-eyed and impatient reader, this procedure can be exasperating, especially with such fertile and penetrating thinkers as belong to the professions of literary theory and language philosophy. However, we have to acknowledge that this is what real understanding is always about—not about reference but about what is beyond reference—the process of renaming.

Major Functions of Naming

We name things all the time. As explained earlier, every substantive term in the dictionary is a designation that has an act of naming behind it. Accordingly, the process of naming goes on and on in any living language, fulfilling a variety of needs and functions. We name our children, our pets, organizations, books, stories, and poems, for a variety of reasons, whether serious, celebratory, or frivolous. Corporations name their products and services to make them sound practical, glamorous, or romantic, as the marketing occasion warrants. We name and rename certain bodily functions, so as to skirt around forms of unpleasantness and taboo. Military commanders give different names to their operations so as to minimize ("protective reaction strike") or maximize ("Operation Shock and Awe") their ferocity. We sometimes even rename ourselves, hoping to signal or even to actuate a change of life and character. When the legendary prizefighter Cassius Clay changed his name to Muhammad Ali, he was certainly signaling such a change.

It would be absurd to try to name all the animals—that is, to sort out all the possible types and uses of naming. Nevertheless, it is worthwhile to identify and put names on four of the largest types and uses of naming, exploring their significance for issues of symmetry and for their value to literary humanism. Ultimately, the hope is, of course, to come to better understand their natures (to use Milton's language) in the process, perhaps in a more modest way than Milton envisioned. Thus far, the goal has been to shake loose, temporarily, the notions of the figurative and the nonliteral from the poetic, so as to emphasize the presence and importance of the naming process in all kinds of human discourse. This shaking loose carries with it, of course, the implication that the process may function differently in various settings. And so I think it will be useful to attempt an inventory of these different functions, if for no other reason than to demonstrate that individual ones of them are not tied to specific kinds or genres of discourse.

Most traditional inventories of figurative language are organized as lists of forms, the products of naming, such as metaphor, symbol, analogy, synecdoche, metonymy, and so on. While such a list is useful, my effort for the present is to focus on the *process* of naming and the different kinds of things that figurative language can do—what people are attempting to accomplish when they give new names to things.

Struggling to express

There can be no doubt that a large majority of those sieges, which Jespersen highlighted above, are due to a lack of—or forgetfulness of—established vocabulary. In regular conversation, when we do not know enough words for what we are trying to express, we have two choices: to fall silent or to move forward with adaptations and recyclings of the words we have. In most circumstances, most of us will keep going. This process is most noticeable in the speech of children, who often charm and delight us with such expressions as "wayback" for the luggage compartment of a station wagon. What the hearers of such talk may consider a hilarious renaming is actually for the speakers a new naming. This is precisely the spontaneous process by which new words come into a language, and the reason why a word's etymology will sometimes reveal a startling figure of speech.

The word "curfew," for instance, derives from the Norman French expression "couvre-feu," meaning "cover fire," which originally named the ringing of an evening bell reminding or requiring medieval villagers to dampen or extinguish their fires. Even in its original meaning, the term was a figure of speech, synecdoche, wherein a part of a thing or process is elected to name the whole. The term was later stretched or turned further, to name a signal (perhaps in some cases the same church bell) requiring individuals to be off the streets. We have no way of knowing, of course, but there may have been an element of playfulness, perhaps of irony at this expression's forming and catching on and eventually settling in as a designation. And so the characterization of this process as a "struggle to express" should not obscure the fact that new expressions do come readily enough to clever minds. There is an element of pleasure and discovery in them. They constitute a kind of natural poetry; and "natural" poetry can eventually cross over into ordinary speech. Sometimes it makes sense and is fun and enlightening to put aside established ways of saying things and to look at them in a new or different way, the way a child or an anthropologist from Mars or Eve or Adam in the Garden of Eden would do, as if for the first time.

Expressing well

With this process we move from a "natural" to a "composed" instance of new naming. In this case the speaker may have at hand a store of existing expressions for a thing, but now the struggle is for something beyond the ordinary: something charming, surprising, inspiring, dignified—not usually all of these things at once, of course, but always something memorable. In many cases, we note, what makes the expression memorable is that the figure of speech will produce an image, like the covering of fire in the example above. This is where the term "imagination" comes from, of course, and poets of the classical and neoclassical schools have tended to understand imagination in precisely this way. Alexander Pope, perhaps the greatest of neoclassical English poets, wrote famously that:

> True wit is Nature to advantage dressed,
> What oft was thought, but ne'er so well expressed;
> Something whose truth convinced at sight we find,
> That gives us back the image of the mind.
> *(An Essay on Criticism,* II, 297–300)

With these lines from Pope's poem, it appears as if we might be headed once again toward an exclusive discourse of the poetic; however, that word "convinced" is a reminder that rhetoricians too have always understood the devices of new naming to be powerful instruments of persuasion as well as delight. From classical times through the Renaissance period, they kept long lists of them for the sake of investing speeches with charm and dignity, the two most commonly recognized effects. They understood that these things could help to sway audiences just as readily as sound arguments. They also knew that the well-turned phrase could on occasion produce that powerful and lasting image that would actually dominate thought on an issue for years to come. When Winston Churchill, with his famous "Sinews of Peace" speech, said that an "iron curtain" was descending upon Europe, he brought to world consciousness a metaphor for the purposeful isolation of countries that had come under Communist control, a lasting and memorable name for the instrument of that isolation, and a persuasive suggestion that the lives of people behind that curtain were lives of imprisonment.

Discovering and rediscovering the world

In the beautiful passage of poetry above, Alexander Pope's celebration of the "ne'er so well expressed" does, for all its sweetness of expression, overlook an important fact: that the bright new image will sometimes bring with it a new conception and a new experience of reality. Here is a legitimate and all-important form of symmetry, the participation of language in the reality it names and the epistemic force of its imaginative deployment. As we have already seen, there can be no conceptual reordering or new understanding of anything in the absence of this process.

The failure to acknowledge and account for this epistemic force is precisely the shortcoming of most traditional (classical and neoclassical) theories of discourse, which are otherwise learned, thorough, and elegant in their expression and practical in their application. It was not until the romantic period, beginning in the late eighteenth century, with such poets and theorists as Samuel Taylor Coleridge, Percy Bysshe Shelley, and Giambattista Vico, that some kind of formal accounting for this force and function was attempted. It is also from this period, interestingly enough, that we can trace the beginnings of the attempt by Western nations to extend the benefits of literacy and formal training in language to a larger portion of their citizenries. This project surely had more to do with new social and economic realities created by the industrial revolution than with new theories of language. But other revolutions—revolutions in understanding—were taking place as well in Europe and America. Expansive and prophetic thinkers like Walt Whitman were bold enough to project and look forward to a new democratization of the human spirit, and in such thoughts a new role and a new challenge were posed for literary humanism.

Shaping reality

Sometimes when we name things we urge them in a certain direction. When parents name their children after great men and women, or after the lovely persons and great achievers of their own families, they do this hoping that the child will "grow into" the name. They also hope, sometimes, that the spirit of that person—the positive elements of character and action that were alive in that person—will live on in the family by virtue of the fact that there is a person in their midst so named. In recognizing this shaping function of language, we are reaching back to the performative principle and the social construction of reality. Once again we meet the astonishing fact that certain kinds of realities are not merely discovered but actually brought into being by language. This is most easily discernible in such overt forms of social construction as pledges, pronouncements, and agreements; but there do exist subtler instances as well—realities of collective feeling and allegiance that are maintained through a process of strong representation.

Much of the figurative language that we encounter in daily life is sentimental and merely ceremonial, but sometimes it has an effect. And "ceremony" itself, as we previously saw, is an important builder of social realities, a promoter and maintainer of values and ways of life (consider how many ceremonies are actually naming ceremonies). There are, of course, realities that are not shapeable by speech. Naming a certain structure "The George Washington Bridge" is certainly not going to affect the load tolerances of the structure itself, but there are a number of social realities that might be affected: a sense of collective pride in the grandeur of the thing (as opposed to misgiving about its massive expense); a sense of confidence in the ability of government (science, technology, or labor) to achieve great things, and a consequent willingness to embark upon new ventures; the hopeful reconnection of social geographies (neighborhoods) that are literally connected by the bridge.

This shaping function is also notable in the dynamics of organizations. The organization that calls itself "The Salvation Army" will in fact organize itself and go about its work, at least initially, in a different way from the one that is named "The Brothers and Sisters of Peace and Mercy." Sometimes organizations, like individuals, will change their names, not just to signal to others a change in character or direction but, in addition, to help bring about change, by nudging the attitudes of their own members in a new direction.

Designating versus Naming as Pilot Analogy

Structural properties of language—most often expressed as oppositions of an x versus y character—"anticipate" or have their analogues in issues of human aspiration, behavior, and culture. These analogues, and not supposed correspondences of form and meaning at any level, constitute the true sources of symmetry in language. An adequate and effective literary humanism will justify and orient itself toward the pilot analogies of language and culture. As we have seen earlier, the cultural analogue of symmetry versus asymmetry is participation versus freedom; the cultural analogue of saying versus doing is contemplation versus action; and the cultural analogue of designating versus naming is tradition versus innovation.

The act of designation belongs to the existing language—the fund of memory and reference that we scroll through to find the appropriate, understandable way of saying things. The act of naming, by contrast, belongs to our individual (sometimes highly personal) extension of that fund into new territory. Designation is what tradition hands us; naming is the new thing we make of it. Designation makes use of a collective fund; naming makes a new use of that fund, sometimes permanently altering the fund itself. Sometimes, as we have seen, naming can involve deliberately rejecting what is in that fund. This happens when humans insist on new ways of saying, conceptualizing, or even constituting things.

It is not difficult to see the parallel movements in the world outside of language: In all of our comings and goings, we are guided by existing structures and existing traditions of how to define ourselves and conduct our business. These structures and traditions constitute a social and institutional langue, the fund of reference for the parole of actions, decisions, and movements in concrete circumstances. In a settled culture, most of our daily actions and interactions take place comfortably and unconsciously within that structure. Other times, however, the actions of individuals will place that structure under considerable pressure, demanding change. Here is an obvious example: Most thoughtful persons at this hour in the twenty-first century have rejected the traditions of racism and racial discrimination in our culture. This did not come about, however, before individuals challenged those traditions. The change was personal and individual before it was collective. It was "in here" before it was "out there."

The notion of structure is a reminder that both designating and naming are processes framed by a larger system of governance—the grammar of a language. This principle of structure also holds in the dynamics of tradition versus innovation. And in that fascinating intermixture of acting out and speaking about our lives, we continuously scroll through the "lexicons" of cultural practice (including literature and discourse), and this will result in our following, altering, or sometimes overturning existing "usage" in particular cases. People ought to be trained to study the "grammars" of cultural practice—that is, the organizing traditions (including philosophy and religion) that aim at an overall understanding of things.

For this reason it is not at all outlandish to think of established ways of doing things—in government, society, religion, and all the arts and sciences—as "languages." Nor is it unreasonable, therefore, to think of accomplishment in the primary medium—language in the literal sense—as fundamental to accomplishment in these substantive areas. Nothing will substitute, of course, for devoted and systematic study of the specific lexicons and specific grammars (methodologies, theories, and so forth) of the various disciplines, or for as much cultural knowledge as one can attain. Training in language, however, has the opportunity of providing more than literacy and communication skills. A practiced sophistication in language and its inner movements can open windows to those outer movements of tradition and innovation, established usage and personal response, that belong to a good life and a good society.

Suggested Reading

Barney, Rachel. *Names and Nature in Plato's Cratylus*. New York: Routledge, 2001. This penetrating study makes better sense than any other, in my opinion, of Socrates's apparent ambivalence about the symmetry of linguistic forms. Barney suggests that Socrates's "conventionalism" (asymmetrism) is about verbal forms or designations, whereas his continuing excitement is about the process of naming in language. This is, of course, exactly the distinction that I have pursued in this chapter.

Harris, Roy. *The Language Machine*. Ithaca: Cornell University Press, 1987. This short book is a devastating critique, taking a historical perspective, of the distinction between langue and parole (or competence and performance) that has both empowered and bedeviled modern linguistics.

Lakoff, George, and Mark Johnson. *Metaphors We Live By*. Chicago: University of Chicago Press, 1980. A very intelligent and remarkably readable study of the ways in which metaphors influence our thinking.

7

Figuring (Out) the World
Tropes and Tropology

It is impossible to talk about ways of thinking and understanding without resorting to tropes—figures of speech, turnings of meaning from one area of experience to another. With the word "area," I have begun with a trope derived from the area of mapping and geography, where some of the most common tropes that humans use to describe thinking and understanding originate. All of our talking and writing, once we get past the simplest and most formulaic transactions, entail something already known (marked and tagged by words ready at hand) and something struggling to be said, a search for words to get it right. As we have seen, this struggle to say a thing well is often, in itself, a struggle to understand that thing and, perhaps, to influence the way others understand it.

Sometimes, we are attempting to find our way to a thing, while other times we are attempting to nudge a thing in a certain direction. Sometimes, the resulting expression will be a judicious selection from an existing vocabulary, either as remembered or researched (searched for) by the speaker, while other times the result will be an extension or stretching (into new space) of that vocabulary. And sometimes, it will be a trope—a turning of regular speech, a dramatization or imagining of the thing, as if it were something else. Many times the result will be merely a clever or colorful way of saying what others have already experienced or already know. Sometimes, however, it will constitute new knowledge, a different, surprising, even shocking way of envisioning the world.

Tropology

Interestingly, what is true of individual speech acts is also true of whole works of discourse and even whole philosophies—comprehensive representations and figurings of the world. In the study of literature, this process of tropological searching and shaping is well-known and understood, because it is highly intentional and a significant part of what authors build into literary works and want their audiences, in turn, to experience. In literary criticism, it is often discussed under the heading of dominant or controlling metaphor. A classic example can be found in Shakespeare's *King Lear,* where the scenic feature of the storm emerges as a trope—an analogy to inner states of mind. This controlling metaphor of the storm suggests a condition of disorder in both exterior and interior worlds. It also serves as a device for exploring the (brief and slender) possibilities for reconstructing order and peace in both worlds.

Not so obvious or well understood, because far less intentional or even acknowledged by philosophers themselves, is the process by which comprehensive understandings of the world, or even significant parts of it (economic and political theories, for example), inevitably make use of powerful, captivating as ifs, or controlling figures of speech. Tropology is a field of criticism that critiques—and yes, to some extent deconstructs—theoretical discourses by examining their "turns" beyond the literal sense of words, identifying the explanatory energy they draw from powerful figures of speech. As it stands, in works of criticism and theory that go by that name, tropology is a highly speculative, sometimes quite abstruse form of analysis that tends to focus on works of history and philosophy of history (see Ankersmit; Kellner; Mellard; and White). My goal in this chapter is to domesticate this field, so to speak, place it within a broader perspective of critical analysis, speak in a clearer voice than its most prominent adherents, and offer some plainer applications to the concerns of literary humanists.

We have examined the process by which any new or different understanding of a thing will put pressures on existing ways of talking about it;

and we have also seen how an individual trope, or figure of speech, can be an exploratory as well as a decorative or dramatizing device. But how is it that a whole theory or philosophy of something will march off in a tropological (metaphorical, "as if") direction? There are several ways of answering this question, and since it is a difficult question, it will be useful to look at more than one of them.

One possible answer can be found if we follow a postmodern course and speak from a position of radical, philosophical asymmetry. In this view, "reality" itself is always either constructed by language or filtered through language; and since there is no essential connection (symmetry) between language and any other kind of reality, there can exist no such thing as literal or solid, obvious, incontrovertible truths. Therefore, all of our understandings of things are tropes, as ifs of one sort or another. The more comprehensive and extensively articulated these understandings are—that is, the more they qualify as philosophies or theories—the more saturated they will become with dominating tropes, and the more likely and extensively they will carry with them prejudices, distortions, and subjectivities of outlook.

There is a more balanced approach to the question, one that preserves a place for symmetry—that is, a more constructive and positive relationship between structures of language and valid understandings of the world. Here we are invited to listen to and learn from language, as opposed to simply being on guard against it. We begin by pointing out that there are vast areas of inner and outer space that we know very little about—so little, in fact, that we lack proper, uncontested designations for them. It is hard to know how to talk about them. They do not consist of "things," objects that can be marked, tagged, weighed, measured, pointed to—designated. Instead, they consist of relations, movements, developments, for which we have to try to develop names. Our attempts to name them can only be stretchings or turnings of words from areas that we do know something about—or think we know something about. All that we can do is imagine them, produce images of them.

A more exact explanation, perhaps, is to point out that theories or philosophies are never—can never be—based upon observations (much less understandings) of all the phenomena they attempt to account for. They are based, rather, on a selection of things that are taken to be most important, most representative of the whole. These selected sets then become models of the whole, providing the vocabularies for describing things that are, strictly speaking, outside those particular sets; and when this happens, those vocabularies are stretched and turned into tropes, figures of speech, or as ifs.

An extreme example of this process involves the Darwinian theories of evolution and natural selection. For purposes of demonstration, please leave aside the contentions of many that even as biological concepts these are "merely" theories. I want to draw attention to the even more controversial extension of these notions beyond the strictly biological realm and into social and economic history. Within the selected data set of strictly biological processes, such terms as "selection," "competition," "mutation," and "evolution" have strictly limited meanings. They are in fact designations of a closely guarded kind. If, however, the biological theory becomes a model for understanding change, development, progress, or evolution in economic or social systems, these terms become tropes, producing some interesting insights, perhaps, but also in this particular case a considerable amount of distortion. I'm tempted to say that they break out of their closely guarded cells and begin to rampage across the countryside, but that would be more metaphorical than the present discussion seems to warrant! A more sober observation would be that, once released in this way, these terms cease to be designations and become namings—"turnings" away from their function as designations. Consequently, they must necessarily enter into a more serious competition with other ways of looking at things than they would in the strictly biological sphere.

A way of observing and assessing the competition among theories, therefore, is to search out the principal tropes on which they are based and the places of experience from which these tropes are derived. Any method of doing this systematically may be termed a tropology. We can define tropology, then, as the intellectual work of figuring out how the different ways of understanding a particular phenomenon (the idea of justice, let us say) are related to different controlling or systematic (this would be Lakoff and Johnson's term for it) metaphors or figures of speech. As the result of this activity, a tropology is a list and a classification of these different metaphors. The critics and intellectuals who devise tropologies are also at pains, usually, to show how these different metaphors relate to—complement and contrast with—each other, based on the known areas from which they derive.

As you will see from the examples that follow, tropologies apply most interestingly to those realms (literature, culture, politics, and so on) where it is most difficult to keep designations under scientific control—although science itself is not free from the turns of language, and the role of metaphor and analogy is by no means insubstantial in scientific discourse (see Black). As noted earlier, tropology is itself a rather speculative activity, and no particular version of it is likely to be completely satisfying. The most well-known theorists of tropology, Hayden White and Hans Kellner to name just two, have attempted to employ a single tropological system derived from Giambattista Vico to develop comprehensive theories of discourse. To be more modest, it seems more likely that multiple tropologies are possible, and a tropology is valuable if it helps us to understand how different theories or ways of understanding things relate to each other. Furthermore, tropologies are also valuable in helping us to understand that different views of reality are based not just upon different observations of the world but also upon different ways of using language.

Stephen Pepper's *World Hypotheses*

Lakoff and Johnson's *Metaphors We Live By* calls attention to the role of "orientational metaphors" in organizing our thinking. (Interestingly though, Lakoff and Johnson are reluctant to apply the notion to a comparison of competing philosophies—which is viewed as a principal task of tropology here.) The directive or orienting power of metaphor is most apparent when we consider those all-embracing philosophical projects that attempt to envision the character of the universe and the place and destiny of human beings within it. One of the first and most interesting attempts to classify philosophical systems on the basis of their controlling or orientational metaphors has been made by the American pragmatist Stephen Pepper in his classic work of philosophical orientation *World Hypotheses: A Study in Evidence*. Pepper begins with the premise that the most important world hypotheses are powerful and brilliant envisionings, always and necessarily based on limited evidence, of how the whole world operates. The farther these theories reach (stretching the existing language with them), the more metaphorical they will become. And the more coherently these philosophies are expressed, the more they will appear to be dominated by a single metaphor or set of metaphors. In Pepper's analysis, most coherent philosophical systems fall into one of four types, each based upon a different "root metaphor" (141).

1. Formism, also known as realism or Platonic idealism, is best represented by Plato, Aristotle, and the medieval scholastic philosophers.

Its root metaphor is the idea of "similarity" or correspondence, as if every material thing in the world were a mirror image or reflection of an idea, an intellectual or immaterial thing (151).

2. Mechanism, also known as naturalism or materialism, is represented by the philosophies of Lucretius, Thomas Hobbes, and John Locke. Its root metaphor is the machine, as if everything that exists (including thoughts and feelings) were part of an interlocking system of causes and effects, stimuli and responses (228).

3. Organicism, also known as absolute idealism, is represented by such philosophers as Georg Wilhelm Friedrich Hegel and Samuel Taylor Coleridge, and has also been very influential in the tradition of romantic literature since the eighteenth century. Its root metaphor is the organism, as if everything were part of a living whole, a "unity above and beyond individual constituents" (280).

4. Contextualism, also known as pragmatism, is presented by the American philosophers Charles Peirce, William James, John Dewey, and Pepper himself. Its root metaphor is dramatic action, the "act in context," as if everything in the world were "a rich concrete thing, in which features interpenetrate." In this view, things (including ideas, religions, and cultures) can only be known in their connection and interaction with other things, each of which may have separate sets of connections (234). Pepper and others especially favor this outlook because in it they see a basis for pluralism, giving everything its due respect in a world struggling to contain its own diversity.

As brilliant and provocative as Stephen Pepper's book is, it is somewhat unsatisfying for the student of language, because Pepper does not pay close attention to the linguistic process of how metaphors work and come to dominate a discourse. Nor does he offer any explanation of why this particular set of metaphors (mirror, machine, organism, and drama), out of all the hundreds of possibilities, emerged in the history of philosophy as root metaphors. More provocative from a linguistic point of view, though certainly more speculative and freewheeling, is Kenneth Burke's dramatistic pentad, the underlying conceptual frame of his famous book *A Grammar of Motives*. In this scheme, serious and comprehensive views of experience—philosophies, social theories, works of literature—can be analyzed according to the relative emphasis they place on one or more of the five essential components of a drama: act, agent, agency, scene, and purpose.

Kenneth Burke's Pentad

Burke is notoriously evasive about his own philosophical leanings, and he is playfully inconsistent in his methods. It is not surprising, then, that commentators have interpreted his pentad in a variety of ways. However, to call the pentad a contextualist tropology would be accurate. Although Burke does not identify himself as a contextualist or pragmatist, he places himself squarely in that corner by consciously adopting the metaphor of dramatic action, both as a world hypothesis, to use Pepper's terminology, and as a paradigm of how people use language to understand the world. It is also implicit in his writings that the world itself—or at least the human experience of it—is "a rich concrete thing, in which features interpenetrate." It is too rich, complicated, and big for anyone to understand all at once.

Out of this massive complexity and richness arises the need to contemplate the whole through the lens of one of its parts—or at best, he says, a linking of two of its parts (act-scene, agent-agency, and so on). The clearest example of this may be seen in returning to the now familiar conflicting understandings of the concept of "justice." In the liberal and individualistic political philosophies that undergird American and European democratic capitalism, justice is viewed from the lens of the agent (or perhaps an agent-act ratio); and so justice is seen as a virtue, a standard for measuring the actions of individuals. It is then theorized that the best society will be a society of just individuals. Although the broader conditions of perfect equality and community that we hope for will continue to elude us in the present, we can work toward those goals. By contrast, in the socialist political philosophy of Marxism, justice is viewed from the lens of the scene (or a scene-agency ratio); and so justice is seen as a desired condition of society as a whole, and the first job is to locate agencies by which that condition can be achieved. It is then theorized that individuals, whose rights and living conditions may be temporarily crushed by those agencies, will be better and better-off in the long run.

Burke does not identify the pentad as a construct derived from the structure of language, nor does he specifically identify its individual "placements" as tropes or metaphors. However, it is clear that Burke is participating in that broad philosophical project of the twentieth century that has been called the linguistic turn (see Rorty; Crusius). This is the movement that has rejected two extremes in thinking about ideas: the philosophical quest for certainty about such concepts as justice, virtue, substance, mind, and God; and the modern, scientific impulse to dismiss discussions about them as mere talk about empty nothings. Thinkers of the linguistic turn have sought to replace both the quest and the dismissal with an understanding that conflicting views about these things are different constructions—different ways of exploiting the potentialities of language. Faced with a conflict about fundamental concepts, our most important question is not about which one is true or more true. The important thing to decide is which one constitutes a more fruitful way of talking about in the present crisis—the rich, concrete, and problematic circumstance that always surrounds us.

There is another way in which the pentad may be viewed as a linguistic construct, and that way lies in Burke's strong insistence that language itself is a form of "symbolic action." Without calling directly upon the speech-act theory of J. L. Austin, Burke nevertheless exhibits a powerful understanding of the performative principle, the principle by which we understand every sentence, and every discourse, as acting as well as saying; hence the success of any discourse depends as much upon its conducting a valid and successful action as upon making a "true" statement. The "placements" of the pentad—lenses for viewing the overwhelming complexity of the world—are also components of the complex set of actions that comprise the linguistic system itself. Burke does not specify any of this; however, it is apparent that here also is a pronouncement of symmetry—the congruence of language to the world. While understanding that the forms of language are arbitrary and discontinuous with the world and ideas about it, Burke also intuits that world hypotheses are constructed out of the basic processes of naming.

Giambattista Vico's Master Tropes

In "Four Master Tropes," a fascinating appendix to *A Grammar of Motives* (503–17), Kenneth Burke introduces an alternate tropology—a more explicitly tropological one than the pentad, in fact—by speculating that among the various figures of speech there are four that are all-important and subsume the others. These master tropes are metaphor, metonymy, synecdoche, and irony. Corresponding to these tropes, there exist four ways of talking about (and therefore of understanding) complex realities. For each of these ways of talking/thinking, one of the master tropes stands as the linguistic starting point and instrument of discovery. Following the terminology developed in the previous chapter, we might call it the generator of new names for things. Although he does not make any direct attributions at this point, Burke is clearly adapting the master tropes concept from the brilliant eighteenth-century rhetorician and philosopher Giambattista Vico, who in his book *The New Science* was attempting to demonstrate in specific ways the importance of language to human civilization and thought. Burke's treatment of the master tropes is in some ways more cogent than Vico's own, and it is therefore worth some special notice here.

It is important to remember that in Burke's treatment, the alignment of master tropes to ways of thinking can be discovered in philosophical and political works as well as in literature. The processes of discovery and thought are not fundamentally different from one genre to another. Their alignments according to Burke are investigated below.

Metaphor—perspective

Metaphor is the trope through which we see a thing in terms of something else. Its corresponding thought or discovery process is that of perspective—that is, we view a field of experience from the perspective of another field. The ancient and Christian idea of the "great chain of being" is perspectivist in orientation because it grades different orders of things (stones, plants, animals, humans, angels) from the perspective of spiritual being (*A Grammar of Motives* 504).

Metonymy—reduction

Metonymy is the trope through which we see a thing by means of a particular physical aspect of the thing. The trope is most noticeable when we characterize a nonconcrete or nonphysical thing (bravery, for instance) by means of a strikingly physical thing (guts). The corresponding thought or discovery process to metonymy is reduction. This is the process through which insubstantial emotional, intellectual, psychic, and spiritual states are made concrete through their association with particular physical manifestations, events, and processes. The physical and behavioral sciences are reductionist in their thought processes, since they characteristically search for what is materially taking place—when someone is said to be "depressed," for instance. Burke is eager to point out, however, that the process of reduction, associated negatively with the social sciences in his day, also belongs to "poetic realism," which seeks to concretize the emotional and spiritual, never pronouncing their commonplace designations but dramatizing them with vivid images, actions, and interactions (*A Grammar of Motives* 506).

Synecdoche—representation

Synecdoche is the trope through which we see a thing by means of a representative part, species, or microcosm of the thing. If we take the Methodist church as typical (a microcosm) of American middle-class Protestantism, we are engaging in a synecdochic or representational line of thought. Scientific and social scientific projects that investigate particular species (fruit flies, for instance) or populations (Methodists in the city of Indianapolis) as representative of larger wholes participate in this process. Literary works (*Moby Dick*, for instance) that represent particular characters (the whale) or actions (Ahab's quest for the whale) as symbolic of broader psychic and spiritual processes are representational in this way (*A Grammar of Motives* 508–9).

Irony—dialectic

Burke is exceedingly vague and digressive about this one, but I am going to give it a try. Irony is the trope through which we see a thing by placing it in contrast or interaction with what it is not. When I said, "You devil, you!" to the loved one who walked into the house yesterday with tickets to the opera, I was engaging in a commonplace sort of irony. I had complained earlier about the high cost of opera tickets, and besides, I had decided that it would be better to stay home and finish writing this chapter. Of course I was delighted to go to the opera, and the "what it is not" part of my saying had a certain applicability—served as an informing contrast—to the reality of the situation. It was of course a way of saying thank you.

Dialectic—the corresponding thought or discovery process to irony—is the process by which we illuminate concepts by contrasting them with (and distinguishing them from) opposing, competing, or related concepts. Consider, for instance, the following kind of discussion: A special committee is attempting to solve a problem involving a person's behavior in a particular institution. He has acted improperly toward a client or co-worker, and the committee has agreed that it is exceedingly important to do the "correct" thing for both sides. It may become crucial in the midst of this discussion to distinguish the "correct" thing from the "kind" thing, the "understanding" thing, or even the "just" thing. On this last note, one of the discussants might object vigorously and say, "Wait a minute! This has gone too far! I will not accept a notion of 'correctness' that separates itself from 'justice.' If that's your idea of correctness, I'm outta here!" At this point, the group will have two choices, if it wants to retain the participation of the objector: accept a notion of "correctness" that includes a consideration of what is just, or agree to look for a solution that is both correct and just. If there's a philosopher in the group, this person might continue to reflect, and possibly write an essay, on the possible differences between correctness and justice. For the others, it will all be the same: "Whatever," they might sigh. What is happening in this hypothetical situation is the process of dialectic, or rational problem solving. This is a process that typically involves the examination of opposing viewpoints through the definition, comparison, contrast, and classification of ideas.

At this point, readers may object, claiming that there is a vast difference between saying what you do not really mean (irony) and rational problem solving, which ought to mean saying exactly what you mean in the clearest and most direct way possible. With Burke's and Vico's extension of the concept of irony, we do seem to have run up against a paradox: we have connected a train of discourse that ideally tries for truth, clarity, and directness to a linguistic locomotive (irony) that is characteristically indirect, evasive, and mendacious. Moreover, whereas we can actually see the tropes of metaphor, metonymy, and synecdoche operating inside the discourses of perspective, reduction, and representation, respectively, there is no corresponding integral instance of irony inside the discourse of dialectic. Whole ethical and political discourses (and whole committee meetings, sadly) do go on without the smallest ironical utterance.

And so, will this train stay on track? Probably not; however, Burke's larger point is both brilliant and correct. Burke is not actually claiming, synecdochically, that every dialectical discourse has within it a nugget of irony, but that every concept eventually gets understood by comparison with what it is not, or what it is up against, or what it may look like but is really not. (Some people might consider the idea of "charity" as always consistent with the idea of "kindness," but many people insistently do not; and they will "sharpen" the concept by distinguishing it from that other concept.) Just as importantly, this dialectical process of concept sorting is as continuously, and sometimes more effectively, at work in poetry, fiction, and drama as it is in nonfiction discourses. But in literary art, one usually does find a substantial nugget of irony at work.

One of the most common types of character in literature is the person who does not know who he or she really is. A classic example is the character of Oedipus. We the audience know who Oedipus is from the beginning of the drama; however, Oedipus does not know his origin. Irony lies in the discrepancy between what we know and what the character knows; and while the action unfolds before us, we are left to ponder the differences between the good that he is trying to represent and the good that is really required of him. In *Antigone,* the sequel to *Oedipus Rex,* the character Creon erroneously thinks that he is a model ruler, working to ensure the stability of the state. But his idea of stability is placed in "dialectical" tension with that of the character Antigone. As it turns out, Antigone is right and Creon's idea of stability in the state has actually been, tragically, a source of its opposite: chaos and ruin. We the audience may not know this from the beginning, but we come to realize it long before Creon does, and so we have time to consider: what does stability really mean, and what are its real sources in our communal life?

Burke's broader point is that there does not exist a poetic or literary language set off from the rational discourse of philosophy, politics, theology, or any other discourse concerned with knowledge or action in the world. Consequently, works of literature are not simply art objects (as the formalist critics of Burke's generation tended to argue). They are also discourses that are subject to the same sort of rational critique as other discourses. A legitimate function of criticism is to enter into conversation with them, sometimes an adversarial conversation, about the ideas they engage. Can literature be beautiful and successful but ideologically "wrong"? Burke certainly thought so. Literature is a kind of discourse, and very few discourses are completely "right."

The Significance of Tropology

Burke's brilliant predecessor in tropology was the eighteenth-century Italian rhetorician and historian Giambattista Vico. It is interesting that Vico himself saw irony as different from the other tropes—one whose influence, or epistemological force, developed later than the other three in the history of the human race. The early language of mankind, Vico speculated in *The New Science,* was a poetic language. All of its significant terms were figures of speech, hence all of early man's outlook on nature and the cosmos was poetic and mythological. This is why the gods of the world's mythologies are in origin the "names" of natural phenomena (Zeus is the sky, Apollo is the sun, and so on). With the discovery and unfolding of irony as a linguistic possibility, humans developed a new, dialectical form of speech and progressed from a mythological to a rational worldview.

Vico's sometimes wild speculations about the origins of language and the development of rational consciousness must be regarded today as they appear, wildly speculative. However, they do remain quite significant because the tropology procedure, which Vico basically invented, remains a useful one for students of language and discourse. It is significant that Vico was himself a student and teacher of rhetoric. As such, he was faced with the task of defending the art of rhetoric against a new set of opponents: leaders of the scientific revolution, who saw human language as the distorter and corruptor of sound knowledge and concepts. Rhetoric was despised as a distraction from rather than the foundation of a useful education. Chief among these detractors were the Frenchman René Descartes and the English philosopher John Locke.

Literary humanism—that project which promotes the study and teaching of language and literature as essential to the success of individuals and the health of society—had from the beginning rested upon a proposition most powerfully articulated by Isocrates: that human knowledge, accomplishment, and social cooperation rested upon the foundation of language (*Antidosis* 325–26, par. 253–57). Platonists and Augustinians had raised powerful philosophical objections to such a thoroughgoing form of symmetry; however, they had not wanted to dismantle rhetoric as a practical program, and the effect of their philosophical objection was not at all to banish rhetoric but rather to demand that the teaching of rhetoric and literature be placed in a bracing tension with the demands of logos—the requirement of reason (for Plato and Aristotle) and the necessity of revelation (for Saint Augustine). The new science, as represented by Locke and Descartes, did propose a dismantling of the entire project—or at best its reduction to the necessary, elementary inculcation of literacy and basic communication skills. And so Vico's project in *The New Science* was to discover new, more specific, and convincing ways in which the old humanist belief about language was true.

In the process, Vico opened up for students of language a new field of speculation about ways in which language was not simply the transmitter but also the originator and channeling agent of thought. Vico borrowed from the followers of the French rhetorician Peter Ramus the idea that there were four all-important figures of speech. The Ramists' purpose had actually been to reduce rhetoric to a more quickly learnable subject, so as to make room for what they considered more important matters. However, Vico peered into the logic of this reduction and saw, to his astonishment, a tropology.

Traditional rhetorics treated schemes and tropes (dozens of them) as ways of departing from ordinary speech. With the tropes convincingly contracted to a system, viewable all at once, Vico was able to see ways in which all speech, even the philosophical speech that distinguished itself most proudly from the rhetorical and poetic, had a strong tropological content. Thus, Vico created a new way of analyzing literature, philosophy, politics—discourses of any kind—as organizations of language. Investigations of this sort are practiced today under such headings as rhetorical theory, discourse analysis, semiotics, and pragmatics. They rest on the assumption, as Frank Ankersmit stirringly puts it, "that language is the principal condition for the possibility of all knowledge and meaningful thinking" (2).

If language does bear such an important relation to thinking, it stands to reason that the analysis of language should contribute handsomely to the job of understanding and critiquing any kind of discourse. And herein lies the other part of Vico's contribution. Tropologies, and indeed other devices for viewing discourse from the standpoint of linguistic structure and process, can be illuminating tools of criticism and analysis. One of the most interesting adaptations of Vico's (and Burke's) specific tropology is Hayden White's *Tropics of Discourse*. White dismisses any idea that histories are objective accounts of what really happened in the past. He then suggests that different traditions of history writing (and the ideological orientations that go with them) match up to the four ways of conceptualizing that are explained by the master tropes. Philosophers and historians have long been aware that historical narratives are not simply about the facts of history but are informed by perspectives and viewpoints. What is interesting about White's analysis is the demonstration of specific ways in which this must be true. What is troubling about it, of course, is the attempt to fit everything—every way of envisioning the history of things—neatly within one of four categories.

The Compass of Discourse

We have examined some different tropologies, each an exciting way of looking at discourses—texts, theories, world hypotheses—but each is nevertheless deficient or not completely satisfying in some way. Stephen Pepper's *World Hypotheses* simply enumerates four different root metaphors without any concern as to whether they form a system. Pepper is satisfied that he has covered all the bases, but we are left with questions: Why just four root metaphors? Why these particular four? Burke's pentad, by contrast, does present us with a tightly closed system, based on the notion of language as dramatic action; and we do know why there are just five "placements." However, the system has a limitation for this very reason. Language is dramatic action, but it is not just dramatic action. There does exist saying as well as doing, contemplation as well as action. Therefore, the pentad is a more exciting instrument for examining the motivations of human systems (literature, economics, politics), rather than for investigating ideas about the natural world or the broader universe, of which humanity is a part. Burke is aware of this, and this is possibly why he turns longingly to an alternate tropology at the end of his book. And the Viconian master tropes, as illuminating as they are, do have their own problems, as we have seen.

The intellectually exciting thing about tropologies is their further confirmation of the principle of structural analogy, which claims that structures and internal patterns of language do have analogues in the broader world of human experience. Conversely, we may take it as axiomatic that significant problems of human understanding and experience have analogues in the structure of language. However, now is precisely the moment to remember that we are dealing with analogies, not things-in-themselves. And so we must also recall a cardinal rule of argumentation: analogies are valid only up to a certain point, past which they become false analogies. They tend to run up against incompatible facts. However, in those discussions that matter most, it is never simply the facts of the case, but rather alternate as ifs, that will replace them. This is why discussion about large matters must always go on; it is also why multiple, complementary, and competing tropologies are possible, useful, and necessary.

Now, a different tropology from what we have seen so far will open up new territory. But first, take a look at the word "territory." This chapter began with the speculation that the most common metaphors we use to explain thinking and talking are directional or geographical. This is all the more remarkable when you consider that the processes of thinking and talking are themselves fundamentally temporal and linear, not spatial at all. They exist in time, not in spaces; they have no physical dimensions. We say or think one thing, and then we "move on" to another. However, we use an abundance of spatial, even geographical metaphors to describe (and cue our listeners to) the ways we are trying to make sense.

Earlier, in saying that analogies are valid *up to a certain point,* I was using a locational metaphor. Spatial and directional metaphors are everywhere, but of course we do not mean them literally. But what do we mean? How else can we say it? Where can we find the words for it? In explaining our thoughts—the ways in which we understand the world—we cannot get by without these ubiquitous as ifs. This omnipresence of directional and spatial metaphors suggests the possibility of another set of root metaphors or master tropes. It is possible that we might find in them some important things about the fundamental directions of our thinking. If this is the case, we will need to do something similar to what Vico had to do with classical rhetoric's large accumulation of tropes: can we reduce them to a manageable, significant number, thus framing a tropology, and identify some fundamental directions that discourses take? Yes, we can, and we can receive assistance from two of our most fruitful pilot analogies: saying versus doing and designating versus naming. Remember that the cultural analogue of saying versus doing is contemplation versus action, and the cultural analogue of designating versus naming is tradition versus innovation.

Saying versus Doing and the Up There/Down Here Axis

The saying/doing analogy derives from the performative principle, which highlights the paradox that all discourses are simultaneously separate from and yet participating in action. At the same time, it is possible to distinguish utterances (and discourses) that lean one way or another. Some are "mostly" saying something or constative in nature ("The square of the hypotenuse of a right triangle is equal to the sum of the squares of the other two sides."), while others are "mostly" doing something or highly performative ("Off with her head!").

It is interesting that nearly all of our spatial and directional metaphors direct the first of these kinds of statements (the constative/contemplative) "upward," while nearly all such metaphors direct the second kind (the performative/active) "downward." Contemplation, the territory of ideas and abstract principles, is thought to reach toward the "upper realms" of thought, "above the fray," toward "higher levels" of generalization and "overarching" principles. Action, by contrast, is "down here," "down to earth." When we are ready to act, we get "down" to business, in the nation "under God," where no one is "above the law." Also, recalling the performative principle, the language of "down here" tends to be more directly participatory, often directly enacting what is to be done. By contrast, the language of up there is less participatory. It is the ideas that are important, and we want language to be as unobtrusive and out of the way as possible. Quite interestingly, some forms of mystical contemplation strive to bypass language altogether.

Considering that some statements will tend toward the extremes while others will be in-between, we can plot the upward and downward movements graphically on a vertical line, with clusters of related linguistic and conceptual terms at either end. Once we do so, it is not difficult to plot the directions of two sorts of philosophies or world hypotheses: those that tend to locate reality (or significance) "up there," in ideas and abstract principles, coincide with the philosophical outlook of "idealism"; and those that locate reality "down here," in concrete facts and circumstances, coincide with the philosophical outlook known as "empiricism."

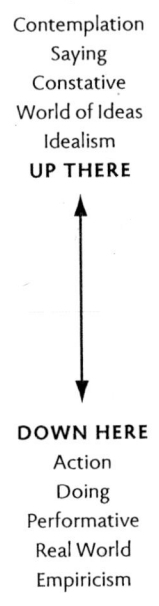

Figure 1. Up There and Down Here directions of language and thought

Designating versus Naming and the Out There/In Here Axis

The designating versus naming analogy states that discourses gravitate at different times toward poles of a different sort: Toward the one pole, we are attempting to use the commonly accepted meanings of words to refer to things that we think of (justifiably or not!) as having an "objective" existence—"out there." Toward the other pole, we are as individuals taking liberties—stretching or turning the accepted language to express things "inside ourselves," realities that are "in here" and hence less tangible or measurable.

As we have seen, however, designating/naming does not always coincide with objective/subjective by any means. The naming function can be scholarly and exploratory as well as personal and expressive. The out there/in here axis is actually associated more with different methods of studying reality—and with conflicting views about which methods are valid—than with different kinds of reality. Out There methodologies stress identifying particular things-in-themselves (objective reference), distinguishing these entities from others (analysis), and making sure that terms refer to distinct facts or events (operational definitions). In Here approaches stress the need to understand things as they have been experienced (perspectivism), to find connections between things that happen in different areas (synthesis), and occasionally to look at things from the standpoint of feeling (personalism).

These different ways of knowing and talking about things have been recognized by linguists and discourse theorists under a variety of nomenclatures. In Burke's adaptation of Vico, this axis is parallel to the distinction between metonymy and metaphor, anticipating reductionist versus perspectivist outlooks respectively. The great philosopher of language Ernst Cassirer speaks of a dichotomy between the "object pole" and the "ego pole" of human consciousness (91). And taking off from Burke, the structural linguist Roman Jakobson has attempted to identify specific features of the "metonymic and metaphoric" poles of meaning in language ("Two Aspects of Language"). As noted above, it might be tempting to add the pair objective versus subjective to this cluster, but it would be misleading to do so. What we can say with confidence is that designating versus naming are associated with different realities (or outlooks on reality), and these in turn are normally characterized as pointing to or coming from Out There as opposed to In Here.

Considering that some discourses will tend toward extremes while others will fall in-between, we can plot the outward and inward movements graphically on a horizontal line with clusters of related linguistic and conceptual terms at either end. Once we do so, it is not difficult to plot the directions of two additional sorts of outlooks: those that insist on methods of factual description, measurement, and analysis of entities (out there) coincide with the general philosophy of realism; and those that insist that things cannot be known except from one or another internal perspective coincide with the general philosophy of relativism.

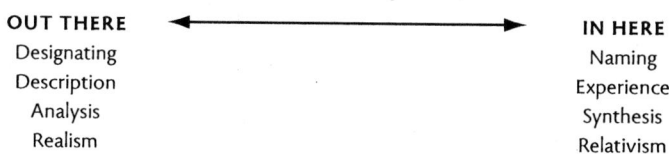

Figure 2. Out There and In Here directions of language and thought

So far, the pilot analogies of saying versus doing and designating versus naming have delivered four basic directions of thought: Up There, Down Here, Out There, and In Here. Furthermore, these four basic directions of thought have four corresponding philosophical placements or ways of knowing reality: idealism, empiricism, realism, and relativism. The pattern of these placements suggests, obviously, an analogy to the compass, our fundamental device for determining where we are or where something is coming from. It also suggests that most of the positions we observe or stand in will be points in-between the four primary directions. These directional placements correspond exactly to the ways of thinking suggested by the Burkean and Viconian master tropes, and they enrich our understanding of these placements by suggesting the states of mind or temperament that correspond both to the four outlooks and to the four characteristic turnings of language:

- The gaze Up There corresponds to irony, the device that distances us from what we are saying, and it suggests a contemplative, idealistic frame of mind.
- The focus Down Here corresponds to synecdoche, the search for concrete examples, and it suggests (in contrast to the contemplative) a down-to-earth, practical temperament.

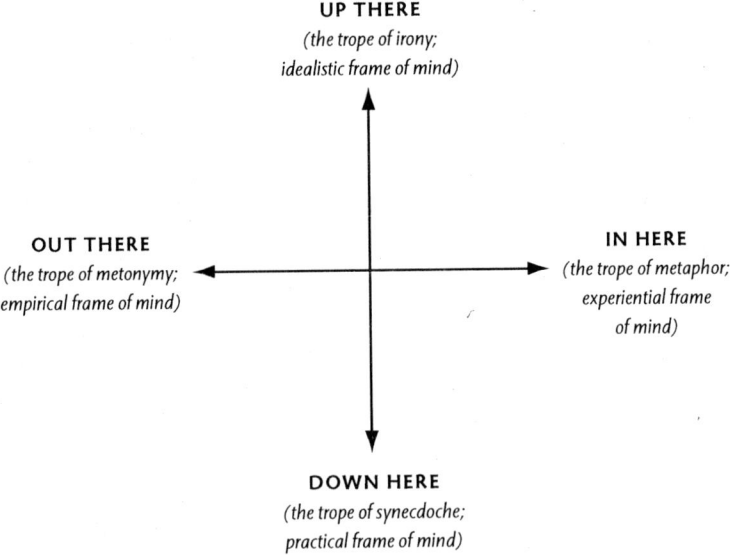

Figure 3. Characteristic uses of language/frames of mind

- The fixed attention Out There corresponds to metonymy, the demand for the tangible, even the measurable, and it suggests an empirical no-nonsense character.
- The attentive listening In Here corresponds to metaphor, a sensitivity to experiential connections, and it suggests a person of feeling with a creative sensibility.

As the preceding diagram emphasizes once again, the compass is an instrument of mapmaking as well as direction finding. Therefore, its usefulness to the understanding of discourse extends even further because acts of discourse are "full" things: no single thing you say exists on just one of these axes; it exists, rather, on both of them at the same time. A statement that occupies a distinct position on the Up There/Down Here axis will also be somewhere on the Out There/In Here scale. You cannot fully understand the statement without understanding both placements. Consider my example of a performative statement, "Off with her head!" from Lewis Carroll's famous *Alice in Wonderland*. This speech act occupies a distinctly downward position on the Up-Down axis (the queen is making a command, not a speculation), but it is also Out There on the other axis: she is commanding a specific group of subordinates to perform a specific action on Alice, right now. Or is she, really? Does she really want Alice executed, or is this just her way of expressing frustration? Or does she intend both things at once? Is she aware of what she is doing? These are questions of interpretation, revealing, among other things, that when you are a queen you ought to be careful about what you say.

Lewis Carroll was intrigued by the mysteries of language, and what his charming but disturbing example illustrates is the general principle that no act of discourse can bring one continuum into play without simultaneously activating the other. So our compass not only finds directions but lays out quadrants, and these quadrants can provide a map of complex placements for those rich and complex discourses that hope for comprehensive understandings of things. If we cross vertical and horizontal lines of the two axes together, we get the four quadrants of a map.

- Up There and Out There: combines idealist and realist orientations (formism)
- Up There and In Here: combines idealist and relativist orientations (organicism).
- Down Here and Out There: combines empiricist and realist orientations (mechanism)

- Down Here and In Here: combines empiricist and relativist orientations (contextualism)

The names of philosophies that are in parentheses after the placements above are precisely those identified by Stephen Pepper. It is exciting because it confirms the basic validity of Pepper's placements, and at the same time challenges his thinking in some ways: Why just four root metaphors? The compass provides an answer. But why these particular four (similarity, machine, organism, and the rich concrete thing)? Well, it does not have to be these particular four, and each of these—like all analogical devices—has distinct limitations in explaining the outlook with which it is associated. The machine, for instance, is a potent analogy for many (particularly modern) forms of empiricist and realist philosophies. However, the device of the machine, with its association of planned function, interlocking parts, and transfer of energy, cannot be said to be an informing or controlling idea for older philosophies such as those of Hobbes and Locke. Not all material interacting is machine-like. Moreover, a number of modern theories of language and mind (notably those of Descartes and Noam Chomsky) are both mechanistic and idealist in implication (see Harris, *The Language Machine*).

Particular philosophies do tend to be rich and creative undertakings, and they do resist pigeonholing. The best that we can do is to plot the different philosophical neighborhoods where different intellectual temperaments, with the different tools and blueprints they typically employ, tend to build their houses. But more specifically important for students of language, what the compass of discourse can do is to lay out dimensions—territories of human interest—where corresponding ways of using language tend to be most relevant and successful. (It's difficult to get past the geographical metaphor, isn't it?) We can also think of these dimensions as areas of specialization, the fields of expertise where highly intentional, planned, and elaborated discourses are typically positioned.

With this particular purpose in mind, our compass allows us to map four basic dimensions, and I offer names for them in the right column of the scheme that follows:

Up There and Out There:	a conceptual dimension
Up There and In Here:	an imaginative dimension
Down Here and Out There:	an operational dimension
Down Here and In Here:	an ethical dimension

These dimensions predict areas of human interest, ways of using language, operations of language, ways of looking at things, and interestingly, the types of temperaments and characters that typically reside in them.

The operational dimension is the area in which we make things happen, get things done, direct activities, make the wheels turn, and organize the show. Typical kinds of language products that turn up here are contracts, laws, technical reports, manuals of instruction, and a multitude of forms. A common character type that resides here is the technician, or sometimes within institutions, the legalist or operative.

The conceptual dimension is the area from which we view the big picture, build theories, comprehensive explanations, overviews, and even tropologies. Typical kinds of discourses, obviously, are scholarly treatises, articles, and textbooks. The typical character is that of the scholar or theorist.

The imaginative dimension is the domain of as ifs, of intuition, where language is stretched and turned (troped) beyond its normal meanings in pursuit of the not yet expressed, or the not so well expressed. It is where things not outwardly or immediately true are made the instruments for viewing inner truths; where worldly things are viewed from otherworldly perspectives. Typical kinds of discourses are works of literature, but great works of religious and political prophecy and inspiration also turn up here. The basic character type is that of the poet or prophet (William Blake is the great modern instance of the two uniquely combined).

The ethical dimension is the arena in which actions must be taken, difficult choices must be made, problems must be solved, and allegiances must be formed, adhered to, or abandoned. And there is another important feature: the choices and answers hinge not merely on what will work (as in the operational dimension) but also on what is right, what is most satisfying to multiple interests, or (rather often) what constitutes the best compromise between conflicting values or points of view. This is the realm of rhetoric, and to it belong all those discourses that are designed to persuade us about what to do, what to value, and how to live. The paradigmatic character type that goes with this set is the statesperson or organizational leader.

All of these dimensions can be mapped. As a reminder, the terms at the top of the vertical and horizontal axes are those of the pilot analogies from which the compass of discourse tropology is composed.

148 FIGURING (OUT) THE WORLD

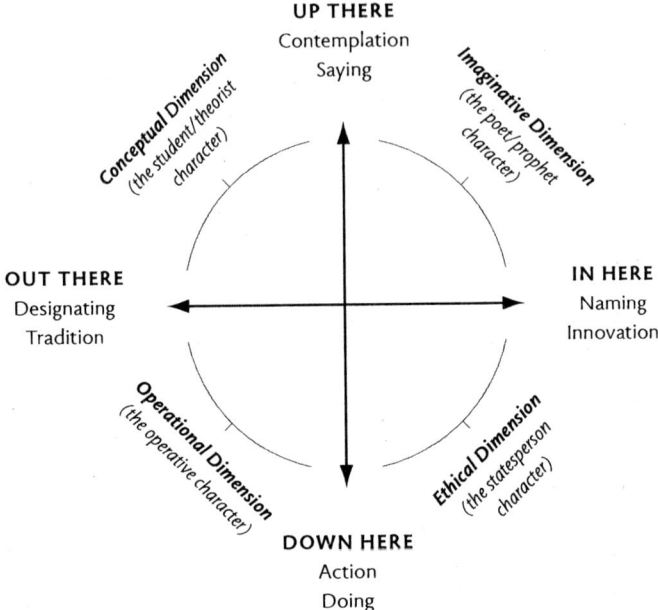

Figure 4. The Compass of Discourse, dimensions of interest and types of characters

Four Processes of Composing Discourse

Since language is microcosmic, it is not surprising that we should discover from the compass of discourse not merely a set of dimensions, and even organizational character types, but also a model of process—in this case, an inventory of the things that we are doing when we speak, write, or compose discourses. Gazing at the four dimensions of the compass, I'm prompted to realize that every time we frame a communication in language we are doing four things at once:

1. We are making something—putting together the various components of language to achieve a specific purpose.
2. We are saying something—conveying a message, with a specific content to an audience.
3. We are exploring or envisioning something—turning (troping) an existing vocabulary or framing a set of imaginative as ifs.

4. And we are doing something—performing one of the numerous acts that utterances and discourses can perform.

Each of these components has a placement in the compass, moving clockwise from the operational to the ethical. In ordinary conversation, of course, all of this comes easily and unconsciously, and our movements in one or another of the quadrants may be so negligible as to seem nonexistent. When we say, "Would you bring me a cup of coffee?" it is only the doing component—requesting something—that is normally a conscious act (although, in some circumstances, the speaker would be wise to choose just the right words and gestures). In longer, more careful, and intentional discourses, all of it becomes more conscious and difficult. And the fact that all of the components come into play at once makes composing an especially stressful task, an art that requires practice and study.

The most significant thing about tropology can be observed in Burke's view of the "placements" of the Burkean pentad. Any person who looks seriously at the world—or alternately at the inner world of language itself—will tend to concentrate on (or look out from the perspective of) one of these placements. In the process, that person will inevitably slight or even distort one or more of the other placements. Even when that person attempts to touch all the bases, he or she will tend to see the others from the perspective of just one or two. Sometimes this creates a remarkable and wonderful new way of seeing things. Other times it is a disaster. Consider what happens when either the technician or the poet or prophet becomes an organizational leader.

The world is a complex and "whole" thing; humans and their societies are whole things. They occupy all of the dimensions at once, but we cannot see them all at once. Most of the time we are not motivated to do so, but even when we earnestly try, we cannot see from every direction at once. Even tropologies, which attempt to produce maps of the whole thing, are perspectivist: Burke's pentad looks out from the perspective of symbolic action; Viconian master tropes apply to all thinking an intuitive reduction of the classic figures of speech; the compass of discourse fashions an instrument out of the pervasive spatial and directional metaphors that we use to make sense of things. Each has its limitations; more tropologies are always possible. What each of them demonstrates, however, is what literary humanists from ancient Greece forward have intuited: language is the complex and whole thing that mirrors, in its various dimensions, the whole thing of the world.

Suggested Reading

Ankersmit, F. R. *History and Tropology: The Rise and Fall of Metaphor.* Berkeley: University of California Press, 1994. Probably because of the powerful example of Hayden White, tropology as an academic pursuit has tended to concentrate on the ideological analysis of historical writings. Ankersmit's book is a masterful review of this enterprise.

Black, Max. "Metaphor." *Proceedings of the Aristotelian Society* 55 (1954–55): 273–94. This is a classic analysis of the role of metaphor in scientific and philosophical discourse.

Burke, Kenneth. *A Grammar of Motives.* New York: Prentice-Hall, 1945.

———. *A Rhetoric of Motives.* Berkeley: University of California Press, 1969. These are now regularly assigned classics by probably the most seminal thinker in modern literary humanism. The term "motives" in each title is something of a puzzle, and Burke almost never defines his terms. I think in light of the chapter just concluded that we can consider "motives" to mean "tropological placements."

Mellard, James J. *Doing Tropology: Analysis of Narrative Discourses.* Urbana: University of Illinois Press, 1987. This is an important book because it takes seriously the idea of multiple tropologies, and therefore of tropology itself as an active methodology of criticism.

Pepper, Stephen. *World Hypotheses: A Study in Evidence.* Berkeley: University of California Press, 1961. This is the classic work in history of philosophy that introduced the idea of philosophical systems as based upon root metaphors.

Vico, Giambattista. *The New Science of Giambattista Vico.* Trans. Thomas Goddard Bergin and Max Harold Fisch. Ithaca: Cornell University Press, 1968. The fountainhead of tropology, a work of energetic exploratory genius. The first Italian edition in appeared 1822, with influential translations into French following in 1824 and 1836.

White, Hayden V. *Tropics of Discourse: Essays in Cultural Criticism.* Baltimore: Johns Hopkins University Press, 1978. White was the first to apply in a rigorous and extended way the implications of Viconian/Burkean tropology to works of history.

8

Style and Virtue

The ancient struggle between Plato and the sophists, the rhetoric teachers of his day, was the opening exchange in the centuries-long debate over the symmetry question in language. Plato considered the sophists dangerous for a variety of reasons, but at the philosophical heart of it was the belief, promoted by some sophists, that there existed parallels and affinities between patterns of language, patterns of thought, and patterns of human society. Plato believed seriously in a competing theory: the good society was supposed to mirror the pattern of the perfect soul, and language had very little to do with it. If the sophists were right, Plato realized, then the form of education they were promoting—rhetoric—might be considered just as important as philosophy and science. The perfection of human society, as Plato's rival Isocrates had openly claimed, would lie within the cultivation of language as much as with reason. That would be a disaster. In Plato's view it already was a disaster.

For Plato, the most astonishing and outrageous advertisement of the sophists was the claim that their teaching would make young men virtuous. In the dialogue *Protagoras,* Socrates visits the sophist of that name in the company of a young man who wants to sign up for instruction.

When Socrates asks Protagoras what a person can hope to take away from the course, the itinerant wise man answers with swaggering confidence: "Young man, if you come to me your gain will be this. The very day you join me, you will go home a better man, and the same the next day. Each day you will make progress toward a better state." When Socrates inquires in just what way the young man is to become "better," Protagoras does not flinch, answering: "The proper care of his personal affairs, so that he may best manage his own household, and also of the state's affairs, so as to become a real power in the city, both as a speaker and man of action." Socrates, clearly surprised, inquires: "Do I follow you? . . . I take you to be describing the art of politics, and promising to make men good citizens." Protagoras claims that is exactly what he professes to do. At such an answer Socrates is completely astonished and driven to irony: "Then it is a truly splendid accomplishment that you have mastered . . . if indeed you have mastered it" (*Protagoras* 318a–19a).

For Plato, the sophistic claim about virtue was outrageous. The public discourse practiced by sophists and their students was widely considered a deceptive and disreputable activity, not a virtuous one; furthermore, the claim was philosophically shallow—the sophists hardly knew what they were talking about when they spoke about virtue. Finally, the sophist's stock in trade was manifestly a verbal discipline, not a philosophical one. In Plato's view, it was dialectic, not the study of words, that might give to individuals the power of better understanding the world, and hence of conducting better lives. But sophistic teaching was based on the cultivation of language and little else.

Plato's student Aristotle may be seen as taking the side of Plato, though only up to a point. His *Rhetoric,* which begins with the famous statement, "Rhetoric is the counterpart of dialectic," presents itself openly as an attempt to yank rhetoric away from an overemphasis on verbal artistry and give it back to reason (1354A). But even with the adjustment toward dialectic, the practical-minded Aristotle is wary of the virtue agenda promoted by the sophists; and he makes no claim in this direction. Actually, it is Plato himself, in his soaring and captivating dialogue *Phaedrus,* who envisions a kind of elevated and noble discourse based upon the cultivation of the soul's innate gravitation toward truth, beauty, and goodness. The virtue agenda does not go away with the shift from language to pure reason. The argument, for Plato, is ultimately about who should be in charge of promoting virtue: the philosopher or the teacher of rhetoric.

Plato devotes the remainder of *Protagoras* to demonstrating that the renowned sophist has no good idea of what "virtue" is; therefore, he cannot possibly be a fit teacher of it. With devastating powers of cross-examination, Socrates demonstrates that Protagoras cannot even defend the proposition that virtue can be taught, much less the proposition that it can be taught through the verbal discipline of rhetoric. Aristotle later takes up the challenge of defining virtue philosophically in his famous *Nichomachean Ethics.* However, in the *Rhetoric* he backs away from any claim at all about ethics. Whether rhetoric is good or bad, he insists, has entirely to do with the intentions of those who practice it, not at all with the art of rhetoric in itself (*Rhetoric* 1355b). Aristotle is especially firm on this point, for he is eager (contra Plato) to emphasize rhetoric's neutrality: There is nothing particularly virtuous about it, but nothing particularly corrupt either. It all depends on who is doing it.

Isocrates, director of a rival school with a much closer affinity to sophism, also greets the virtue agenda with an initial sneer in his tract *Against the Sophists*: "But these professors have gone so far in their lack of scruple that they attempt to persuade our young men that if they will only study under them they will know what to do in life and through this knowledge will become happy and prosperous" (165, par. 3). Isocrates is actually more attracted to the virtue agenda, however, than either Plato or Aristotle. In the later and probably more serious work entitled *Antidosis,* Isocrates presents the more idealistic view that, since there can be no absolute science of knowing how to live well,

> people can become better and worthier if they conceive an ambition to speak well, if they become possessed of the desire to be able to persuade their hearers, and finally, if they set their hearts on seizing their advantage—I do not mean 'advantage' in the sense given to that word by the empty-minded, but advantage in the true meaning of that term. (337, par. 274–76)

You will notice the considerable caution with which Isocrates, in contrast to Protagoras, expresses these views, and it is entirely possible, by the way, that the actual, historical Protagoras was more moderate in his expression than Plato's literary caricature of him. The reasons for caution on such a topic are obvious: not everyone who becomes a skilled speaker turns out to be a virtuous person. Conversely, there have been many wise and good persons who were ineffective speakers and writers. Furthermore, it is obvious, without the benefit of Platonic philosophy, that there are significant differences between style and substance—on occasion rather embarrassing ones. And finally, it's obvious that particular forms and particular strategic choices of language have no intrinsic morality to them. To darken the picture even further, it is not so obvious at all what particular connections may exist between the cultivation of eloquence and becoming a better person.

Nevertheless, the virtue agenda did not go away in classical rhetoric, and it was the Isocratean tradition of moderate symmetrism, emphasizing the simultaneous development of the skilled speaker and the ethical person, that won out in ancient teaching. This viewpoint is expressed elegantly (though again cautiously) by Cicero; propounded more explicitly and confidently by Quintilian; then sternly rejected some centuries later by the fierce early Christian asymmetrist, Saint Augustine. In his great work *De Oratore,* Cicero uses the dialogue form to good advantage, orchestrating the interplay of different literary voices to create a balanced and nuanced view of the situation. Listening to these different voices, we come to understand that wisdom, virtue, and skill in speaking are separate though interrelated characteristics of Cicero's ideal citizen, the orator statesman. It is interesting, nevertheless, that Cicero's principal spokesperson in that dialogue does at one point assign something of a primary role to rhetoric itself:

> [E]loquence is so potent a force that it embraces the origin and operation and development of all things, all the virtues and duties, all the natural principles governing the morals and minds and life of mankind, and . . . expresses everything that concerns whatever topic in a graceful and flowing style. (III. xx)

Quintilian, who knew Cicero's *De Oratore* well, developed this sentiment further into an educational doctrine: an individual could not become a "truly good" speaker without also becoming a wise and virtuous person; and conversely, in what seems a return to the full confidence of Protagoras, rhetorical training in itself was a maker of the virtuous person. The result would be, in Quintilian's well-known definition of the ideal orator, "the good man speaking well."

At such high-flying moments as these in the texts of Cicero and Quintilian, one wishes for a Socrates to step in and ask, "What do you mean by virtue? And what specific connections do you allege to exist between virtue (or specific virtues) and the arts of language?" There are possibly two sets of answers to these questions. The first stems from a faithful explanation of ancient attitudes, and the second stems from a more speculative discussion of ancient and modern intimations of symmetry.

Virtue, Strength, and the Performative Principle

The virtue agenda of classical rhetoric was not based on the idea that certain kinds of linguistic choice were better than others, ethically or otherwise. Nor, though no one would have denied the proposition, was it based on anything like the eighteenth-century belles lettres idea that improvements in character would lead to elevated taste or refinements in the use of language. It was based, rather, on an understanding of public discourse as public action and on a concept of virtue itself as a kind of readiness for public action.

Discourse as public action invokes the performative principle, which states that every utterance is a doing as well as a saying. Even though classical rhetoricians lacked an adequate theory of language to back them, they did have a strong sense of this principle. They did not define the various kinds of speeches as different registers of language, or even different ways of organizing language. They thought of them as different kinds of public action, to be performed in well-defined circumstances:

exhorting and dissuading, in legislative assemblies

accusing and defending, in courts of law

praising and blaming, in public festivals and ceremonies

These are Aristotle's famous definitions of the three kinds of rhetoric: deliberative, forensic (or legal), and epideictic (*Rhetoric* 1358b). To be a good speaker meant that you were prepared to perform these actions as needed. Chief among the elements of preparation for conducting these public actions were the following:

the linguistic resources to produce coherent and impressive speeches

the logical resources to create persuasive arguments

the imaginative resources to connect to the emotions and aspirations of audiences

the social resources to be a believable character and to speak in an appropriate way

It is significant that the last three of these are encompassed in Aristotle's classic formulation of the three basic "appeals" or ways of generating belief: the rational appeal, the emotional appeal, and the ethical appeal. The first of them, however—what could be termed the stylistic appeal—is omitted as a formal category of "pistis" or belief making in Aristotle. This omission is perhaps owed to Aristotle's commitment to make rhetoric the "counterpart of dialectic." Siding with Plato in this instance, Aristotle continues to view style as an after-the-fact, not a generative, component of the composing process. The basic training of the orator should be conceptual, not linguistic.

The notion of training carries us to the second important concept of this discussion, "aretē" or virtue. For with the idea of training lies the important connection to rhetoric. Virtue is a term that moderns have come to associate either with inner inclinations toward goodness or with outward demonstrations of clean living. If we turn to specific forms of behavior, we are likely to think in terms of avoiding certain vices, maintaining a clean record, and deserving a decent reputation. In the ancient outlook, however, the concept of virtue has far more of an orientation toward public leadership, and a far greater association with action and results. There is something athletic about it; it implies competition and training (see Hawhee, "Agonism and Aretê"). There is also, at least on the surface, something exclusively male and aristocratic about it (see especially Gleason, *Making Men,* for an application specifically to training in rhetoric). In the relations between style and virtue, virtues such as justice have a deep structure that transcends the injustice of particular societies, and hence a relevance to all the citizens of a decent political order. In sum, virtue in the ancient world means excellence, strength, readiness, and the ability to do the good things that should be done for the public good. To have virtue means to have that readiness, to be in possession of those strengths that make a strong citizen and leader. In classical thought, these are not so much dispositions to be cultivated as they are skills or types of performance in which to be trained.

Chief among the virtues were what came to be known in classical and Christian teaching as the cardinal virtues: justice, or right and fair dealing; prudence, or practical wisdom and decision making; fortitude, or courage; and temperance, or self-control and appropriate behavior. In claiming to embrace virtue, the teachers of rhetoric were claiming that their teaching helped to promote these and other skills or qualifications of public leadership. Virtue is about deciding what to do and how to do it; rhetoric is about deciding what to say and how to say it. And since discourse is itself a form of public action, the education of a good speaker must be related to the education of a virtuous person. This is the moderate form of the argument. As noted above, the most enthusiastic promoter of the virtue agenda in the ancient world was Quintilian, who made explicit connections and did not hedge his bets:

How will an orator succeed in eulogy, unless he has a clear knowledge of what is honorable and what is disgraceful? Or in persuasion, unless he understands what is advantageous. Or in judicial pleadings, unless he has a knowledge of justice? Does not oratory also demand fortitude, as the orator has often to speak in opposition to the turbulent threats of the populace? (II.xx. 8)

Justice, prudence, fortitude, and temperance were the strengths not only of individuals but also of states. They constituted the values that would inevitably be appealed to in both private and public decision making. It made sense, therefore, that the best and most effective speaker would be the person who had attained these virtues. The best leader would have attained them also. Public speaking is not only an aspect of leadership, in this view, but an important training ground in the virtues themselves. Are individual character, native ability, and general culture not also important, even primary? Of course they are, but it is precisely their requirement that helps to develop the total package, "the good man speaking well." Such a development is entirely feasible, says Quintilian, and literary humanism should be arranged to facilitate it.

The Virtues of Style

Quintilian's is the strong case. Interestingly, if you will look over his blocked quotation above, you will see specific connections between rhetorical activity and the virtues, but no specific connections to forms, processes, or particular ways of using language. This is a fact of particular significance, because it allows us to recognize that, even in its strong form, the virtue agenda did not allege strict symmetries between the forms of language and the strengths of the effective person. From time to time in the history of literary humanism, teachers have had to pull back from an overemphasis on correctness, acceptability, or elegance of linguistic choice as the marks of effective discourse, and perhaps of character as well.

Nevertheless, ancient rhetoricians did develop a substantial lore of the excellences or virtues of style. And they did make occasional striking reference to connections between these virtues and corresponding excellences of the good man. What would be the basis of such connections? Certainly, one connection would be that the processes of achieving stylistic and real-world virtue were considered to be similar and, in some cases, identical. In the *Institutes,* Quintilian makes reference to Stoic philosophers who made direct connections of this sort, and who considered discourse itself a "positive virtue" (II. xv. 20). It is unfortunate that these writings, as well as most of the writings of the Greek sophists, are now lost to us. If we had them, we would be in possession of a good deal more speculation from the ancients on these matters, and possibly some attempts to frame a comprehensive theory.

No such comprehensive theory exists, but a very striking instance has its beginning in Book III of Aristotle's *Rhetoric*. It has to do with the stylistic virtue of "prepon"—what would later be termed "decorum" or "propriety." In discussing this stylistic virtue, Aristotle remarks that the way to achieve it is to discover, for the individual occasion, a happy medium between a style that is too plain and one that is too flamboyant or extravagant (1404b). What is interesting about this procedure is its similarity to the one that Aristotle recommends for the virtuous person in *Nichomachean Ethics*. In that treatise, such virtues as courage, justice, and temperance are theorized as the capability of finding means between extremes of action and feeling. The virtue of courage, for instance, is considered a mean between the extremes of cowardice and a careless bravery.

As I noted above, Aristotle was not expressly interested in the virtue agenda; however, later rhetoricians and philosophers have quite reasonably concluded that, in stressing the correlation to dialectic, Aristotle was really emphasizing the virtue of prudence or practical wisdom, that is, the ability to apply right reason to human problems. The virtue agenda is in fact inescapable if you consider the inescapable fact that speech is an important form of human action and is bound up in every human action. In the *Nichomachean Ethics,* Aristotle does, after all, identify decorum—appropriateness—as an aspect of wisdom and happiness. And so later generations of humanists, well into early modern times, have understood decorum as an excellence of both style and of character, connected to the broader virtue of practical wisdom (see Self; Garver; Pender).

One of the earliest and most influential of these humanists was Cicero, who seized upon Aristotle's very point about decorum, taking it farther than Aristotle would have. In his treatise *Orator,* while discussing the choices a speaker must learn to make among high, middle, and low styles, Cicero makes explicit the connection between decorum and practical wisdom:

> Now the man who controls and combines these three varied styles needs rare judgment and great endowment; for he will decide what is needed at any point, and will be able to speak in any way which the case requires.

> For after all the foundation of eloquence, as of everything else, is wisdom. In an oration, as in life, nothing is harder than to determine what is appropriate. The Greeks call it prepon; let us call it decorum or propriety. . . . From ignorance of this mistakes are made not only in life but very frequently in writing, both in poetry and in prose. (*Orator* xxi. 70)

In his own ethical treatise, *On Duty,* Cicero elaborates further on decorum as an ethical virtue, defining right action in the world as the action that is appropriate to a human being. At one point he even goes so far as to proclaim: "What is proper is morally right, and what is morally right is proper" (I. xxvii. 93). Obviously, in such a view, decorum goes beyond politeness: in all things, human beings should behave in ways appropriate to their nature as rational creatures, made for cooperation and society, for subordinating impulse to reason, for remembering the past, for planning for the future, and "for order, for propriety, for moderation in word and deed" (I. xl.142). In his comprehensive work *Roman Literary Theory and Criticism,* J. F. D'Alton points out that, in Cicero's highly influential formulation, the doctrine of decorum combines ethical, aesthetic, and philosophical principles in a single moment (369). Living well and writing well are in this respect not only connected but merged into one another.

As we have already seen, the more explicit elaboration of the virtue agenda into an educational ideology would come from Quintilian. However, Quintilian was drawing upon a well-established tradition that saw public discourse as an important form of social action, and hence the person of strong character as the best qualified to conduct that action. This was a tradition that included canons of invention and disposition (the conceptualizing and arranging of discourse) as well as (to a lesser degree) delivery and memory. In Aristotle, for whom rhetoric is the counterpart of dialectic, the role of invention is clearly primary. However, the Isocratean tradition was eventually more influential than the Aristotelian. In the Roman period, rhetoric became more and more a preparatory course, focused less on direct training in adult, real-world discourses, and more on exercises and disciplines that would develop in young people the general capacity and potential for such things.

A natural consequence of this development was a more extensive and intense focus on language—on smaller units and operational processes of composing—and a particular focus on style. In such a context, it is no accident that the virtues of style developed in such a way as to mirror comprehensively the virtues of discourse at large—invention and arrangement as well as style. They also were put forward in such a way as to mirror those kinds of appeals (ways of generating agreement) identified by Aristotle: the logical, the emotional, and the ethical, in addition to the appeal generated by the beauty and well-madeness of a discourse itself.

Among the ancient world's different classification of the virtues of style, the most comprehensive and influential was constructed by Aristotle's student Theophrastus. It was later adapted and extended (sometimes with different terminology) by Cicero, Quintilian, and others, but in most applications what emerged was a fourfold structure: the stylistic virtues of correctness, clarity, ornament, and decorum. Because this classification was meant from the beginning to be comprehensive in character, each of these terms came to pack in more than what immediately meets the eye.

Correctness (Well-madeness)

Correctness (sometimes "purity," "Hellenism," or "Latinity") means using language that is "normal" and readily understandable to an audience, and this includes following accepted conventions and patterns of sentence construction. However, a better term would probably be well-madeness, for this category went beyond what we call correctness to include making a discourse that is graceful, pleasing, and even beautiful (insofar as the subject and occasion will allow). It was well understood that these effects were not only virtues in their own right but they also contributed to the overall effectiveness of a discourse. In its extension to the medium of writing, this category would include a making a discourse that is highly readable and visually pleasing. In principle, for both writing and speechmaking, it would include elements of structure beyond the sentence, such as the organizing of paragraphs and whole discourses.

Clarity

Clarity goes far beyond presenting a discourse that is readily understandable or readable. It means being faithful to certain conceptual content while at the same time pointing the audience in right directions: choosing the right words, presenting definitions, distinctions, and examples where necessary, and arranging things so that they present a clear and convincing path of discovery. A distinction between two different issues of word choice might well illustrate the difference between correctness and clarity: The choice between "infer" and "imply" is usually one of correctness. The words do mean two different things, but that difference is not what is at stake. The issue arises most of the time because the word "infer" is "incorrectly" put in the place of "imply." By contrast, the choice between "imply" and "insinuate" does involve an issue of clarity. The words do mean related things, but unless you want to point your audience toward an understanding of underhanded, malevolent behavior on the part of the person doing the insinuating, you should refrain from using that word.

An important pattern is beginning to emerge. As with the virtue of correctness, achieving clarity starts with a consideration of words and sentences but then goes beyond that: it inevitably comes to include considerations of what to say and use in a discourse (definitions, distinctions, examples, illustrative narratives, visual aids, and so on) as well as how to shape and organize that discourse. In fact, the criterion of clarity directs us back to the canon of invention—that is, the discovery of content. In formal rhetorics, this canon is usually considered prior to style altogether, but it is difficult to keep them apart.

Ornament (Power)

Ornament is clearly the least aptly named of the stylistic virtues in classical lore. This virtue gets its name from the fact that it bears a direct reference to the use of schemes and tropes—those captivating syntactic arrangements and figures of speech that rhetoricians made such long lists of and encouraged their practice and imitation. The eighteenth-century rhetorician Hugh Blair gives an excellent example of the difference between plain and ornamented discourse, in his lecture on the "Origin and Nature of Figurative Language":

> [T]o say, "It is impossible, by any search we can make, to explore the divine more fully," is to make a simple proposition. But when we say, "Canst thou, by searching, find out God? Canst thou find out the Almighty to perfection? It is high as heaven, what canst thou do? Deeper than hell, what canst thou know?" This introduces a figure into style; the proposition being not only expressed, but admiration and astonishment being expressed together with it. (Vol. I, 273)

As Blair's example directly illustrates, in any serious discourse there is much more at stake with schemes and tropes than ornamenting or prettifying its language. Cicero's term for it was dignity, but that still does not quite express what is at stake. It fails to capture the sense of the power of eloquence to sweep up an audience in feeling, and it does not address the issue of where that extra element of expression and audience appeal comes from. Plato's rival Gorgias ascribed something like magical, mesmerizing powers to a language of elegant complication and grandiosity, but his formulation failed (as Plato knew) to distinguish between true and false—truly moving versus merely impressive—variants of ornament. The Greek rhetorician Longinus proposed the notion of "the sublime." Longinus argued forcefully that sublimity could not be achieved through skillful manipulations of language alone, but only by a great and sensitive soul under the influence of powerful emotion.

Sublimity comes closer than dignity, but I think the term "power" most aptly names the process and the effect we are talking about. The term eloquence has often been a substitute over the centuries, but that term also serves as a general concept for all the virtues combined. Power fits a wider range of discourses than does the notion of sublimity, and it does express that we are talking simultaneously about a way of using language, an element of inspiration and feeling behind that use, and an ability to carry an audience into that inspiration and feeling. That stern asymmetrist Saint Augustine added a distinctly un-Ciceronian bit of understanding to the notion of power, by pointing out that a truly moving and inspirational discourse need not require the grand style at all: "O eloquence, so much the more terrible as it is so unadorned; and as it is so genuine, so much the more powerful" (*On Christine Doctrine* IV. 30). Augustine is defending the inspirational power of the Bible, whose language is often not at all artful in the classical sense; he also has in mind the capacity of an unadorned but emotionally authentic sermon or confession to move an audience. The true source of power in discourse, as Augustine understood it, was not language at all but revelation; and such a thing could be powerfully expressed in the simplest of language, the plainest of styles.

Decorum (Appropriateness)

Decorum is the ability to match language to situations—to say things in an appropriate way, at the appropriate time, with an appropriate mixture of clarity and power and politeness, under the circumstances. As with the other virtues, this means choosing the appropriate words and phrases and ways of joining sentences together, but it intends a great deal more. More broadly, it includes choosing the most appropriate things to say under the circumstances, organizing these things in the most appropriate way, and (in situations of speechmaking) conducting oneself appropriately while doing so. Consider the following example: A possible argument for government support of private schools might be feared to weaken the power of teachers' unions. Consequently, if you're attempting to gain or retain the support of teachers themselves, it might be best to "minimize" (Aristotle's term) this consequence, or perhaps to avoid it altogether and save this topic for the question/answer session. Decorum is the virtue most directly related to broader fields of human conduct. Cicero and Quintilian made this connection directly, pointing out the relation of decorum to the virtue of prudence, or practical wisdom; and they implied that decorum in language was an important training ground for the larger virtue. It is not surprising, then, that decorum acquired a kind of governing role among the stylistic virtues. Correctness is a virtue, but there will be times to sacrifice it in favor of clarity. Both clarity and correctness may have to bow to power, but then power, especially when it has been summoned by lofty and bombastic phraseology, must be moderated very often in favor of clarity and decorum.

How about decorum itself? Are there times to let it go? This is analogous, of course, to the logical conundrum of whether moderation should ever be moderated. Cicero does not anticipate such a possibility. He goes so far as to say that what is right is decorous, and what is decorous is right (*De Officiis* I. xxvii, 94). However, we must certainly allow for the possibility, in general behavior as well as in speech (keep in mind now that we are talking about virtues in the ancient sense of abilities that underlie right action). Simply put, there are times when we do have to break decorum. History and individual experience have demonstrated repeatedly that there are times when decorum, insofar as that term implies settled, acceptable, and polite ways of accomplishing things, must be sacrificed to a higher virtue. Obvious cases in point: the rhetoric of demonstrations and civil disobedience. In a given circumstance, it may be prudence itself that dictates this, it may be inspiration (a broader virtue that connects to power in discourse), it may be reason (the broader virtue that connects to clarity), or it may even be a higher sense of correctness, the law, a higher law, or justice (for an excellent example involving the struggle for women's rights, see Oravec).

The Virtues and the Compass of Discourse

The compass of discourse, you will recall, is based upon the irretrievably "directional" cast of all our verbalization of experience. In constructing the compass of discourse, I mapped four quadrants of conceptualization—four fields of experience, ways of understanding and talking about experience: an operational field (in the down-here/out-there quadrant), a conceptual field (in the up-there/out-there quadrant), an imaginative field (in the up-there/in-here quadrant), and an ethical field (in the down-here/in-here quadrant).

A matter of signal importance for the current project is that the compass of discourse does not merely confirm the work of Pepper, Burke, and others on the elaboration of world views and social philosophies; it also anticipates and finds placements for the four basic processes that we are engaging in when we compose a fully elaborated work of discourse: we are making something (in the operational field); we are saying something (in the conceptual field); we are exploring or envisioning something (in the imaginative field); we are doing something (in the ethical field).

As a clarifying recapitulation, I am reproducing and expanding the diagram that maps these relations. In the familiar figure below, you will notice that the compass of discourse now includes the placement of the four classical virtues of style: well-madeness in the operational field, clarity in the conceptual field, power in the imaginative field, and appropriateness in the ethical field. Four corresponding virtues in the world of action have also been placed in the fields to which they belong: practical competence in the operational field, clear thinking in the conceptual field, inspiration in the imaginative field, and good judgment in the ethical field.

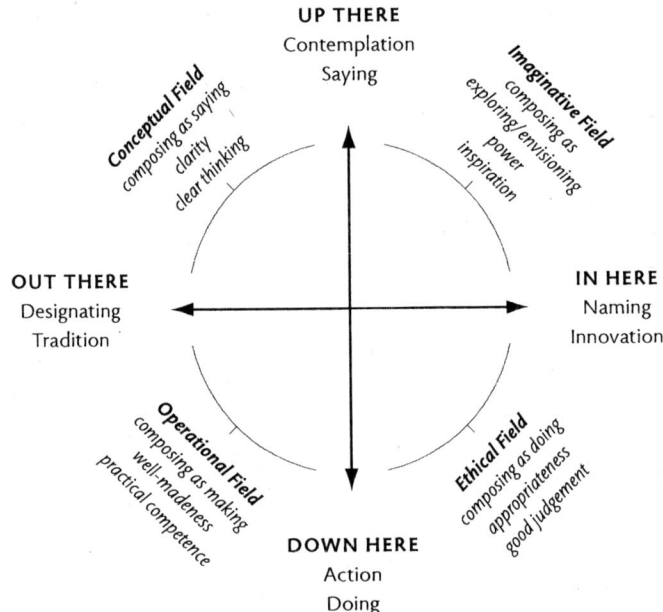

Figure 5. Fields of Experience, Processes of Composing, Virtues of Style

These virtues, I claim, are the practical or world-of-action correlates of well-madeness, clarity, power, and appropriateness of style. With respect to style, I have been claiming (with Theophrastus, Cicero, and Quintilian) that the concepts of well-madeness, clarity, power, and decorum do constitute a fairly comprehensive inventory. No such claim of comprehensiveness can be made with respect to virtue in the larger sense. Nevertheless, these particular virtues (strengths and abilities of mind and character) are exactly what the successful practice of discourse requires most. These, accordingly, are the virtues to whose development the study of discourse can most readily contribute. This claim is warranted not only by theory but also by the aims and practices of most English teaching as we know it. We help students to produce and value a discourse that shows practical competence, intellectual strength, inspiration, and good judgment.

We study and provide instruction in the craft of making discourse. In doing so we acknowledge and claim—even when our study and practice is centered on the literary and impractical—that skill in this craft is an important part of a person's ability to succeed in society. We also study and teach the processes of reasoning: assisting in the attainment of the intellectual resources necessary for planning, organizing, and thinking through a successful discourse. In doing so we claim that we are contributing to students' critical thinking, problem solving, and reasoning abilities in general.

We know that inspiration, intellectual and spiritual commitment, and the personal ownership of ideas are important components of success in discourse, as well as in life. Therefore, we promote the meditative and self-exploratory potentialities of writing, both as a means of self-development and an avenue toward power in making discourse. We also study and teach works of inspired literature, both as models and sources themselves of inspiration. We also study and teach the lore of literary and rhetorical strategy, including questions of what to say, how to say it, and in what order to say it in particular situations, to particular audiences. In doing so, we claim that we are contributing to the development of good judgment in general.

The Teleologies of Virtue

In the Platonic dialogue *Protagoras,* the character of Protagoras was able to produce some rather eloquent statements about the value of discourse education to individuals and society, but he was not able to persuade Socrates that he understood what virtue was, philosophically, or that he had a firm grasp of how it related to language. Socrates would probably not be satisfied either with the rather optimistic outline presented above about the virtues of English teaching. Socrates would perhaps look for an avenue of attack that involved categorizing the values of practical competence, intellectual strength, inspiration, and good judgment as processes only. To put it in grammatical terms, they are basically verbs without objects, and those objects could be good things or bad things, constructive things or destructive things. Unless, we could move beyond the simple statement of processes to a statement about ends, Socrates would not be satisfied.

Earlier in this chapter I pointed out that the tradition of moderate symmetrism (that of Isocrates and Cicero) did take care to state the virtue agenda rather modestly. Isocrates did not say that a person would be made virtuous by the practice of skillful speaking, but rather by the ambition to do so. And only in the case of decorum did Cicero make a strong, one-to-one correlation of style to virtue. It was only Quintilian who pressed hard for the intuition of symmetry. He would not accept that a successful and moving speech promoting the destruction of a city and massacre of its inhabitants could be termed as "inspired" or arranged with "good judgment." He would accept that it was exceedingly clever and executed with a remarkably good strategy. However, it is not possible that inspiration or good judgment, in the proper sense, could be aimed at such a dreadful outcome.

I am going to support Quintilian and provide an answer to Socrates. This is not because I believe such an answer is necessary to the fate of literary humanism. I think the various classical formulas work just fine, and I rather like the outline of rhetorical virtues presented in the preceding section. However, there is an important final point to be made about the symmetry question and about our characteristic ways of thinking about public discourse. For here as elsewhere, while direct attributions of symmetry—that is, in this case, the match-up of structures of language and structures of behavior—are disputable and even mistaken, the broad intuition of symmetry is never simply wrong. There is a way in which Protagoras and Quintilian were right, and the compass of discourse can help us to discover it.

You will recall that the basic coordinates of the compass are directional: they point to directions of conceptualization and quasi-geographical fields or dimensions of interest and motivation. Socrates requires that we connect objects to our verbs—reasons, ultimately, for what we are doing, end points, or teleologies of the virtuous processes we have identified. We can meet that requirement by asking an additional question: are there further directions (on or off the compass) in which these processes take us? Since we are talking about tendencies—long-range rather than practical ends—it is just as valid to ask: are there further directions in which we characteristically want them to take us? I believe that there are. Each of them requires some explanation and commentary, however.

The teleology of clear thinking is truth

Do not think right away about epistemology or abstract principles. Think about the simple act of telling the truth, sentence by sentence. Even when you are engaged in an overall act of evasion or deception, are not the vast majority of your sentences true? As a practical matter, truth is as essential to intelligibility as clear pronunciation. Without the assumption of it, we could not follow from one sentence to the next. What we are hearing would not make sense. Truth telling is a deep principle of discourse and a requirement of successful interchange, even at the most basic levels. This is why habitual or compulsive liars are considered people that you simply cannot talk to, and they are either shunned or taken as candidates for treatment. With this point established, we can move forward to the issue of finding and communicating the truth. This is what the rules of clear thinking should help us to do. Truth is a principal value on which cases are made, and also a desired outcome of any kind of discursive exchange. Isocrates recognized this point when he said that:

> The power to speak well is taken as the surest index of a sound understanding, and discourse which is true and lawful and just is the outward image of a good and faithful soul. With this faculty we both contend against others on matters which are open to dispute and seek light for ourselves on things which are unknown. (*Antidosis*, par. 254–66)

Socrates was unwilling to grant this point, as Cicero pointed out in *De Oratore,* because truth as an end point, in Socrates' thinking, needed to be incontestable truth, and rhetorical discourse could not produce that.

The traditional answer to Socrates has been that there are whole arenas of human concern where incontestable truth is not available, but where an approximation to it is valuable. Perhaps the performative principle can also assist us here: there are some truths that are themselves constructed, maintained, modified, and sometimes overturned through acts of discourse (for an application specifically to public morality, see Condit). In this case, the chief requirement of clear thinking is to construct acts of discourse with as much skill, thoughtfulness, and integrity as possible.

The teleology of inspiration is ultimate value

This teleology is the most difficult to name and talk about (although the connection is itself not a difficult one), because it is so variously understood in different communities of belief. It has many names: the ultimate, ultimate reality, the absolute, absolute beauty, God, the most high, the most deep (profoundest), *ground* of all being, the soul, the oversoul, the Holy Spirit, the transcendent. The list could go on. One of its names in the Western tradition is Logos—The Word. It is no accident that in much of traditional thinking it is conceived as a voice—speaking from without or from within the human psyche.

The teleology of good judgment is wisdom

Ordinary speech does not even require good judgment, much less wisdom. It does require, however, the use of memory to frame a harmonious relation of parts. Judgment (decorum) in discourse requires the use of memory to frame a harmony of the other virtues—structural, intellectual, and inspirational—into a successful communication in specific situations. Wisdom is exactly parallel to judgment in its role as coordinator or umpire among other virtues. It is composed of them, and it works with them. Wisdom may be defined, therefore, as the harmonious application of practical working, truth, and ultimate value to human problems. This is not the deepest sort of wisdom; that belongs to "ultimate value." This is practical wisdom, what the Greeks termed "phronesis," and the Romans translated "prudentia."

The teleology of practical competence is justice

This connection is the least intuitive and the implications are the most controversial. Practical competence is the most difficult of the virtues to attach to something deeper; however, the connection turns out to be one of the most interesting for that reason and, as it happens, one of the most intelligently discussed in modern rhetorical theory.

How does practical competence take us in the direction of justice? Practical competence is the practice of right making and right ordering, with due consideration to the requirements of the tools and materials at hand. Justice, on the other hand, is the principle of acting and responding rightly, of giving to things and people their due consideration. One of the meanings of just is "straight"; the connection is preserved in such phrases as "going straight" and "the straight and narrow." It is also preserved in such craft terms as the "just corner" in carpentry and "justified type" in printing.

The modern rhetorical theorists Chaïm Perelman and Lucie Olbrechts-Tyteca have written more penetratingly than any others about the connections of justice to public discourse, most notably in *The New Rhetoric*. Justice in their view (and this is the principal contribution of their theory) is not merely a principal topic and point of value for rhetorical discourse; it is also a principle of successful ordering in discourse itself. Even at the sentence level, there is a requirement that certain grammatical and conceptual slots must be given their due by the structures that are owed to them. The blank in the following string must be filled in with a noun or noun phrase of human category: That man up on the podium is a _____. This requirement may be seen as a microcosm of justice: things must be given their due. At higher levels of organization, more freedom of choice appears, of course, and with it a greater possibility of just and unjust choices. Perelman and Olbrechts-Tyteca do not claim, however, that the practice of discourse will in itself lead to a refined sense of justice. Their analysis helps to explain the sense of extreme violation, sometimes horror, that everyone feels when a well-made and beautiful (on the surface) discourse is pointed at unjust ends.

There is something else, not discussed by Perelman and Olbrechts-Tyteca, that justice shares with the correspondent virtue of practical competence, and that is justice's surprisingly dependent relation to the other virtues. It is easy to think of justice as the most basic of the teleologies, perhaps foundational to the others. Justice is after all the simple principle of this-for-that ("an eye for an eye"), treating equivalent things equally; making a fair trade; putting things in their right places. However, justice is never that simple, and that is why there is endless wrangling in the courts about the legitimacy of practices, the severity of sentences, and the disposition of settlements.

Here is a complicated case: Should state legislatures have the right to force public employee unions to gain the consent of nonmembers before making political contributions from union dues? Before you answer, consider the following: the nonmembers are required to pay union dues, even though they don't belong to the union (the rationale is that they are being represented by the union); the nonmembers could easily attain the right to be consulted at no additional cost, simply by joining the union; there is the additional question of whether public employee unions should be allowed to contribute to political campaigns at all; and there is the additional question of whether legislatures should be allowed to regulate the unions at all, in which case the nonmembers should have to sue for the right to be consulted. (In 2007, the U. S. Supreme Court ruled that the Washington state legislature did have such a right.)

Not only are individual cases complex, but practices that were at one time considered to be just are always turning out upon review—historical, judicial, and otherwise—not to have been just after all. And that is why any good society will, like any good legal system, open itself to review, change, and even reversal in response to higher claims of truth, wisdom, and ultimate value. A classic modern example of the appeal to a higher law may be found in Martin Luther King, Jr.'s "Letter from a Birmingham Jail":

> Since we so diligently urge people to obey the Supreme Court's decision of 1954 outlawing segregation in the public schools, it is rather strange and paradoxical to find us consciously breaking laws. One may well ask: "How can you advocate breaking some laws and obeying others?" The answer is found in the fact that there are two types of laws: There are *just* and there are *unjust* laws. I would agree with Saint Augustine that "An unjust law is no law at all." Now, what is the difference between the two? How does one determine when a law is just or unjust? A just law is a man-made code that squares with the moral law or the law of God. An unjust law is a code that is out of harmony with the moral law. (70)

Although the connection may at first seem far-fetched, the pattern is the same with practical competence in discourse: the ways of making (rules of correctness, good usage, and basic coherence and organization) are, to borrow King's and Augustine's language for a moment, lower laws. It is easy to think of them as foundational to the other virtues of intellectual strength, inspiration, and good judgment. However, as most students of composition know very well, well-madeness is never that simple, either in the well-making of individual discourses or in the development of practical competence in individual writers and speakers. The protocols of making (sentence, paragraph, and the formal requirements of different discourse genres) are only marginally productive in the creation of successful discourse. Like actions that at first (or long ago) seemed to be just, they are always subject to review, revision, and reversal. Even in the case of set generic forms (the Shakespearian sonnet, for instance), the success of the discourse will depend on accommodation and relevance to thought, inspiration, or judgment rather than on the discrete beauty or integrity of form itself. It is true that form is primary in the sense that it is tangibly and practically indispensable. It must be attended to. The same is true of simple justice. Departing from it too broadly, or too thoughtlessly, always leads to trouble.

The State of Public Discourse

A particularly ardent spokesperson for the virtue agenda has been the eighteenth-century Scottish professor Hugh Blair, whose works were influential in Europe and America throughout the nineteenth and early twentieth centuries. Blair's composite term for stylistic excellence was "taste," and in the first of his *Lectures on Rhetoric and Belles Lettres*, he had this to say about it:

> I will not go so far as to say that the improvement of taste and of virtue is the same; or that they may always be expected to co-exist in an equal degree.... At the same time, this cannot but be admitted, that the exercise of taste is, in its native tendency, moral and purifying.... One thing is certain ... that, without possessing the virtuous affections in a strong degree, no man can attain eminence in the sublime parts of eloquence. He must feel what a good man feels, if he expects greatly to move or to interest mankind. (Vol. I, 13)

To put it mildly, such a pronouncement is no longer acceptable. Modern people have experienced too much exploitation and degradation of public discourse. In addition, we are painfully aware that society has excluded too much (and too many) of the un-tasteful, in actual violation of justice, truth, wisdom, and ultimate value. When we reflect upon things of this sort, it is time to protest. It is obvious that successful writers and speakers are not always the best or wisest people, and that discrepancies between form and substance dominate our public lives and discourse. Asymmetries abound. In and of themselves, the virtues of style do not reflect and will not lead to real virtue, even in the classical sense. Isocrates understood this, rejecting a formalistic regimen and proposing instead a program of general culture accompanied by models, coaching, and practice.

As modern students of composition have learned, a fixed concentration on forms will not even lead to good writing. There are essential things to be learned about the characteristic author to audience relations, conceptual strategies, and organizational patterns of the different genres of discourse. Most modern composition pedagogies do embrace the priority of social, intellectual, and emotional development over correctness, clarity, and decorum as traditionally understood. Saint Augustine did likewise, insisting that the real sources of power in discourse were the end points—particularly the end point of ultimate value—and certainly not the stylistic forms and features associated with eloquence.

However, the intuitions of symmetry that fueled the virtue agenda were not simply mistaken. The surest sign of this is that debates about rhetoric, ever since Plato picked the first quarrel, are ultimately about the character of public discourse and the good society. The one is an example—but more than that, a microcosm—of the other; this is the reason that we are bitterly dismayed and frightened when skillful and moving discourses do not come from justice, truth, wisdom, and ultimate value. Pedagogically, to hold that rational understanding is the cause and not the effect of clarity is still to uphold the connection. And this proposition can be taken to each of the other quadrants of the compass—to practical competence, inspiration, and judgment, as well as to justice, ultimate value, and wisdom. Symmetry acknowledges the connection, in theory and in hope. Asymmetry demands that neither side, style nor virtue, be left unattended. They can instruct each other, but their happy coalescence does not just happen.

Suggested Reading

Atwill, Janet M. "Rhetoric and Civic Virtue." *The Viability of the Rhetorical Tradition.* Eds. Richard Graff, Arthur E. Walzer, and Janet Atwill. Albany: SUNY Press, 2005. 75–92. This interesting article offers a different theoretical perspective from the one I have presented in this chapter. Instead of the relations among language and individual virtues, Atwill focuses on different theories of the state, ancient and modern, and the different kinds of virtue that their discourses might promote or embody.

Condit, Celeste Michelle. "Crafting Virtue: The Rhetorical Construction of Public Morality." *QJS* 73 (1987): 79–97. An excellent article emphasizing not only rhetorical performance as a form of virtuous action and a test of virtue, but also the agency of public rhetoric in shaping the understanding of virtue itself.

Hariman, Robert, ed. *Prudence: Classical Virtue, Postmodern Practice.* State College: Penn State University Press, 2003. An important collection of essays, a number of which explore the connections between prudence and the arts of language. See especially Hariman's "Theory Without Modernity"; Robert Cape's "Cicero and the Development of Prudential Practice at Rome"; and Christine Oravec's "Fanny Wright and the Enforcing of Prudence: Women,

Propriety, and Transgression in the Nineteenth Century Public Oratory of the United States."

Hawhee, Debra. "Agonism and Aretê." *Philosophy and Rhetoric* 35 (2002): 185–207. Defines virtue as classical teachers of rhetoric would have understood it, particularly as the "accomplishment" (as opposed to the disposition) of a public person, achieved through competitive experience.

McIntyre, Alasdair. *After Virtue: A Study in Moral Theory.* 3rd ed. Notre Dame: Notre Dame University Press, 2007. A great ethical treatise, steeped in sympathetic knowledge of the cardinal virtues as understood in the classical world, particularly in the works of Aristotle.

Miller, Thomas P. *The Formation of College English: Rhetoric and Belles Lettres in the British Cultural Provinces.* Pittsburgh: University of Pittsburgh Press, 1997. An excellent source for investigation of the transformation of the ancient virtue agenda into the modern tradition of belles lettres in higher education.

Nussbaum, Martha C. *The Fragility of Goodness: Luck and Ethics in Greek Tragedy and Philosophy.* New York: Cambridge University Press, 2001. A great scholarly work on the virtues, particularly justice, locating primary issues in debates of the ancient world.

Pender, Stephen. "The Open Use of Living: Prudence, Decorum, and the 'Square Man.'" *Rhetorica* 23 (2005): 363–400. A penetrating investigation of the basis in Aristotelian ethics of the virtue agenda in classical rhetoric.

Conclusion

The Love of Words

Literary humanism is any conscious program of scholarship and teaching that combines the study of language, rhetoric, and literature, working toward greater competence, character, and wisdom in the individual and, hence, toward a better society. The credibility of this enterprise, and the viability of its hopes, are greater if there exist correspondences or analogues between structures of language and those of human knowledge, character, and social aspiration. Herein lies the importance of the symmetry question. An overarching purpose of this book has been to examine ways in which different traditions and different practices of literary humanism are based upon different answers to (and intuitions about) that question.

This has not been a dispassionate, on-the-sidelines examination. I have advocated three propositions: that while specific attributions of symmetry are often incorrect, leading to all sorts of futile pedagogical practices, the basic intuition of symmetry is never wholly wrong—language is worth listening to and learning from; symmetry and asymmetry are not opposing philosophies but reciprocal and complementary agencies within language itself; and a successful literary humanism can be legitimately based on the assertion of powerful correspondences between structures of language and structures of human life in society. In chapters four through eight, I've presented different versions of such correspondences. This conclusion provides a coda to these arguments, taking the form of a meditation on a feeling more basic than any proposition from linguistics or the philosophy of language—the love of words.

Almost universally, past and present, literary humanists profess the love of words, and they hope that this love, when carried forward into the disciplines of language, rhetoric, and literature, will be useful to society. (In the old days, the nineteenth century, they were actually called philologists, word lovers.) When they gather to celebrate this love, they rather often commiserate about their failure to pass it along to students. Later, when they fall to bickering about matters of theory, criticism, or pedagogy, it often becomes apparent that they do not all love the same things. Then again, most in the profession would be hard put at any given moment to say exactly what we mean by the love of words. This is not a disgrace. Perhaps all love is this way. However, I think that after eight chapters on symmetry and asymmetry one ought to be able to answer these questions: What are the various things we mean by the love of words? If there are different kinds of love, what are they? And since love has been known to be a dangerous and frustrating, as well a beautiful and empowering thing, how can these kinds of love (ways of loving) be ordered and managed?

Ought love to be managed? After your first set of student essays, well, maybe. As an opening exercise in the management of this love, I ask you to consider this rather beautiful statement by Dylan Thomas:

> I wanted to write poetry in the beginning because I had fallen in love with words. The first poems I knew were nursery rhymes, and before I could read them for myself I had come to love just the words of them, the words alone. What the words stood for, symbolized, or meant, was of very secondary importance. What mattered was the sound of them as I heard them for the first time. . . . I realise that I may be, as I think back all that way, romanticising my reactions to the simple and beautiful words of those pure poems; but that is all I can honestly remember, however much time might have falsified my memory. I fell in love—that is the only expression I can think of—at once, and am still at the mercy of words, though sometimes now, knowing a little of their behaviour very well, I think I can influence them slightly and have even learned to beat them now and then, which they appear to enjoy. ("Notes on the Art of Poetry" 185–86)

Dylan Thomas's rapturous testimony suggests there can be such a thing as the pure, unqualified love of words, individually considered and without any care for what they mean. Can there really? On sober reflection we realize—do we not?—that what he really means by "the sound of them" is the music they produce in artful combination, which they do not really possess by themselves. We can go further and suggest that the role of meaning was probably not inconsiderable in the courtship of the young Dylan by words. Even with an imperfect apprehension (indeed sometimes a misapprehension) of specific meanings, children will generally add to the playful sounds a sense of playful semantic goings on. I think we can take a step further still and suggest that it wasn't really words as things that young Dylan loved but words as linguistic acts—marvelous sayings and tellings, the acts of little dramas in which individual, isolable words are only the poor players.

But now you might protest: Haven't we gone too far in suggesting to Dylan Thomas what he actually meant? He has said after all that it was "just the words of them" he was in love with (you do not fall in love with an action!), and even that he has learned to beat them! However playful and metaphoric all of this may be, the fact remains that Thomas is thinking of words as things, even individual things, the love of which turned him into a poet.

It is important to acknowledge that such a love as Thomas remembers does exist, and not to be embarrassed about it. Words are to some extent discrete, sensory things, and it is certainly possible to be charmed by them—the sound of them in the air and the sight of them on paper. However, such an acknowledgement is no sooner made, with the image it conjures of words as individual objects of delight, than it almost immediately asks for qualifications. Look again, and you will see qualifications in Thomas's own statement. He is careful to portray this love as a first love, an initiatory dizziness, as it were. Moreover, although he implies that he loves words individually, he speaks of them consistently in the plural, as a community, somewhat reminiscent of a child's storybook village of charming little people.

In reality, Thomas would surely acknowledge, it was not words as individual entities that he loved, and it was not words separate from the images and memories that they evoked—especially as his relationship with them progressed and matured. In fact, it was the enchanting evocation of images and memories through a musical overflow of words together that became Dylan Thomas's signature accomplishment:

> Now as I was young and easy under the apple boughs
>   About the lilting house and happy as the grass was green,
>   The night above the dingle starry,
>   Time let me hail and climb
>   Golden in the heydays of his eyes,
>   And honoured among wagons I was prince of the apple towns
>   And once below a time I lordly had the trees and leaves
>   Trail with daisies and barley
>   Down the rivers of the windfall light.
>   (*Poems of Dylan Thomas,* "Fern Hill" 195, 1–9)

This beautiful opening stanza from "Fern Hill" is both an auditory and a visual feast. It is the totality of it, however, and its conjuring of a sacred childhood memory, that makes it something to love. The sight of it on the printed page, moreover, brings up another caution about the status of words: the very notion of words as discrete entities is something of an illusion, fostered and intensified by the technology of writing. On the written page you can see passages of discourse segmented into paragraphs, paragraphs into sentences, sentences into words, and words themselves into letters or discrete sounds. The primary oral and auditory experience of language is rather different, however, and this is strikingly true with respect to words.

Linguistic definitions of the concept "word" always include as a defining feature the word's freestanding character or its separability from the stream of speech. However, words almost always come in batches, wrapped in bundles as it were. Words always depend upon the words around them, and even the sentences around them, for their actual significance. Why is this? The basic unit of discourse in any language is not the word itself or even the sentence but the speech act—the act of reminding, the act of warning, of asking, of directing, well-wishing, greeting, saying good-bye, and on through the copious inventory of the things we do when we speak or write. Words, phrases, and sentences are only the surface components of such acts. As transformational grammarians have eloquently demonstrated, these components in any given instance are rearrangeable and interchangeable with other components. Just as importantly for the present purpose, many of these surface components come in prepackaged phrasal form: "with a grain of salt," "on the other hand," "for the time being," "all things considered," "and so on."

Many so-called words, as a matter of fact, do not even meet the separability criterion. Function words such "a," "an," "the," "this," "that," "some," "any," "in," and "to" never occur alone. They can never stand alone, and no other words can be inserted between them and the nouns that they go with. (Some traditional grammars use the term "modify" rather than "go with," but that is hardly an apt identification of what they do.) In fact, in many languages these functions are performed by inflections (word endings or prefixes) rather than entities that look like separate words.

An analogous situation exists with regard to compound words. What combinations get to be one word, while others have to remain two? Linguistically it is easy: terms such as railroad train, cirrus cloud, sales booth, table wine, airline pilot, and thousands of other pairings are grammatically single words (just like blackboard, handbag, keyboard, and all the others), and their appearance as separate words is entirely an artifact of writing. Scribal or printing customs (or whims, actually) in the English-speaking nations where they first gained currency gave letter contiguity to some compounds but not to others. Among the Germans, who are much more consistent in these matters, all of the terms above are written as single words.

I am building a case for the proposition that the love of words is not a literal affection for words in the particular but some broader, more important thing. However, I want to acknowledge another form of word adoration that my arguments so far have not touched. There is another cult of words in which I personally must confess membership, and this is the cult of word origins and word histories. The priests, priestesses, and acolytes of this cult love to peer into the lives of words, and it is definitely individual and particular words that they love. They keep multiple dictionaries always close at hand; their "favorites" caches on the Internet are topped with lexicographical databases; they subscribe to "Word of the Day" electronic newsletters and receive daily emails about interesting, out of the way words. These cultists sometimes interrupt serious conversations to consult a dictionary. They will even add to their billable time with an attorney to inquire into the meaning and origin of such an ungainly term as "precatory letter."

This sort of love sends a few individuals into serious careers as linguists and lexicographers. Like Dylan Thomas, many of them would describe it as a first love, an opening infatuation that led to something deeper. Outside of this small circle of professionals, and sometimes even within it, there does seem something rather eccentric about it. A negative caricature of the philologist, the hapless and eccentric Professor Dr. Moritz-Maria von Igelfeld, author of *Portuguese Irregular Verbs*, is satirized mercilessly by Alexander McCall Smith, in a hilarious novella of that title. The reason for this impression of eccentricity, as Alexander Smith narrates pointedly, is that this sort of attention is something of a distraction from regular business. And the reason for this, in turn, is that the relationship between words and the things they name is, for the most part, asymmetrical. If there is knowledge to be had there, it is a distinctly limited and fragmentary knowledge. There are occasions when the etymology of a concept tells us something important about the concept we are about to explore. Most of the time, however, this love of words is an unrequited love. It is interesting to know that "curfew" derives from the medieval practice of "covering the fire" at curfew time, but in most of our talking and writing we actually need to forget this kind of information. We do and we have.

There is something serious and revealing about this particular love, however. The love of word origins derives from an intuition of symmetry that is worth paying attention to. In peering into the origins of words, we are trying to reach back into their infancy and early childhood, when they might still have been names rather than designations. Etymologists, especially amateur ones, are very often mistaken about particulars; but still, what they love is the process of naming and renaming, in which there is a kind of coming to know. There is a kind of poetry in it, and there is a parallel movement in poetry itself. You can see it at work in the stanza from Dylan Thomas's "Fern Hill." Pervasive in this stanza, which is about childhood, are new namings and renamings, new terms coming to life: "honoured among wagons," "prince of the apple towns," "once below a time," "rivers of the windfall light."

Here is definitely not an unrequited love, for there is both beauty and wisdom in return. It is not, however, in a sober articulation, simply a love of words. The French philosopher Voltaire is said to have quipped (and there was something to it) that linguistics is a science in which consonants count for very little and vowels for nothing at all (Müller 258). With respect to the widely professed love of words, a parallel observation applies: Words as individual entities count for remarkably little. We do not love them all that much, or for all that long.

By now, it should be clear that what we really love is acts of discourse—including both the process of producing them and the results they achieve. "Act of discourse" is a better translation of logos than "word." In early Christian writings, the Latin "sermo" (act of speech) was a competing and a better translation than "verbum" (Lombardi 3). These acts and processes are various, and we do not love them all in the same proportion or with the same intensity. Different individuals do not practice, teach, or learn them all equally well. We do have instruments for talking about them precisely, such as the compass of discourse. Peering into respective quadrants of the linguistic and discursive landscape, we identify four sorts of activity in which we are engaging when we conduct any kind of intentional discourse:

1. We are *making* something—arranging units and subunits of language and discourse into intelligible and attractive whole things.

2. We are *saying* something—conveying a message, with a specific content to an audience.

3. We are *exploring* or *envisioning* something—reaching for something beyond what is literally being said; sometimes making a special connection to, or impression upon, an audience; sometimes discovering for ourselves, or with our audience, what we are looking for.

4. We are *doing* something—performing one or more of the numerous acts that utterances and discourses can perform.

One should be able to realize that literary humanists have in modern times loved best the first and third items in the list above—the making and exploring arts of discourse. They love the making, reading, and hearing of beautiful and arresting, wonderfully made discourse; and they love the pleasures and the wondrous insights of the literary imagination. The fields of expository, investigatory, and rhetorical discourse have traditionally belonged for most English teachers in the category of activities that pay the bills. But these too have their attractions, and many of us take deep satisfaction in the study and the practice of them. For here too, as we have seen, the world is always being renamed and remade.

Historians of rhetoric are quite aware that preferences in love have not always been what they are today. In the ancient world and in the European Renaissance, the literary imagination took a back seat in schools to rhetoric, the art of doing the world's business with words. In the classical periods of Greece and Rome, the masterful public speaker emerged as a cultural hero—the individual who accomplished great things with persuasive and captivating language—supplanting the warrior kings of their distant past. The formal study of literature was relegated to the equivalent of elementary school. In every age, however, the love of making has been the stormiest romance. Many a literary humanist has seen the love of words sour into the hatred of student writing. Beautiful and well-crafted discourse is both the easiest thing to love and the most difficult thing to teach. In any curriculum, the craft of discourse must be given its due, and it is very often a stumbling block. It was a stumbling block in schools of the European Renaissance, where the classical ideal of the citizen-orator clashed with the laborious pounding of Latin into preadolescent schoolboys. It is a stumbling block in schools today, when matters of purpose, message, and value must wait for the acquisition of the "basics" of grammar and composition.

The love of making is at its most basic level a sheer delight in the artful articulation and framing of speech acts and larger continuous discourses. Here lies the pleasure we take in the well-turned phrase or sentence, the well-ordered paragraph or passage, the cleverly or pleasingly arranged whole discourse. Here are all the schemes (antithesis, antimetabole, and anadiplosis, to name a few favorites) and the tropes as well. Here also are well-crafted verses, ingeniously told narratives, arresting and unified dramas. (I cannot resist reminding you, lover of words that I am, that "making" is the older English word for composing literature, a translation of the Greek "poiesis," from "poiēin," "to make"). This is the art of composition in the strict sense, set off from considerations of discovering what you want to say and why.

Symmetry tells us that the greatest lovers of making are poets, and many of them are symmetrists of a rather mystical sort. Their playing with language, their search for beautiful, satisfying, and unique ways of saying things are more than just craft. They believe that language itself can deliver up secrets about the world, and they are sometimes right. Certain realities are actually made with language, and certain realities are fully grasped only in the process of naming or renaming them.

For many purposes, there are time-tested ways of saying things and arranging discourses. Smarter and more skillful people than the rest of us have already discovered many of these forms, and so you ought to try to learn from them. You can do this by imitating models of really successful discourse, and also by studying precepts or rules derived from the study of these models. Doing this will not only make you a better writer and speaker; it will actually lead you to a clearer and quicker discovery of what it is you want to say. This is an important matter since, as everybody who has tried it knows, you never know fully what you are going to say until you start saying it. The choice of a medium (speech, writing, telephone, email, live, taped, and so on) or stylistic register (formal, informal, standard, ethnic, and so forth) is an important part of any message or discursive action. It will enable you in certain ways, restrict you in others.

Asymmetry, however, claims that it is a mistake to think that mastery of form at any level will generate competent, effective, eloquent, or beautiful discourse. Form is sometimes a clever and indispensable servant to message and purpose, but it remains a servant. It is a mistake to lock forms into meanings, at any level. It is a mistake to think that dialects, media, formal levels, or registers are inherently confined to or even best for specific types of messages or specific confines of meaning, except under specific circumstances. It is as wrong to say that "school language" is confined to (best for) authoritarian messages, as it is to say that African American Vernacular English is confined to (best for) messages of emotional liberation, that German is best for philosophy, or that Latin is best for baptisms.

The four loves—of making, saying, envisioning, and doing—have attached themselves in modern times to distinct language arts (the arts of composition, critical thinking, literature, and rhetoric, respectively) and in each there are legitimate features of both symmetry and asymmetry. One of these arts is not more basic than another, and the love of words to which they all belong is after all a single love. Specific attributions of symmetry are often mistaken, but the intuition of symmetry is never wholly wrong. The corollary of course is that, while intuitions of symmetry are never wholly mistaken, specific attributions are rather often wrong. Love is a difficult thing to manage, but the important thing is to listen to and learn from language intelligently, in the specific moment.

Works Cited

Aarsleff, Hans. *The Study of Language in England, 1780–1860*. Princeton: Princeton University Press, 1967.
Ankersmit, F. R. *History and Tropology: The Rise and Fall of Metaphor*. Berkeley: University of California Press, 1994.
Aristotle. *The Basic Works of Aristotle*. Ed. Richard McKeon. New York: Random House, 1941.
———. *On Rhetoric: A Theory of Civic Discourse*. Trans. George A. Kennedy. 2nd ed. New York: Oxford University Press, 2007.
Auden, W. H. *The Complete Works of W. H. Auden*. Ed. Edward Mendelson. Princeton: Princeton University Press, 1988.
Augustine, Bishop of Hippo. *St. Augustine's Confessions*. Trans. William Watts, 1631. 2 vols. The Loeb Classical Library. Cambridge: Harvard University Press, 1961.
———. *De Dialectica*. Trans. B. Darrell Jackson. Dordrecht: D. Reidel, 1975.
———. *On Christian Doctrine*. Trans. D. W. Robertson, Jr. New York: Liberal Arts Press, 1958.
———. *Sermons on Selected Lessons of the New Testament*. Trans. By members of the English Church. Vol. 2. A Library of Fathers of the Holy Catholic Church. Oxford: John Henry Parker, 1844.
———. *The Teacher. The Free Choice of the Will. Grace and Free Will*. Trans. Robert P. Russell. Washington: Catholic University of America Press, 1968.
———. *The Trinity*. Trans. Stephen McKenna. Washington: Catholic University of America Press, 1963.
Austin, J. L. *How To Do Things with Words*. Cambridge: Harvard University Press, 1962.
———. *Philsophical Papers*. Ed. J. O. Urmson and G. J. Warnock. 2nd ed. Oxford: Clarendon Press, 1970.
Bacon, Francis. *The New Organon and Related Writings*. Ed. Fulton H. Anderson. New York: Macmillan, 1985.

Bailey, Richard W. *Images of English*. Ann Arbor: University of Michigan Press, 1991.
Barney, Rachel. *Names and Nature in Plato's Cratylus*. New York: Routledge, 2001.
Beale, Walter H. *A Pragmatic Theory of Rhetoric*. Carbondale: Southern Illinois University Press, 1987.
———. "Rhetorical Performative Discourse: A New Theory of Epideictic." *Philosophy and Rhetoric* 11 (1978): 221–45.
Berlin, James. "Contemporary Composition: The Major Pedagogical Theories." *The Writing Teacher's Sourcebook*. Eds. Gary Tate, E. P. J. Corbett, and Nancy Myers. 3rd ed. New York: Oxford University Press, 1994. 9–21.
Bizzell, Patricia, and Bruce Herzberg, eds. *The Rhetorical Tradition: Readings from Classical Times to the Present*. Boston: Bedford Books, 1990.
Black, Max. "Metaphor." *Proceedings of the Aristotelian Society* 55 (1954–55): 273–94.
Blair, Hugh. *Lectures on Rhetoric and Belles Lettres*. Ed. Harold F. Harding. 2 vols. Carbondale: Southern Illinois University Press, 1965.
Bloomfield, Leonard. *Language*. New York: Holt, Rinehart & Winston, 1933.
Bolinger, Dwight. *Language: The Loaded Weapon*. London: Longman, 1980.
Brown, Peter. *Augustine of Hippo: A Biography*. Berkeley: California University Press, 1969.
Burke, Kenneth. *A Grammar of Motives*. New York: Prentice-Hall, 1945.
———. *A Rhetoric of Motives*. Berkeley: University of California Press, 1969.
———. *The Rhetoric of Religion*. Boston: Beacon Press, 1961.
Burrow, John. "The Uses of Philology in Victorian England." *Ideas and Institutions of Victorian Britain*. Ed. R. Robson. London: G. Bell & Sons, 1967. 180–204.
Cape, Robert W., Jr. "Cicero and the Development of Prudential Practice at Rome." *Prudence: Classical Virtue, Postmodern Practice*. Ed. Robert Hariman. State College: Penn State University Press, 2003. 35–65.
Cassirer, Ernst. *The Logic of the Humanities*. Trans. Clarence Smith Howe. New Haven: Yale University Press, 1961.
Chase, Stuart. *The Tyranny of Words*. New York: Harcourt Brace, 1938.
Cicero. *Brutus*. Trans. G. L. Hendrickson. *Brutus. Orator*. Cambridge: Loeb Classical Library, 1960.
———. *De Officiis*. Trans. Walter Miller. Cambridge: Loeb Classical Library, 1968.
———. *De Oratore, Books I and II*. Trans. E. W. Sutton and H. Rackham. Cambridge: Loeb Classical Library, 1959.
———. *De Oratore, Book III. De Fato. Paradoxica Stoichorum*. Trans. H. Rackham. Cambridge: Loeb Classical Library, 1960.
———. *Orator*. Trans. H. M. Hubbell. *Brutus. Orator*. Cambridge: Loeb Classical Library, 1960.
Cole, P., and J. L. Morgan, eds. *Speech Acts*. New York: Academic Press, 1975.
Cole, Thomas. *The Origins of Rhetoric in Ancient Greece*. Baltimore: Johns Hopkins University Press, 1991.
Coleridge, Samuel Taylor. *Biographia Literaria, or Biographical Sketches of My Lit-

erary Life and Opinions. Eds. James Engell and W. Jackson Bate. Princeton: Princeton University Press, 1983.

———. *The Statesman's Manual. Lay Sermons. The Collected Works of Samuel Taylor Coleridge.* Ed. R. J. White. Vol. 6. Princeton: Princeton University Press, 1972. 3–114.

Collins, Billy. *Sailing Alone Around the Room: New and Selected Poems.* New York: Random House, 2002.

Condit, Celeste Michelle. "Crafting Virtue: The Rhetorical Construction of Public Morality." *QJS* 73 (1987): 79–97.

Conley, Thomas M. *Rhetoric in the European Tradition.* New York: Longman, 1990.

Corbett, Edward P. J. *Classical Rhetoric for the Modern Student.* 3rd ed. New York: Oxford University Press, 1990.

Crowley, Tony. *Standard English and the Politics of Language.* 2nd ed. New York: Palgrave Macmillan, 2003.

Culler, Jonathan. "Philosophy and Literature: The Fortunes of the Performative." *Poetics Today* 21 (2000): 479–502.

D'Alton, John Francis. *Roman Literary Theory and Criticism: A Study in Tendencies.* London: Longman, Green, and Co., 1931.

Dante Alighieri. *Dante Alighieri's Divine Comedy.* Trans. Mark Musa. Bloomington: Indiana University Press, 1996.

———. *De Vulgari Eloquentia.* Ed. and trans. Steven Botterill. Cambridge: Cambridge University Press, 1996.

Davidson, Donald. "What Metaphors Mean." *Critical Inquiry* 5 (1978): 31–47. Rpt. in *Inquiries into Truth and Interpretation.* Ed. Donald Davidson. Rev. ed. Oxford: Clarendon Press, 2001.

Derrida, Jacques. *Of Grammatology.* Trans. Gaytria Spivak. 2nd ed. Baltimore: Johns Hopkins University Press, 1976.

———. "Signature Event Context." *Glyph* 1 (1977): 172–97.

Dominik, William J., ed. *Roman Eloquence: Rhetoric in Society and Literature.* London: Routledge, 1997.

Eco, Umberto. *The Search for the Perfect Language.* Trans. James Fentress. Oxford: Blackwell, 1995.

Enos, Richard L. *Greek Rhetoric before Aristotle.* Prospect Heights: Waveland Press, 1993.

Ferry, Anne. *The Art of Naming.* Chicago: Chicago University Press, 1988.

Foucault, Michel. *Discipline and Punish: The Birth of the Prison.* Trans. Alan Sheridan. 2nd ed. New York: Vintage Books, 1995.

Frye, Northrop. *The Great Code: The Bible and Literature.* Ed. Alvin A. Lee. Toronto: University of Toronto Press, 2006.

Fulkerson, Richard. "Four Philosophies of Composition." *CCC* 30 (1978): 343–48.

Garver, Eugene. *Aristotle's Rhetoric: An Art of Character.* Chicago: Chicago University Press, 1994.

Genette, Gerard. *Mimologiques: Voyage en Cratylie.* Trans. Thais E. Morgan. Lincoln: University of Nebraska Press, 1995.

Gleason, Maud W. *Making Men: Sophists and Self-Presentation in Ancient Rome.* Princeton: Princeton University Press, 1995.

Glenn, Sheryl. *Rhetoric Retold: Regendering the Tradition from Antiquity through the Renaissance.* Carbondale: Southern Illinois University Press, 1997.

Gorgias. "Helen." Trans. George A. Kennedy. *Readings from Classical Rhetoric.* Eds. Patricia P. Matsen, Philip Rollinson, and Marion Sousa. Carbondale: Southern Illinois University Press, 1990. 33–36.

Gorman, David. "The Use and Abuse of Speech-Act Theory in Criticism." *Poetics Today* 20 (1999): 93–119.

Graddol, David, Dick Leith, and Joan Swann. *English: History, Diversity, and Change.* New York: Routledge, 1996.

Grafton, Anthony, and Lisa Jardine. *From Humanism to the Humanities: Education and the Liberal Arts in Fifteenth- and Sixteenth-Century Europe.* Cambridge: Harvard University Press, 1986.

Hariman, Robert, ed. *Prudence: Classical Virtue, Postmodern Practice.* State College: Penn State University Press, 2003.

Harris, Roy. *The Language Machine.* Ithaca: Cornell University Press, 1987.

Havelock, Eric A. *The Literate Revolution in Greece and Its Cultural Consequences.* Princeton: Princeton University Press, 1982.

Hawhee, Debra. "Agonism and Aretê." *Philosophy and Rhetoric* 35 (2002): 185–207.

Hayakawa, S. I. *Language in Thought and Action.* 4th ed. New York: Harcourt, Brace, Jovanovich, 1978.

Hobbes, Thomas. *Leviathan.* Ed. Richard Tuck. Cambridge: Cambridge University Press, 1991.

Holloway, John. *The Victorian Sage: Studies in Argument.* London: Archon Books, 1962.

Isocrates. *Against the Sophists.* Trans. George Norlin. *Isocrates, Vol II.* The Loeb Classical Library. London: Heinemann, 1929. 160–80.

———. *Antidosis.* Trans. George Norlin. *Isocrates, Vol II.* The Loeb Classical Library. London: Heinemann, 1929. 181–367.

Jaeger, Werner. *Paideia: The Ideals of Greek Culture.* Trans. Gilbert Highet. 3 vols. New York: Oxford University Press, 1934–44.

Jakobson, Roman. "Quest for the Essence of Language." *Selected Writings II: Word and Language.* The Hague: Mouton, 1971. 345–59.

———. "Two Aspects of Language and Two Types of Aphasic Disturbances." *Fundamentals of Language.* Roman Jakobson and Morris Halle. 2nd ed. The Hague: Mouton, 1971. 69–96.

Jarratt, Susan C. *Rereading the Sophists: Classical Rhetoric Refigured.* Carbondale: Southern Illinois University Press, 1991.

Jespersen, Otto. *Mankind, Nation, and Individual, from a Linguistic Point of View.* Cambridge: Harvard University Press, 1925.

Johnson, Samuel. *Johnson's Dictionary: A Modern Selection.* Eds. E. L. McAdam, Jr. and George Milne. New York: Pantheon Books, 1963.

Joseph, John E. *Limiting the Arbitrary: Linguistic Naturalism and its Opposites in Plato's* Cratylus *and in Modern Theories of Language.* Amsterdam: John Benjamins, 2000.

Kastely, James L. *Rethinking the Rhetorical Tradition: From Plato to Postmodernism.* New Haven: Yale University Press, 1997.
Kaster, Robert. *Guardians of Language: The Grammarians and Society in Late Antiquity.* Berkeley: University of California Press, 1988.
Kellner, Hans. *Language and Historical Representation: Getting the Story Crooked.* Madison: University of Wisconsin Press, 1989.
Kennedy, George A. *Classical Rhetoric and Its Christian and Secular Tradition from Ancient to Modern Times.* 2nd ed. Chapel Hill: University of North Carolina Press, 1999.
Kerford, George B. *The Sophistic Movement.* Cambridge: Cambridge University Press, 1981.
King, Martin Luther, Jr. "Letter From a Birmingham Jail." *Why We Can't Wait.* New York: New American Library, 2000. 64–84.
Knowles, Gerry. *A Cultural History of the English Language.* London: Arnold, 1997.
Krapp, George Philip. *The Knowledge of English.* New York: H. Holt, 1927.
Kristeva, Julia. *Language—The Unknown: An Initiation into Linguistics.* New York: Columbia University Press, 1989.
Lacan, Jacques. "The Instance of the Letter in the Unconscious, or Reason Since Freud." *Écrits: The First Complete Edition in English.* Trans. Bruce Fink. New York: W. W. Norton, 2006. 412–44.
Lakoff, George. "Linguistics and Natural Logic." *Semantics of Natural Language.* Eds. D. Davidson and G. Harmon. Dordrecht: Reidel, 1972. 545–665.
Lakoff, George, and Mark Johnson. *Metaphors We Live By.* Chicago: University of Chicago Press, 1980.
Lanham, Richard. *The Electronic Word: Democracy, Technology, and the Arts.* Chicago: University of Chicago Press, 1993.
Law, Vivien. *History of Linguistics in Europe from Plato to 1600.* New York: Cambridge University Press, 2003.
Lee, Benjamin. *Talking Heads: Language, Metalangage, and the Semiotics of Subjectivity.* Durham: Duke University Press, 1997.
Lombardi, Elena. *The Syntax of Desire: Language and Love in Augustine, The Modistae, Dante.* Toronto: University of Toronto Press, 2007.
Lunsford, Andrea, ed. *Reclaiming Rhetorica: Women in the Rhetorical Tradition.* Pittsburgh: University of Pittsburgh Press, 1995.
McDonald, Russ. *Shakespeare and the Arts of Language.* Oxford: Oxford University Press, 2002.
McIntyre, Alasdair. *After Virtue: A Study in Moral Theory.* 3rd ed. Notre Dame: Notre Dame University Press, 2007.
Maddox, Kristy. "Finding Comedy in Theology: A Hopeful Supplement to Kenneth Burke's Logology." *Philosophy and Rhetoric* 39 (2006): 208–32.
Mailloux, Stephen, ed. *Rhetoric, Sophistry, Pragmatism.* New York: Cambridge University Press, 1995.
Markus, R. A. "St. Augustine on Signs." *Phronesis* 2 (1957): 60–83. Rpt. in *Augustine: A Collection of Critical Essays.* Ed. R. A. Markus. Garden City: Anchor, 1972. 61–91.

Matsen, Patricia P., Philip Rollinson, and Marion Sousa, eds. *Readings From Classical Rhetoric*. Carbondale: Southern Illinois University Press, 1990.

Meier, A. J. "Apologies: What Do We Know?" *International Journal of Applied Linguistics* 8 (1998): 215–31.

Mellard, James J. *Doing Tropology: Analysis of Narrative Discourses*. Urbana: University of Illinois Press, 1987.

Mellon, John C. *Transformational Sentence-Combining: A Method for Enhancing the Development of Syntactic Fluency in English Composition* (NCTE Research Report No. 10). Urbana: National Council of Teachers of English, 1975.

Miller, Thomas P. *The Formation of College English: Rhetoric and Belles Lettres in the British Cultural Provinces*. Pittsburgh: University of Pittsburgh Press, 1997.

Milton, John. *The Complete Poems*. Ed. John Leonard. New York: Penguin, 1998.

Müller, F. Max. *My Autobiography: A Fragment*. New York: Charles Scribner's Sons, 1901.

———. *The Science of Language*. 2 vols. London: Longmans, Green, and Co., 1891.

———. "Semitic Monotheism." *The Essential Max Müller: On Language, Mythology, and Religion*. Ed. Jon R. Stone. New York: Macmillan, 2002. 25–42.

Murphy, James J. *Rhetoric in the Middle Ages: A History of Rhetorical Theory from Saint Augustine to the Renaissance*. Berkeley: University of California Press, 1974.

———, Richard A. Katula, Forbes I. Hill, and Donovan J. Ochs. *A Synoptic History of Classical Rhetoric*. 3rd ed. Mahwah: Hermagoras Press, 2003.

Nänny, Max. "Iconicity in Literature." *Word and Image* 2 (1986): 199–208.

———. "Introduction." *Word and Image* 2 (1986): 197–98.

Norris, Christopher. "Structuralism." *Oxford Companion to Philosophy*. Ed. Ted Homeric. New York: Oxford University Press, 1995. 855.

Nussbaum, Martha C. *The Fragility of Goodness: Luck and Ethics in Greek Tragedy and Philosophy*. New York: Cambridge University Press, 2001.

O'Hare, Frank. *Sentence Combining: Improving Students Writing Without Formal Grammar Instruction* (NCTE Research Report No. 15). Urbana: National Council of Teachers of English, 1973.

Olson, Gary. "Social Construction and Composition Theory: A Conversation with Richard Rorty." *JAC* 9 (1989): 1–9.

Ong, Walter. *Orality and Literacy: The Technologizing of the Word*. London: Methuen, 1982.

Oravec, Christine. "Fanny Wright and the Enforcing of Prudence: Women, Propriety, and Transgression in the Nineteenth-Century Public Oratory of the United States." *Prudence: Classical Virtue, Postmodern Practice*. Ed. Robert Hariman. State College: Penn State University Press, 2003. 189–225.

Pearson, Justus R., and James Robert Reese. "Project Grammar: The Linguistic and Language Preparation of Secondary School Teachers of English. Interim Report." 1969. Educational Resources Information Center (ERIC): #ED031500. <http://eric.ed.gov/ERICDocs/data/ericdocs2sql/content_storage_01/0000019b/80/35/0e/2a.pdf>

Pender, Stephen. "The Open Use of Living: Prudence, Decorum, and the 'Square Man.'" *Rhetorica* 23 (2005): 363–400.
Pepper, Stephen. *World Hypotheses: A Study in Evidence.* Berkeley: University of California Press, 1961.
Perelman, Chaim, and L. Olbrechts-Tyteca. *The New Rhetoric: A Treatise on Argumentation.* Trans. John Wilkinson and Purcell Weaver. Notre Dame: Notre Dame University Press, 1969.
Pitcher, George. "Austin: A Personal Memoir." *Essays on J. L. Austin.* Sir Isaiah Berlin, et al. Oxford: Clarendon Press, 1973. 17–30.
Plato. *The Collected Dialogues of Plato.* Ed. Edith Hamilton and Huntington Cairns. Princeton: Princeton University Press, 1969.
———. *Cratylus.* Trans. Benjamin Jowett. *The Collected Dialogues of Plato.* Ed. Edith Hamilton and Huntington Cairns. Princeton: Princeton University Press, 1969. 421–74.
———. *Gorgias.* Trans. W. D. Woodhead. *The Collected Dialogues of Plato.* Ed. Edith Hamilton and Huntington Cairns. Princeton: Princeton University Press, 1969. 229–307.
———. *Protagoras.* Trans. W. K. C. Guthrie. *The Collected Dialogues of Plato.* Ed. Edith Hamilton and Huntington Cairns. Princeton: Princeton University Press, 1969. 308–52.
———. *Republic.* Trans. Paul Shorey. *The Collected Dialogues of Plato.* Ed. Edith Hamilton and Huntington Cairns. Princeton: Princeton University Press, 1969. 575–844.
Poster, Carol. "The Task of the Bow: Heraclitus' Rhetorical Critique of Epic Language." *Philosophy and Rhetoric* 39 (2006): 1–21.
Poulakos, John. *Sophistical Rhetoric in Classical Greece.* Columbia: University of South Carolina Press, 1994.
Pratt, Mary Louise. *Toward a Speech Act Theory of Literary Discourse.* Bloomington: Indiana University Press, 1977.
Quintilian. *Institutio Oratoria.* Trans. H. E. Butler. 4 vols. The Loeb Classical Library. Cambridge: Harvard University Press, 1959–63.
Ringer, Jeffrey. "Faith and Language: Walter Hilton, St. Augustine, and Poststructural Semiotics." *Christianity and Literature* 53 (2003): 3–18.
Roberts-Miller, Patricia. "Post-Contemporary Composition: Social Constructivism and Its Alternatives." *Composition Studies* 30 (2002): 1–13.
Robinson, Douglas. "Linguistics and Language." *The Johns Hopkins Guide to Literary Theory and Criticism.* Eds. Michael Groden, Martin Kriswirth, and Imre Szeman. Baltimore: Johns Hopkins University Press, 1997.
Rorty, Richard, ed. *The Linguistic Turn: Recent Essays in Philosophical Method.* Chicago: University of Chicago Press, 1967.
Sapir, Edward. *Language.* New York: Harcourt Brace, 1921.
Saussure, Ferdinand de. *Course in General Linguistics.* Eds. Charles Bally and Albert Sechehaye. Trans. Roy Harris. La Salle: Open Court, 1986.
Schiappa, Edward. *Protagoras and Logos: A Study in Greek Philosophy and Rhetoric.* Columbia: University of South Carolina Press, 1991.

Searle, John R. *Consciousness and Language*. New York: Cambridge University Press, 2002.
———. *The Construction of Social Reality*. New York: Free Press, 1995.
———. *Mind, Language and Society: Philosophy in the Real World*. New York: Basic Books, 1998.
———. "A Reply to Derrida." *Glyph* 1 (1977): 198–208.
———. *Speech Acts: An Essay in the Philosophy of Language*. London: Cambridge University Press, 1969.
Sedgwick, Eve Kosofsky. "Queer Performativity: Henry James's The Art of the Novel." *GLQ* 1 (1993): 1–16.
Self, Lois S. "Rhetoric and Phronesis: The Aristotelian Ideal." *Philosophy and Rhetoric* 12 (1979): 130–45.
Shelley, Percy Bysshe. *A Defence of Poetry. Percy Bysshe Shelley: The Major Works*. Eds. Zachary Leader and Michael O'Neill. Oxford: Oxford University Press, 2003. 674–701.
Smith, Alexander McCall. *Portuguese Irregular Verbs*. New York: Anchor Books, 2005.
Smitherman, Geneva, and Victor Villanueva, eds. *Language Diversity in the Classroom: From Intention to Practice*. Carbondale: Southern Illinois University Press, 2003.
Sprague, Rosamond K., ed. *The Older Sophists*. Columbia: University of South Carolina Press, 1972.
Thomas, Dylan. "Notes on the Art of Poetry." *Modern Poetics*. Ed. James Scully. New York: McGraw Hill, 1965. 185–91.
———. *The Poems of Dylan Thomas*. Ed. Daniel Jones. New York: New Directions, 1971.
Thoreau, Henry David. *Winter: From the Journal of Henry David Thoreau*. Ed. H. G. O. Blake. Boston: Houghton Mifflin, 1887.
Todorov, Tzvetan. "The Birth of Western Semiotics." *Theories of the Symbol*. Trans. Catherine Porter. Ithaca: Cornell University Press, 1982. 15–59.
Vendler, Zeno. *Linguistics in Philosophy*. Ithaca: Cornell University Press, 1967.
Vickers, Brian. *In Defence of Rhetoric*. Oxford: Clarendon Press, 1987.
Vico, Giambattista. *The New Science of Giambattista Vico*. Trans. Thomas Goddard Bergin and Max Harold Fisch. Ithaca: Cornell University Press, 1968.
Weaver, Constance. *Teaching Grammar in Context*. Portsmouth: Boynton/Cook, 1996.
Weaver, Richard. "Scholars or Gentlemen?" *College English* 7 (1945): 72–77.
White, Hayden V. *Tropics of Discourse: Essays in Cultural Criticism*. Baltimore: Johns Hopkins University Press, 1978.
Whorf, Benjamin Lee. *Language, Thought, and Reality: Selected Writings*. Ed. John B. Carroll. Cambridge: MIT, 1956.
Williams, William Carlos. *The Collected Poems of William Carlos Williams*. Eds. A. Walton Litz and Christopher MacGowan. 2 vols. New York: New Directions, 1986.
Wordsworth, William. *The Poems*. Ed. John Hayden. New Haven: Yale University Press, 1981.

Index

Aarsleff, Hans, 61, 62
Alice in Wonderland (Carroll), 90–91, 145
allegorical interpretation, medieval, 31–32
analogy. *See* structural analogy
analogy-anomaly question, 19
Ankersmit, F. R., 127, 139
appropriateness, as stylistic virtue, 162–63. *See also* decorum
arbitrariness, 5–25, 32–44, 54, 71, 117, 133. *See also* asymmetry
Aristotle, 49, 130–31, 138; *De Interpretatione*, 49; ethics, 153, 158; logic, 25, 49–51; *Nichomachean Ethics*, 153, 158; philosophy of knowledge, 10; *Poetics*, 24, 94; *Rhetoric*, 24, 152–60
asymmetry: defined, 5–6, 104; as freedom from reference, 35; linguistics and, 5–6; of names, 108–9, 117; philosophical, 128–72; Plato and, 18–26; reciprocity with symmetry, 35, 39, 41, 66; Saint Augustine and, 26–35; versus symmetry, 13–16, 37–66, 182. *See also* arbitrariness; symmetry
Auden, W. H., 13–14, 103
Augustine, Saint: as asymmetrist, 26–35, 70–71, 83, 85, 108, 138; *Confessions*, 27, 29, 34, 83; *De Dialectica*, 26; *De Magistro*, 29; eloquence and, 26–28, 33–34, 162, 172; *On Christian Doctrine* (*De Doctrina Christiana*), 32–33, 162, 172; *On the Trinity* (*De Trinitate*),
29–32, 83–84; *Sermons*, 34; virtue agenda and, 154; the Word and, 28–35, 77, 83, 138
Austin, J. L., 68, 85–93, 97, 102, 133

Babel. *See* Tower of Babel
Bacon, Francis, 14
Barney, Rachel, 35, 125
Beale, Walter H., 85, 90
Berlin, James, 98
Bible, the, 27, 30, 33, 41, 61, 63, 162. *See also* Word, the
binary opposition, 71–72, 74, 78, 110
Black, Max, 130
Blair, Hugh, 161, 171
Blake, William, 147
Bolinger, Dwight, 54–55, 66
Burke, Kenneth: approach to language study, 38–39; *Grammar of Motives, A*, 132–37, 140; master tropes, 133–37, 143; pentad, 131–33, 139–40, 149; recognition of performative principle, 86, 133; *Rhetoric of Religion, The*, 31, 68, 70; structural analogy, 30–31, 68, 70–72
Burrow, John, 66

cabala, 31
Cape, Robert W., Jr., 172
cardinal virtues, 156–57
Carroll, Lewis, 90–91, 145
Cassirer, Ernst, 143

categories, logical, 49–51
Chase, Stuart, 15
Chomsky, Noam, 146
Christianity: hegemony of Latin and, 10; logos and, 30–31, 83. *See also* Augustine, Saint
Cicero, 12, 26, 34, 68, 154–59, 160–63, 166; *De Oratore*, 154; *On Duty* (*De Officiis*), 159; *Orator*, 158–59
clarity: as virtue of discourse, 160–61
coherence: in discourse, 55, 72, 170
Coleridge, Samuel Taylor, 25, 28, 38, 63, 122, 131
Collins, Billy, 73
comparative linguistics. *See* comparative philology
comparative philology, 56–60, 65, 66
compass of discourse, 144–49, 163–64, 166–67, 172, 180
composition, composition studies: academic field of, 1, 4, 20–21, 65–66; belles lettres conception of, 171–72; grammar and, 47, 55, 181; "making," well-madeness, 170, 181–82; opposing ideals of, 80; problem of coherence, 55; social constructivism and, 107; sophistic rhetoric and, 20–21
Condit, Celeste, 168, 172
Confessions (Augustine), 27, 29, 34
Conley, Thomas M., 16
continuum, as design feature of discourse, 74–76. *See also* structural analogy
Corbett, Edward P. J., 3
correctness: as stylistic virtue, 160–61, 163, 170, 172; justice and, 135–36. *See also* well-madeness
Cratylus (Plato), 24–26, 40, 44
criticism, importance of, 105–6
Crowley, Tony, 3, 20
Crusius, Timothy, 82, 132
Culler, Jonathan, 85, 103, 106
culture, language and, 42, 55–60; structural analogy and, 69–82. *See also* pilot analogies
D'Alton, John Francis, 159
Dante Alighieri, 8–9, 63
Davidson, Donald, 112

decorum: as stylistic virtue, 34, 158, 160, 162–63; prudence and, 158–59, 163, 166; wisdom and, 168. *See also* appropriateness
deconstruction, 106, 107
De Dialectica (Augustine), 26
De Doctrina Christiana (Augustine). See *On Christian Doctrine*
De Oratore (Cicero), 154
Defence of Poetry, A (Shelley), 60–63, 91
De Interpretatione (Aristotle), 49
De Trinitate (Augustine). See *On the Trinity*
Derrida, Jacques, 29, 35, 36, 100, 102, 106, 107
Descartes, René, 138, 146
designation: versus naming, 110–25, 129, 179; versus signification (Genette), 45. *See also* reference; sign; structural analogy
Dewey, John, 131
diagrammatic iconicity, 53–55, 92
dialectic: alternative to rhetoric (Plato), 49, 152; component of the medieval trivium, 21–22; "counterpart" to rhetoric (Aristotle), 152, 155–59; formulation by Aristotle, 49–51; irony and, 135–37; literary humanism and, 15. *See also* logic
dignity: as stylistic virtue, 33, 161, 162. *See also* ornament; power

Eco, Umberto, 27, 62
"Encomium to Helen" (Gorgias), 23
English studies, 1–4
etymology, 45–46, 109, 120, 179

figurative language: Blair on, 161; naming and, 111–112; role in classical rhetoric, 33; romantic view of, 64; traditional inventories of, 120. *See also* literal/figurative distinction; trope; tropology
Fish, Stanley, 85, 102–3, 107
form/meaning analogy, 68–70
formalism, in teaching, 53
formism (worldview), 130–31
Frye, Northrup, 31
Fulkerson, Richard, 61

Garver, Eugene, 158
general semantics, 15
genitive case, 10, 48–49
Genette, Gerard, 12, 16, 25, 40–41, 45, 85, 111
Gleason, Maud W., 156
Goethe, Johann Wolfgang von, 84
Gorgias, 22–24, 161
Gorman, David, 103
Grafton, Anthony, 16–17
grammar: analogy to cultural practice, 124; ancient teaching of, 47; component of medieval trivium, 9–10; identification with study of Latin, 7–12, 47, 51; and logic (thought), 50–52; modistic, 11, 47; structural, 71; symmetry of, 47–53; teaching of vernacular, 3, 10, 49, 52–53, 181; transformational, 69, 177; universal, 28, 32
Grammar of Motives, A (Burke), 132–37, 140
grammar schools, Renaissance, 7, 9, 12, 60

Hariman, Robert, 172
Harris, Roy, 118, 125
Hawhee, Debra, 156
Hayakawa, S. I., 15
Hegel, Georg Wilhelm Friedrich, 131
Heraclitus, 18
Hobbes, Thomas, 38, 131
Holloway, John, 59
Humphrey, Hubert, 99

illocution, illocutionary acts, 89, 97, 100–101
iconicity. *See* diagrammatic iconicity
imagination: connection to "image," 121; literary, 180; symmetry of, 60–66; versus literal language, 112. *See also* romanticism
irony: as figure of speech, 115; as master trope, 133, 144; connection to dialectic, 135–37
Isocrates, 138, 151, 153, 166–67, 171

Jakobson, Roman, 54, 143
James, William, 68, 131

Jardine, Lisa, 16
Jespersen, Otto, 117–18, 120
Johnson, Mark, 112–13, 125, 129–30
Johnson, Samuel, 13, 14, 16, 28
justice: as teleology of discourse, 168–71

Kant, Emmanuel, 62
Kellner, Hans, 127
King, Martin Luther, Jr., 170
Knowles, Gerry, 12
Krapp, George Philip, 25
Kristeva, Julia, 42

Lacan, Jacques, 29, 35
Lakoff, George, 90, 112–13, 125, 129, 130
langue and parole, 117
Latin: assumed superiority of, 6–13, 64–65; attacks on, 41; Bible in, 41; identification with "grammar," 51–52
Law, Vivien, 15–16; 26
Lee, Benjamin, 60
Leibniz, Gottfried, 62
linguistics: asymmetrism of, 38–39, 42; comparative, 56–60; place in English studies, 2–6; pragmatics, 85–86
linguistic relativity, 59–60
linguistic turn (in modern philosophy), 68, 132–33
literal/figurative distinction, 72, 111–20. *See also* figurative language; tropes; tropology
literary humanism: Augustinian, 32; dialectic in, 15; defined, 4–5, 138, 174; hegemony of Latin in, 6–12; impact of comparative linguistics, 60; in poetry, 113–14; in relation to performative principle, 97; in relation to structural analogy, 74, 123; in relation to symmetry question, 5–6, 37–39; in relation to virtue agenda, 157; sophistic, 23–24; weaknesses of classical, 77
Locke, John, 61–62, 131, 138, 146
logic: Aristotelian, 25, 49–50; Augustine's view of, 28; component of medieval trivium, 9–11; in Renaissance education, 12, 15; romantic view of, 63–64. *See also* categories; dialectic

logos: concept of, 27, 30–34, 82, 84, 138, 168, 179
Lombardi, Elena, 27, 30
Longinus, 162

McIntyre, Alasdair, 173
making: as operation of discourse, 83, 148, 181
Markus, R. A., 36
Marxism, 132
master tropes, 133–37, 139–41, 144, 149. *See also* tropology; Vico, Giambattista
Meier, A. J., 87
Mellard, James J., 127
Mellon, John C., 51
Meno (Plato), 29
metaphor: as instrument of discovery, 121–22; as instrument of expression, 120–21; as instrument of shaping reality, 122–23; master trope of, 134, 139, 144–45; orientational (Lakoff and Johnson), 130; and reference, 112–117; romantic view of, 63–64; "root metaphors" (Stephen Pepper), 130–31, 144–46; and scientific discourse, 130; spatial and directional, 126, 130–31, 140–41, 149. *See also* figurative language; literal/figurative distinction; tropes; tropology
metonymy: master trope of, 134–36, 144–45; trope of, 120
medieval age, Middle Ages: drama in, 92; grammar in, 47, 52; role of Latin in, 6–12; scholasticism in, 130–31
Miller, Thomas P., 173
Milton, John, 27, 81–82, 108–10, 119
modistae grammarians, 11, 47
monotheism: and history of language, 58–59
Müller, F. Max, 58–59, 179
Murphy, James J., 21
mythology: and history of language, 57–59

naming, process of, 110–11; versus designation, 110–25. *See also* designation
Nänny, Max, 53
nationalism: in language study, 60

nature versus convention, 19–20
Nazism: in language study, 59
Nichomachean Ethics (Aristotle), 153, 158
Norris, Christopher, 68
Nuckolls, Janis B., 66
Nussbaum, Martha C., 173

Odyssey, The, 64
O'Hare, Frank, 51
Olbrechts-Tyteca, L., 169–70
Olson, Gary, 85, 98
On Christian Doctrine (Augustine), 33
On Duty (Cicero), 159
On the Trinity (Augustine), 29–32, 83–84
"one and the many," problem of, 70
onomatopoeia, 41
Orator (Cicero), 158–59
Oravec, Christine, 163, 172
ordinary language philosophy, 68
ornament: as stylistic virtue, 161–62. *See also* power

Paradise Lost (Milton), 27
Pearson, Justus R., 2
Peirce, Charles S., 53, 131
Pender, Stephen, 158
pentad (Kenneth Burke), 131–33, 139–40, 149
Pepper, Stephen, 130–32, 139, 146, 150, 164
Perelman, Chaim, 169–70
performatives, performative principle, 83–108, 117, 123, 133, 141–45, 155–57, 167
Phaedrus (Plato), 24, 26, 152
Philebus (Plato), 70, 96
philology, 2, 60; and English studies, 60. *See also* comparative philology
philosophical language, attempts to construct, 24, 62–63
phonetics, 57. *See also* sounds
pilot analogy. *See* structural analogy
Pitcher, George, 97
Plato: active versus contemplative life, 96; allegory of the cave, 95–96; *Cratylus*, 24–26, 40, 44; formism (idealism), 130–31; *Meno*, 29; *Phaedrus*, 24, 26, 152; *Philebus*, 70, 96; philosophy of knowledge, 10–11; *Protagoras*, 151–53, 165–66; quarrel with sophists, 20–24,

77, 151–53; *Republic, The*, 95; symmetry question in, 18–26, "the one and the many," 70
Poetics (Aristotle), 24
Pope, Alexander, 121–22
power: as stylistic virtue, 161–62. *See also* ornament
pragmatics, 42, 85, 89, 139
pragmatism: American philosophy, 68, 131–32
Poster, Carol, 18
Pratt, Mary Louise, 85
Prodicus, 23
Protagoras, 22–23, 151–54, 165–66
Progatoras (Plato), 151–54, 165–66

Quintilian, 26, 154–63, 165–66. *See also* virtue agenda

Ramus, Peter, 138
reference, referential function: connection to truth and validity, 100–101; connection to the literal, 112; freedom of language from, 35, 79; impossibility of, 35; in larger discourses, 113–19; to ideas, 19, 30; versus expression and imagination, 63; versus the performative function, 83–89; weakness of language in, 32, 62. *See also* arbitrariness; asymmetry; figurative language
realism versus nominalism debate, 11
Rees, James Robert, 2
Reformation, 9
relativism, 22, 24, 143–44
Renaissance, 4–5, 7–9, 12, 52, 60, 121, 180–81
Republic, The (Plato), 95
Rhetoric (Aristotle), 24, 152–60
rhetoric: ancient, 20–22, 77–78, 97, 151–69; Enlightenment attacks upon, 138–39; in Augustine, 26–28, 33–34; in Renaissance humanism, 12
Rhetoric of Religion, The (Burke), 30, 31, 68, 70
Ringer, Jeffrey, 36,
Roberts-Miller, Patricia, 98, 107
Robinson, Douglas, 3, 17, 39
Romance of the Rose, The, 8

romanticism, romantic period, 28–29, 60–66, 122, 131
Rorty, Richard, 68, 82, 132

Sapir, Edward, 59
Saussure, Ferdinand de, 36, 42, 71, 117–18
saying, as operation of discourse, 83–89, 93–101, 141–42, 148–49
Schiappa, Edward, 20, 36
Searle, John R., 85, 99–106
Sedgwick, Eve Kosofsky, 107
Self, Lois S., 158
semantic change, 46, 109
semantics, philosophical, 38–39
semiotics, 29
sentence-combining, 51
Shakespeare, William, 96–97, 101–5, 115–16, 127
Shelley, Percy Bysshe, 60–63, 68, 91, 122
sign, signification: arbitrariness of, 37; Augustine on, 27–35; Peirce on, 53; Saussure on, 71; traditional philosophy of, 84–85. *See also* designation; reference
Smith, Alexander McCall, 179
Smitherman, Geneva, 3
social construction of reality, 98–106
Socrates, 22. *See also* Plato
sophistic rhetoric, sophists, sophistry: legacy of, in Augustine, 26, 34; Plato and, 20–24, 77, 151–53. *See also* Gorgias; Protagoras
sounds, symmetry of, 39–43
speech act(s): as basic component of discourse, 52, 177; relation to whole discourses, 127; theory of, 85–107. *See also* Austin, J. L.; Searle, John R.; performatives
speech-act theory. *See* speech act(s)
Stoics, stoicism, 18, 22, 30, 32, 157
structural analogy, 67–82, 123–24, 140; continuum analogy, 76, 78; designating/naming, 123–25, 142–43; form/meaning analogy, 68–70; saying/doing, 83–89, 93–101, 141–42; sequence/pattern, 72–74; symmetry/asymmetry, 79–82; "the one and the many," 70; structuralism and, 67–68

style, classical theory of, 33; competing ideals of, 80; component of classical rhetoric, 21; in sophistic rhetoric, 21; Platonic/Aristotelian view of, 156; relationship to "real virtue," 171; traditional virtues of, 160–65
Swift, Jonathan, 62
symmetry: comparative philology and, 55–60; defined, 1–2; Latin and, 6–13; question of, 4–18; reciprocity with symmetry, 35, 39, 41, 66; six claims of, 37–66; versus asymmetry, 13–16. *See also* asymmetry
symmetry question. *See* symmetry
synecdoche, 120; as master trope, 135–36, 144

Theophrastus, 160, 165
Thomas, Dylan, 175–79
Thoreau, Henry David, 116–17
Todorov, Tzvetan, 29
Tower of Babel, 27–28, 61
transformational grammar, 69, 177
trivium, 9, 12, 47
trope, figure of speech, 110
tropology, 126–150; defined, 129. *See also* compass of discourse; master tropes; pentad (Kenneth Burke)

Varro, 47
Vendler, Zeno, 82
vernacular languages: assumed inferiority to Latin, 7–12; literary humanism in, 60, 64; teaching the grammar of, 52–53
ultimate value: as teleology of discourse, 168
Vico, Giambattista, 122, 130, 133–34, 137–39, 141, 149–50

Wallis, John, 41
Weaver, Constance, 49
Weaver, Richard, 75
well-madeness: as virtue of style, 160, 164. *See also* correctness
White, Hayden V., 127, 130, 139
Whorf, Benjamin Lee, 59–60
Wilkins, John, 62
Williams, William Carlos, 113–14
wisdom: as teleology of discourse, 168
Wittgenstein, Ludwig, 68
Word, the: concept of, 26–35, 77, 83–85, 168. *See also* logos
Wordsworth, William, 13–14, 16, 64
writing: instruction in, 47, 52, 65–66, 78, 171–72; medium of, 65–66, 72–73, 80, 160, 165, 177–78. *See also* composition